ALSO BY

CLIFFORD H. POPE

REPTILES ROUND THE WORLD   1957

THE REPTILE WORLD   1955

TURTLES OF THE UNITED STATES AND CANADA   1939

THESE ARE BORZOI BOOKS

PUBLISHED BY *Alfred A. Knopf* IN NEW YORK

THE GIANT SNAKES

Serata and normal Indian Python. Serata has been called a partial albino because she does not have pink eyes. Her skin obviously lacks all pigment cells that are responsible for dark elements of the pattern. In the normal Indian python the light areas are blended shades of grayish and yellowish brown, whereas reddish and blackish browns are blended in the blotches. Iridescence is evident over the entire animal. (Courtesy Staten Island Zoo. Photograph by Jack Muntzner)

THE GIANT SNAKES

THE NATURAL HISTORY
OF THE BOA CONSTRICTOR,
THE ANACONDA,
AND THE LARGEST PYTHONS,

including comparative facts about other snakes
and basic information on reptiles in general

CLIFFORD H. POPE

NEW YORK ALFRED A. KNOPF
1967

L. C. catalog card number: 61–16736

THIS IS A BORZOI BOOK,

PUBLISHED BY ALFRED A. KNOPF, INC.

PUBLISHED NOVEMBER 13, 1961
SECOND PRINTING, OCTOBER 1965
THIRD PRINTING, NOVEMBER 1967

TO SYLVIA

a superior serpent

who inspired this study

Foreword

THIS BOOK is about six of the most spectacular, exciting, and, to some, fearful of animals. These giant snakes are commonly seen in zoos, where they attract much attention, but in spite of their popularity there has been no general account of them. Although written from a strictly scientific point of view, this natural history is addressed primarily to the general reader.

The visitor to the zoo, gazing in amazement and disappointment at the great snake lying motionless in its cage, wonders how such a sluggish creature could give rise to so many fantastic tales of incredible power. One of my objects is to show that though the tales are suspect, the giants' way of life is actually even more fascinating than the tales would have us believe; and that a vast amount of serious and difficult study will have to be carried out before we can fully appreciate that way of life.

Writing this book has entailed scrutiny of hundreds of technical books and papers, in many languages, published during the last century and a half. I have been able to select only a small amount from this vast reservoir of knowledge. The bibliographies at the end of the book indicate sources and suggest supplementary reading.

Acknowledgments

THIS IS a joint endeavor, even though my wife, Sarah H. Pope, refuses to have her name on the title page. She has checked all the facts, criticized the style, written the bibliographies, typed the manuscript, and helped in small ways too numerous to mention. Mere acknowledgment of indebtedness to her seems wholly inadequate.

For bibliographic assistance I am especially grateful to Hazel Gay, of The American Museum of Natural History; Meta P. Howell, Eugenia Bernoff, M. Eileen Rocourt, and Ruth Andris, all of the Chicago Natural History Museum; and Sue Osmotherly and George G. Babcock, of the Winnetka, Illinois, Public Library.

My old friend Carl F. Kauffeld, Curator of Reptiles, Staten Island Zoo, presented several photographs and much interesting information about their subjects. To him and the Staten Island Zoological Society, I wish to express my deep gratitude.

Appreciation of additional aid with the illustrations is due to Charles R. Hackenbrock, of the Staten Island Zoo; Frank E. Fenner, of the World Book Encyclopedia; Walker Van Riper, of the Denver Museum of Natural History; David R. McPhee; William Hosmer; and William B. Allen, Jr., of the Highland Park Zoo, Pittsburgh. Lillian A. Ross gave a great deal of editorial advice;

Acknowledgments

Fritz Haas translated Dutch articles and helped in other ways; Lew Johnson sent data on Sylvia.

I also wish to thank Audrey F. and Edward C. Porter, Janet G. Wright, William J. Beecher, Robert E. Charles, John Moyer, Jane Statham, of the Library of International Relations, Charles E. Shaw, Anthony D. Lilly, Isabelle Hunt and Roger Conant, David H. Corkran, Stephen J. Copland, and Charles M. Bogert.

Information on captive giant snakes was kindly sent me by these herpetologists: J. Lear Grimmer, National Zoological Park; Roger Conant, Philadelphia Zoological Garden; James A. Oliver, New York Zoological Park; R. Marlin Perkins, Lincoln Park Zoological Gardens; Robert Snedigar, Brookfield Zoo; Moody J. R. Lentz, St. Louis Zoological Park; Carl F. Kauffeld, Staten Island Zoo, and Charles E. Shaw, San Diego Zoological Gardens.

The following friends have also been helpful: Austin L. Rand, Emmet R. Blake, Melvin A. Traylor, Jr., Robert F. Inger, Hymen Marx, Philip Hershkovitz, Karl F. Koopman, Loren P. Woods, Henry S. Dybas, Rainer Zangerl, D. Dwight Davis, and Betty O'Blenis, all of the Chicago Natural History Museum; Esther F. Brown, Longstreth H. Brown, Charles Béart, A. Villiers, George Cansdale, Sherman A. Minton, Jr., J. D. Romer, the Richard S. Cutlers, Henry L. Hirschhorn, and Whitney Pope; Tom Olechowski, and William B. Allen, Jr., Highland Park Zoo, Pittsburgh.

Contents

INTRODUCING THE GIANTS   I

   Sylvia   3

   The Big Six   10
      SOME CHARACTERISTICS OF THE BIG SIX
      A GEOGRAPHICAL KEY TO THE GIANTS

   The World of the Giants   19
      MEANS OF DISPERSAL
      DISTRIBUTION OF THE GIANT SNAKES
      ZOOGEOGRAPHIC REGIONS
      HABITATS
      DISTRIBUTION AND HABITATS OF THE GIANTS

MEETING THE WORLD   33

   Senses   35
      VISION
      HEARING
      HEAT-SENSITIVE LABIAL PITS
      JACOBSON'S ORGAN AND CHEMORECEPTION
      SENSE OF TOUCH; SUMMARY

   Strength and Constriction   44
      HANDLING GIANT SNAKES

Contents

1. POWER OF CONSTRICTION
2. FLEXIBILITY OF THE VERTEBRAL COLUMN
C. *Intelligence*   51
D. *Locomotion*   56
    1. OVERLAND SPEED
    2. SWIMMING AND CLIMBING
E. *Activity*   62
    CHARACTERISTICS OF THE SIX GIANTS
F. *Shedding*   68
    1. FREQUENCY OF SHEDDING
    2. THE PROCESS OF SHEDDING

III FUEL   75

What They Eat—and How Much   77
    FOOD PREFERENCES OF THE SPECIES
    SIZE OF PREY
    CAPACITY OF THE BIG SIX
    FREQUENCY OF FEEDING

Feeding Habits   90
    FINDING FOOD
    SEIZING PREY
    SWALLOWING PREY

INTERNAL ECONOMY   97

Digestion   99
    DIGESTIVE JUICES
    ELIMINATION
    EFFECT OF TEMPERATURE

Use of Water   105
    RETENTION AND LOSS
    DANGER OF DEHYDRATION

Temperature   110

Contents

IV REPRODUCTION AND GROWTH   115

  A. *Sex and Mating*   117

    1. SEX RECOGNITION

    2. COURTSHIP

    ORGANS OF REPRODUCTION

    3. COPULATION

    4. FREQUENCY AND TIME OF BREEDING

    5. HYBRIDIZATION AND DELAYED FERTILIZATION

    INTERNAL DEVELOPMENT

  B. *Laying, Brooding, Hatching, and Birth*   128

    BEHAVIOR OF WILD FEMALES

    BEHAVIOR OF CAPTIVE FEMALES

    1. LAYING

    LAYING SEASON AND PRE-HATCHING PERIOD

    2. HATCHING

    THE EGG

    3. SIZE OF CLUTCHES

    4. BROODING AND INCUBATION

  C. *Growth, Maturity, and Length*   148

    MEASUREMENT

    1. GROWTH BEFORE AND AFTER MATURITY

    2. MAXIMUM LENGTH

    GROWTH OF THE SIX GIANTS

    GIANT SNAKES OF AGES PAST

  D. *Longevity*   166

DESTROYERS OF THE GIANTS   171

  Enemies and Defense Against Them   173

    DEFENSES

  Parasites and Sickness   183

    PARASITES

    MITES AND TICKS

Contents

INTERNAL PARASITES

PROTOZOA

FLUKES

TAPEWORMS

ROUNDWORMS

LINGUATULIDS

PARASITISM IN THE GIANTS

TUBERCULOSIS

MOUTH ROT

"ENTERITIS" AND OTHER DISEASES

V. RELATION TO MAN   197

    Man's Study of the Giants   199

    A. Worship   204

        1. IN AUSTRALIA AND SOUTHERN ASIA

        2. IN THE NEAR EAST

        3. IN THE NEW WORLD

        4. IN AFRICA

    B. Beliefs   212

    Encounters with Giant Snakes   218

        ANACONDA

        BOA CONSTRICTOR

        AFRICAN ROCK PYTHON

        INDIAN PYTHON

        RETICULATE PYTHON

        SUMMARY

    C. Attacks on Man   226

    Fear of Giant Snakes   230

        FEAR IN OTHER PRIMATES

    D. Uses by Man   236

        1. USE AS LEATHER

        2. USE AS FOOD

Contents

USE IN MEDICINE

THE SNAKE AS AN AID TO AGRICULTURE

USES IN EDUCATION AND ENTERTAINMENT

ZOOLOGICAL GARDENS

MUSEUMS

LECTURERS

CIRCUSES, CARNIVALS, AND "CHARMERS"

ROADSIDE EXHIBITS

SNAKE CHARMERS OF AFRICA AND ASIA

THEATRICALS

HOBBY GROUPS

THE PRESS

Giant Pets   261

SUGGESTED REFERENCES   265

INDEX   *follows page* 290

Illustrations

Serata and normal Indian Python		FRONTISPIECE
1. *Sylvia at the bath*	FACING PAGE	12
2. *Sylvia and a friend*		12
3. *Anaconda*		13
4. *African Rock Python*		44
5. *Ball Python*		44
6. *Reticulate Python*		45
7. *Reticulate Python*		45
8. *Brood of infant Boa Constrictors*		76
9. *Habitat of Amethystine Python*		76
10. *13-foot Amethystine Python*		77
11. *Head of Amethystine Python from Queensland*		77
12. *Head of Carpet Python from Queensland*		108
13. *Carpet Python*		109
14. *Diamond Python*		140
15. *Constriction on a small scale*		140
16. *Skeleton of Reticulate Python*		141
17. *Pupil that closes to a vertical slit*		172
18. *Round pupil*		172
19. *Head of Boa Constrictor*		173
20. *A conveniently shaped meal*		204
21. *African Rock Python after swallowing a goat*		204
22. *Reticulate Python brooding eggs*		205
23. *Boa Constrictor*		236
24. *Anaconda arrives at zoo*		237

CONVERSIONS OF
WEIGHTS AND LINEAR MEASUREMENTS

1 OUNCE   28.35 GRAMS

1 POUND   0.453 KILOGRAMS

1 INCH   25.4 MILLIMETERS

1 FOOT   0.305 METERS

Introducing
the Giants

✳

Sylvia

BEFORE LAUNCHING into the subject of the six species of giant snakes, I want to explain how this book came to be written and also to introduce a special Indian python named Sylvia. I became so fascinated by Sylvia's unusual habits that the plan of a book on the giant boas and pythons began to take shape. Sylvia certainly deserves what fame has come her way and the tribute given her here. Moreover, it is probable that most pythons will respond to care and attention in much the same way that Sylvia does.

Even if she were human, Sylvia could not recall the events of the first weeks of her life in northeastern Burma. She was found there on October 3, 1945, behind the sugar barrel in the mess hall of an army laboratory. Belief that she was a cobra caused a big rumpus; it was not until close examination proved her to be an infant Indian python, and therefore harmless, that quiet was restored.

She was brought to the United States by a colleague, who arrived at the Chicago Natural History Museum with her in December 1945. By February 10, 1946, Sylvia was 3 feet 5 inches long and growing at the rate of approximately three inches a month, which indicates that she was only a few weeks old when caught in Burma; at birth, Indian pythons are about 2 feet long.

Sylvia was so docile that, soon after her arrival at the museum, she even stopped trying to bite, and her tameness caused me to pay particular attention to her. So little is known about the growth of the giant snakes that I hoped to discover much by studying her. Sylvia has co-operated beautifully ever since.

Those first weeks of Sylvia's life were eventful. They involved getting used to man, leaving her home to travel halfway around the world by plane, and then learning to eat domestic rats rather than a variety of wild animals native to Burma. If she had remained in Burma, she probably would have passed her life within a mile of the spot where she was hatched.

During the second period of her life, from December 1945 through September 1951, her time was divided between the laboratory of the Division of Reptiles of the Chicago Natural History Museum, where there was difficulty in keeping her warm at night, and my home, where she lived in her box by the furnace in the basement. In both places she was handled daily in order to keep her tame and co-operative.

She responded by becoming so tractable that a three-year-old child could pull her around in perfect safety. Leaving her alone with such a child was dangerous, but only for Sylvia. Danny Hessey, a child only nine months old, visited us when Sylvia was over 10 feet long, and the two used to play a game. Sylvia would crawl along, with Danny in pursuit. As soon as he was within reach, Danny would give her tail a pull. This stimulated her to draw up the last few feet of her body and thus free herself from his tiny hand. Danny, of course, thought that it was fun and would pursue Sylvia about the living room. Searching for this game in a book of "activities for children" would be a waste of time.

As soon as the neighbors learn that you have a growing python in the home, they become divided into groups; some are anxious to pay her a visit, some swear that they will never set foot in your house, and a few even become aggressive. One of our friends sheepishly admitted that she had barely restrained herself from calling the police. Suspecting that someone might do that, I had planned to ask two small neighborhood girls, who were enamored of Sylvia, to introduce her to the policemen. After Sylvia had been with us for some time, we heard of steps the Village Hall had taken to warn meter readers and others; on our card in its files was a brief notation: "Snake in basement." A visiting friend once complained that we had been careless about introductions; apparently, as he went down the steps from his room on the third floor, he met Sylvia coming up from her home in the basement. It was something of a shock for him, but we had no report from her.

Pythons have a way of getting into the most unexpected places, and that's why they cannot be allowed the run of a home. When Sylvia moved across any surface—such as a mantel, the top of a table, or a bookshelf—she pushed things off with the exaggerated movements she had to make in an effort to get a purchase on a smooth surface; she was as effective as a broom.

Her tendency to crawl into dark corners and holes resulted in an uncanny ability to disappear; there was no telling where she would turn up. One day Sylvia was nowhere to be found; she had managed to get out of the bathroom after her regular bath. We searched high and low without success. Finally, one of us noticed a small pile of unusual dust under the bed in which my wife and I slept. Above the pile was a short tear in the ticking of the box spring. We soon found that Sylvia, then about 8 feet long, was reposing in the heart of the box springs. Getting her out required a lot of careful maneuvering, and revealed an alarming accumulation of dust in the springs, much of which came out with Sylvia. My wife then recalled that, while dozing on the bed before the search, she had been vaguely conscious of activity in the springs below her but had dismissed the sensation as some sort of sleepy hallucination. This is a fine example of what is to be expected; experiences like this induce the python owner to keep his pet confined except when it is being watched.

We never dared take Sylvia into the yard because we knew that her escape could cause a furor. No declaration of her harmlessness would calm a mother of small children, and the dogs of the immediate vicinity would be in grave danger, not to mention the cats. It is highly unlikely that such a tame snake would ever attack a human being, but possibly a person might suffer a serious shock upon meeting a python. In the winter, the danger would be to the python herself; she would quickly succumb to severe cold.

Since Indian pythons have aquatic tendencies, we were careful to give Sylvia a good soaking in the bathtub at frequent intervals. She obviously liked this. Sometimes she was left alone to enjoy her bath. One day, soon after she had started, we heard water running and hurried to discover that, by crawling across the basin, she had turned on the hot water full force. It was already very hot, and Sylvia would have given herself and the bathroom a good steaming had she not been rescued.

Taking measurements of Sylvia was a regular event that relieved the monotony of her life. Reptile men have written at great length of the difficulties of such a procedure; few giant snakes will allow themselves to be stretched out absolutely straight. With Sylvia there was no problem. Like other reptiles, she felt most content when in contact with a wall or anything resembling one. We had only to put her on the floor near a wall and she would slowly straighten herself out against it. With a little coaxing and patience, an exact measurement could be taken.

It was always a temptation to see how friends would react to Sylvia, but, of course, all experiments had to be carried on with the utmost caution. It has ever been a hard and fast rule with me never to frighten persons with snakes of any kind. One evening I broke this rule. An agent had been trying to sell me insurance for an hour, and I had become weary. It happened to be the time when my son, Whitney, put Sylvia away for the night. This involved taking her from the second floor to the basement past the living-room door.

A sudden daring and experimental desire hit me just as I heard Whitney approaching. Sylvia was draped about his neck with head and tail almost reaching the floor; she was about 8 feet long then.

Saying nothing to the agent, I quietly called to Whitney to step into the living room. He rounded the door to appear with startling suddenness, immediately in front of the agent. I held my breath, expecting a violent reaction that I might live to regret. But I was badly fooled. The agent did not turn a hair or show any sign of alarm. In a calm voice he remarked: "What a nice pet your son has!" It was a demonstration of self-control I never expect to see duplicated.

In strong contrast was the behavior of a photographer sent by a newspaper. He asked how dangerous Sylvia might be. I remarked as casually as possible: "Well, the last man she got around we managed to get free in about an hour." It did not take the photographer long to decide that he had more important pictures to take.

Sylvia's fame began in 1947, when I wrote an article entitled "A Python in the Home," which appeared in the *Chicago Natural History Museum Bulletin*. The *Bulletin* has only a limited circulation, but the Chicago papers were attracted by the idea and published numerous articles, most of them humorous. Newspapers of other cities took up the story, and Sylvia became known from coast to coast. But she reached even greater heights of fame when, on May 8, 1950, *Life* published a short article about her, "Python Is a Boy's Pal." There was a great deal of preparation for the story, and I co-operated to the extent of working for two afternoons with the photographer and his assistant. They took some excellent photographs showing Sylvia crawling about the living room, taking a bath, being measured, and even climbing the stairs. The original plans for the article did not materialize; so only two pictures with eight lines of text appeared, and these on the last page of the issue.

Before going on to the third period of Sylvia's life, I shall try to answer the question: "Did Sylvia ever learn to respond to you?" This cannot be answered categorically, although I would hazard an affirmative answer. My difficulty is that I lack direct scientific evidence and cannot claim to have detected anything but a docile attitude toward everyone. A snake's reactions are much more difficult to analyze than are those of a mammal, let us say, but this is only negative evidence. A snake is handicapped by being unable to move parts of the face, which means that the expression is fixed. Under questioning, the criminal would like to be as expressionless as the snake.

Recent experiments prove that a rattlesnake reacts violently to the odor of a human being through a highly sensitive nose ("olfactory chemoreceptive alerting mechanism" for those who like to be technical). There is no reason to doubt that Sylvia, too, is keenly aware of the presence of human beings. Whether she readily distinguished me from others is a question that calls for further investigation.

Sylvia began the third period of her eventful life on September 27, 1951, when I turned her over to Lew Johnson in Pekin, Illinois. Mr. Johnson is a lecturer dedicated to promoting conservation of wildlife and the "understanding of misunderstood creatures." He had written to ask where he might get a python tame enough for use in lectures. I had by then kept Sylvia for nearly six years and had secured accurate records of her early growth; my son was paying less and less attention to her as a pet. I also realized that she could be of great service to Mr. Johnson. So I agreed to lend Sylvia to him long enough to see how well she would suit his purpose.

I was so impressed by Mr. Johnson's work that I extended the loan indefinitely, and Sylvia has been taken on regular lecture tours ever since. For example, during the school year of 1956–7, Mr. Johnson's program called for delivery of his lecture, "Your Friends the Snakes," in 140 schools of six midwestern states. Also, during eight and a half consecutive years she was shown to school, college, club, and church audiences totaling nearly 800,000 persons. Television audiences have been thrilled by her more than once. Circus pythons have been seen by hundreds of thousands of persons, but I doubt that any other traveling python has been presented to as many people for the purposes of education.

Mr. Johnson practices what he preaches; his animals are given the best of care. While on the farm near Ashland, Wisconsin, Sylvia lives in the parlor of Mr. Johnson's home; when on the road, she rides on foam rubber in a special trailer.

The Big Six

THE PROPER SUBJECTS of this book are the six largest of living snakes: the anaconda, the boa constrictor, and the Indian, reticulate, amethystine, and African rock pythons. With the exception of the boa constrictor, these form a distinct size group among the snakes of the world.

The boa constrictor, with a maximum length of 18.5 feet, is noticeably smaller than the other five. Yet it is large enough to be included as a giant. The only other snake that has a maximum length approaching that of this lesser giant is the king cobra, which sometimes grows to be a little over 18 feet long. This highly venomous Asiatic reptile, not a relative of the big six, is so slender that its weight is nowhere near that of the boa constrictor.

The following facts will show how wide is the gap between the seven longest snakes and the remaining 2,500 or more living species. Taking 12 feet as a limit, I find that only a few other boas and pythons and four snakes of other families ever attain it; three of the four do so *very* rarely. These four are a highly dangerous mamba (largest of the four, it has a maximum length of 14 feet and lives in Africa), the bushmaster (a pit viper of tropical America), and the dhaman and keeled rat snake (both harmless species of southern Asia).

The frequent presence of one or more of the giants in snake exhibits is responsible for the belief that all boas and pythons (the family Boidae) are big snakes. The truth is that only about 15 per cent of the sixty-five or more species of Boidae (including, of course, the six giants) do attain the 12-foot limit. No other family of snakes has more than two 12-footers. The rich snake fauna of the United States has only four (the coachwhip, the indigo snake, the bull snake, and a rat snake) that attain or come within a few inches of 9 feet. An overwhelming majority of all species never exceed a yard in length. A large python or anaconda may be 50 times as long and 65,000 times as heavy as some adult worm snakes (families Typhlopidae and Leptotyphlopidae).

Our giants share certain characteristics that set them off from other animals. Indeed, I venture to say that no other group of creatures has a greater array of extraordinary qualities. The great boas and pythons are the longest of existing land animals, as well as the lightest of the big ones. They are characterized by slender, highly flexible bodies that enable them to throw constricting coils about their prey and their enemies. They are the only large vertebrates without useful appendages; their tiny spurs are but remnants of lost hind legs.

The giant snakes are about the only big terrestrial creatures without a vocal apparatus. They are unable to produce a sound above a hiss. Also, having no external ears, they lack sensitivity to air-borne sounds. They depend on vision to a limited degree and perceive mainly through organs of smell and, in some cases, heat-sensitive labial pits. Thus, they are well adapted to nocturnal as well as daylight activity.

The big snakes, with few exceptions, move (or crawl) more slowly and more silently than do other large terrestrial (as opposed to marine) creatures. No other large animals, though, are so much at home in water as well as on land. The big snakes are superior in the water because of a transparent, watertight eye covering, their undulatory motion, and their ability to hold the breath for a long time. Only one of the great snakes, the anaconda, takes much advantage of this amphibious ability, but all enter water freely when the opportunity arises. They readily climb trees, too, and crawl among branches that will support their weight.

No other large land animals swallow objects approximately as large as themselves, as our six giants can, or devour whole animals the size of a man. (Fortunately this last feat is something that the great snakes rarely attempt.) This swallowing capacity means that they can take in at one time much more fuel (relative to weight) than other land animals. They are able to consume in one meal as much as four hundred times their daily energy need, so periods of fasting sometimes last well over a year.

The ability of a giant snake to crush a victim by constriction has been exaggerated in the public mind. After seizing its prey in vise-like jaws, the serpent coils its body about its opponent and squeezes. The muscular pressure is sufficient to keep the chest from expanding and thus halt the ability to breathe. Bone-breaking exertion, therefore, is unnecessary.

The word "constrictor" is often used to designate any member of the family Boidae. But the habit of constriction is found here and there among other snakes of the world. The king snakes (*Lampropeltis*), for example, are familiar constrictors of the United States and other parts of the New World, though in no way related to the Boidae.

The giants, like other snakes, are "cold-blooded," or, more properly termed, ectothermic. That is, they have no internal heat-producing mechanism, so their temperature remains close to that of their surroundings. As the Boidae prefer a limited range of warm temperatures, all are found within or close to the tropical regions of the world.

We do not know just how often giant snakes breed. The anaconda and boa constrictor are viviparous, bringing forth their young fully formed as mammals do. The pythons lay and brood eggs but rarely incubate them. The young grow rapidly until they

Sylvia at the bath. Sylvia's vital statistics when this photograph was taken were approximately as follows: Age 4½ years, length 10½ feet, weight 35 pounds. (Courtesy *Life*. © 1950, Time, Inc. Photograph by George Skadding)

Sylvia, about eighteen months old, with Whitney Pope, almost twelve years old. (Photograph by John T. Booz)

Anaconda. The ground color is dark green; the conspicuous dark spots are black or blackish. (Courtesy Staten
Island Zoo. Photograph by Jack Muntzner)

reach sexual maturity, after which the rate of growth continues, but much more slowly. It is next to impossible to measure the length of life in the wilds, but captive giants have been known to live twenty years and a little longer.

In early life, when they are no larger than many other snakes, boas and pythons fall victim to many kinds of predatory animals. Upon reaching maturity they have far fewer enemies to fear. Their chief enemy is man—not solely because of hunting but also because of the encroachment of civilization, which destroys their habitats. The snakes are also victims of many common parasites and maladies.

Many are the tall tales that have been built up around giant serpents—in myth, in folklore, in religion. Often they have been feared by man out of all proportion to the danger they present. Their instinct is to give man a wide berth, and there have been few verified accounts of attacks on human beings.

Giant snakes are useful to man in many ways. They yield a durable, waterproof leather, and in some parts of the world they are valued as food. They have been semi-domesticated in the tropics to rid farmland of rodents and other pests. They provide entertainment in circuses and carnivals and in the hands of professional "snake charmers." They serve educational purposes in zoological gardens, museums, and schools. And for owners who are not concerned with strong emotional attachment, they make good pets.

The entire family of Boidae has been traditionally divided into the boas (Boinae) and the pythons (Pythoninae), but recent research suggests that much more must be learned about the anatomy of these snakes before they can be properly divided into subfamilies.

Our six giants fall into simple geographical groups: the two boas of the New World and the four pythons of the Old World and the Australian region. This convenient distribution does not apply to all of the Boidae, however. Many smaller species of boas are found in various parts of the Eastern Hemisphere.

SOME CHARACTERISTICS OF THE BIG SIX

Following is a more detailed discussion of each of the six giants, including a few words about its range and habitats, its maximum length, and certain other characteristics. More complete information on many of these points will be covered in the chapters that are to follow.

Boa constrictor: As the most familiar of the six giants, the boa constrictor deserves treatment first. This species illustrates the extremely rare circumstance of an animal with a common name that is also its technical name. The latter is usually written with an initial capital letter and in italics: *Boa constrictor.* The term "boa constrictor" is often used in a broad sense to mean just any huge snake, but such an extension of the meaning creates ambiguity and should be discouraged.

The range of the boa constrictor reaches from Argentina to the northern Mexican states of Sonora and Tamaulipas, both adjacent to the United States; thus, it is the only giant that lives near us. It is the smallest of the six giants, as I have said, and reaches a maximum length of 18 or 19 feet. It is also the most adaptable of the big snakes in being able to live in various types of country. In Mexico, for instance, it thrives in mild deserts. Yet elsewhere it is at home in wet tropical forests, open savanna, and cultivated fields, from sea level to moderate elevations. The baby boa constrictor occasionally reaches this country in shipments of bananas.

Students have detected marked differences in boa constrictors in certain parts of the boas' range and have given these different types technical names as subspecies. The subspecific name most often encountered is *imperator.* The population for which it is used is found from extreme northwestern South America through Central America and into northern Mexico. Subspecific distinctions do not concern us here: we shall merely think of the species as a geographically variable one.

Anaconda: The next of our six, the anaconda (*Eunectes muri-nus*), of South America, is probably the giant among the giants. A 37.5-foot specimen has been reported, and the species is greater in girth than the other Boidae.

The word "anaconda" is of doubtful origin. Some scholars, tracing it to Ceylon, say it is derived from the Tamil words *anai*, which means "elephant," and *kolra*, which means "killer." On Ceylon the name must have been applied to the Indian python, one of the meanings given to "anaconda" in *Webster's New International Dictionary*. Though the word does not appear in old South American literature, it is now universally applied to the New World snake, not the Indian python.

The anaconda is also known as the water boa because of its aquatic habits. It frequents permanent bodies of water which have enough vegetation in them to afford cover and ensure a supply of food. Though a tendency toward aquatic habits is noticeable in the other giants, this is the only one that can be called truly aquatic. I do not mean that the anaconda cannot crawl about on land as well as the other great snakes; it merely prefers to spend most of its time in water and never to stray far from it. Other names commonly used for the anaconda in South America are *sucuriú* and water kamudi. There are several different spellings of both these words.

Since the anaconda, like the boa constrictor, is a variable species, it has been given a number of technical names, each applying to individuals found in a certain part of the range. The most familiar of these, *gigas*, is given to a population widely distributed in northern South America.

The anaconda has only one close relative, which is also in the genus *Eunectes—Eunectes notaeus* of Paraguay and adjacent regions. This anaconda, a different species, is too small to be rated among our six giants. I shall call it the southern anaconda.

African rock python: Turning to the four Old World giants, all pythons, we shall first consider the African rock python (*Python sebae*). This species, reaching a record length of 32 feet, is often exhibited in zoos. It is the only one of our six with a range that does not overlap that of another. It is widely distributed throughout Africa, except in the great deserts. A need for humidity is presumably what keeps it out of the deserts. It prefers the savanna type of country and has been found at high altitudes. All stories of huge African snakes must stem from this lone giant. The few other pythons of Africa are small species with relatively limited ranges.

The fact that its common English name is widely used, coupled with the snake's isolation, makes identification of the African rock python easy. The only cause of confusion is calling the common python of India and Pakistan the Indian rock python rather than simply the Indian python.

There can be little doubt that man has been in close association with the African giant longer than with any other. If, as is probable, man evolved in Africa, he must have "grown up" with the python. Little wonder that python worship today reaches its height there with this giant as a common symbol.

Indian python: The Indian python (*Python molurus*), sometimes called the Indian rock python, is not only the second most widely known of all the giants but the species about which appreciable scientific information was first acquired. This information resulted from the early stimulation of scientific investigation by the British in India.

Because it is popular with the snake charmers of India and Pakistan, the Indian python is seen constantly, not only by the people of those countries but by many tourists. The zoos of the world stock it regularly even though, being a small giant, it is less spectacular than most of the others. Its greatest known length is about 20 feet.

The Indian python is widely distributed on the mainland of southeastern Asia, including southern China, and, to a very limited extent, the East Indies. It frequents jungles as well as regions devoid of forests and rivals the African rock python in reaching higher

16

elevations. In the eastern part of its range this species differs enough to be set off as a subspecies by a technical name, *bivittatus*.

Reticulate python: The reticulate python (*Python reticulatus*) is often called the giant among great snakes, though there is a strong tendency now to give the honors for size to the anaconda. Its accepted maximum length stands at 33 feet. In any case, the reticulate python has always been a favorite with zoo and circus men. It lives well in captivity and has a striking color pattern.

The range of the reticulate python starts in Burma and extends eastward (south of China) and southeastward to include the Philippine Islands and Timor (just north of Australia). Thus, all the humid tropics of Asia, as well as the great archipelago to the southeast of it, are inhabited by either the Indian or the reticulate python or by both.

Amethystine python: The "dark horse" of the giant snakes is the amethystine python (*Liasis* or *Python amethystinus*). Though it was introduced to science as long ago as 1801, there is still much confusion over its proper name, the exact spelling of the technical one, the snake's maximum size, and the extent of its range. Opinions also differ in regard to its relationships, some students putting it in the genus *Python*, others in the genus *Liasis*. This difference of opinion indicates a need for further anatomical studies.

The amethystine python has been known to reach lengths of at least 22 feet. It is distributed from northeastern Australia to the Philippine Islands. It has shown a preference for riverbanks in wild country, but it is also found near human habitations. Few people in the United States ever have a chance to see the species alive, as our zoos seldom exhibit it. Though not a rare snake, it is, nevertheless, an elusive one.

A GEOGRAPHICAL KEY TO THE GIANTS

NAME	DISTRIBUTION
Family: Boidae	
Boas (Boinae)	New World
boa constrictor (*Boa constrictor*)	Tropical North and South America
anaconda (*Eunectes murinus*)	Tropical South America
Pythons (Pythoninae)	Old World
African rock python (*Python sebae*)	Africa (except deserts)
Indian python (*Python molurus*)	Southeastern Asia and a few islands of the East Indies
reticulate python (*Python reticulatus*)	Extreme southeastern Asia and the East Indies
amethystine python (*Liasis* or *Python amethystinus*)	Northeastern Australia to the Philippine Islands

The World of the Giants

THE STUDY of animal distribution (zoogeography) is a venerable branch of biology, intimately connected with the rise of worldwide interest in the scientific approach to the study of wildlife. Charles Darwin and Alfred Russel Wallace both gained their insights into evolution through concentration on zoogeography. The latter's great work on animal distribution, which he published in 1876, is still valid.

The central problem concerning the distribution of land animals is to explain how related species happen to be abundant on all the continents in spite of seemingly impassable ocean barriers. Since their dispersal took place in ages gone by, we must resort to theories. The most plausible one holds that the continents have long been separated by oceans much as they are today. This means that animals must have, as opportunity afforded, crossed straits and short, narrow land connections between islands and continents.

Many minor changes in land configuration have taken place in comparatively recent ages. For example, geologists have shown that in Eocene times (about fifty million years ago) Sumatra, Java, and Borneo formed part of the Sunda Shelf, which was in turn part of the mainland of Asia. When the Sunda Shelf was broken up, countless species of animals—including giant snakes, no doubt—became isolated on one resulting island or another. The isthmus now joining North and South America has not always existed; when it submerged, the animals of these two continents could not move freely from one to the other. Many additional cases could be cited, but these two are especially pertinent for living reptiles. As climates are no more permanent than some islands, migration from Asia to Europe or vice versa has been possible for reptiles during geologic times when tropical temperatures prevailed in northern latitudes.

MEANS OF DISPERSAL

Although water does seriously interfere with dispersal, land animals often manage to cross wide stretches of it in one of three ways: in currents of air, on floating rafts of vegetation, and by aid of other animals, including man.

Everyone has heard of storm winds carrying objects great distances, and insects, including wingless adults, spiders, and mites, are commonly dispersed in this way. It is little wonder that all islands capable of supporting animal life are inhabited by insects. The surprising fact is that the ability to fly has little to do with the dispersal of light creatures; the less they use their own strength, the better for dispersal. There is a whole literature on "rains of frogs," and all alleged cases cannot be laughed off. Frogs would be the first of the higher animals to be lifted by a cyclone because they so often live in shallow water. Small fresh-water snakes might also be sucked up, but not giant snakes.

Dispersal by floating vegetation is most important for reptiles. The records are replete with examples of animals floating across wide stretches of sea on masses of matted vegetation. These masses sometimes bear erect trees of good size. Animals such as the giant snakes, with arboreal and aquatic tendencies, as well as the ability to live months without food or water, would be first in line for transportation via such rafts. The bottleneck is not so much in the start as in the finish: the chances of landing on an inhospitable shore are great; an animal might live well enough on the raft, which most likely is a bit of its original home, but perish on a barren beach before reaching suitable terrain.

One observer saw in the seas between Celebes and Borneo many floating islands with lush green vegetation, including palm trees 20 to 30 feet high. The most famous report involving a giant snake is that made by Wallace: a boa constrictor arrived in good health on the island of St. Vincent after floating 200 or more miles from South America. An Indian python at least 18 feet long was carried approximately as far down the Godavari River of India to Kotapalli, an island lying across one of the river's mouths.

We have profited greatly from studies made after the stupendous volcanic explosion of Krakatoa, one of a group of three tiny islands lying in the Sunda Strait, between Java and Sumatra. The animal life of these islands was destroyed by the eruption, which took place in 1883. Yet by 1908 the reticulate python was found on Krakatoa; some ten years later it was common there; and still a little later it was living on all three islands. K. W. Dammerman has given a detailed account of the return of the animals, and Willy Ley has drawn a brief but dramatic picture of this catastrophe that accounted for the death of tens of thousands of human beings as well as millions of animals. Incidentally, students of animal and plant dispersal were provided with an experiment conducted on a scale impossible before the development of atomic bombs. The volcanic explosion of Krakatoa, heard 2,968 miles away, made sea waves estimated to be 80 feet high and two sound waves that met on the opposite side of the globe; dust hurled into the air created spectacular sunsets for all mankind to enjoy.

There is no question that man also has moved and continues to move the giant snakes about in one way or another. The wonder is rather that these snakes still seem to have reasonably "natural" ranges.

21

DISTRIBUTION OF THE GIANT SNAKES

So much for history and theories; let us see what can be said about living reptiles in general and giant snakes in particular. The present pattern of reptile distribution is the result of complex evolution. Reptiles are primarily land creatures confined to the warmer regions, yet some are tough enough to cross considerable water barriers. They seem to have moved outward from the tropics of Africa and Asia, but this does not mean that they have deserted these regions; on the contrary, they are still as abundant there as anywhere. A number of dominant reptile groups have moved from the Old World to America, whereas it is not certain that any have done the reverse. The place where snakes originated is unknown, as are the courses of their earliest dispersals, but more recently they have spread out from the tropics of the Old World.

The boas and pythons belong to an ancient family of snakes. Fossils belonging to this family have been found that date from the Eocene epoch, which began some sixty million years ago. This fossil record is all too scanty, but it does show that these snakes were once widely distributed in Europe and temperate North America, regions where they are now all but absent, presumably because of the relatively severe climates. Their wide ancient distribution explains their abundance in such well-separated parts of the world as South America, Africa, tropical Asia, and Australia.

The boas and pythons are now overwhelmingly tropical reptiles with a family distribution not much greater in extent than the combined ranges of our six giants, except in Australia, where small pythons are found in the extreme south as well as in the northern tropical areas.

ZOOGEOGRAPHIC REGIONS

Philip Lutley Sclater, for thirty-three years director of the London Zoological Society, made a fundamental contribution to the study of zoogeography by dividing the world into six regions, each having its characteristic bird fauna. This division serves not only for birds but for other non-marine animals as well. Our giant snakes are largely concentrated in four of the regions: the Ethiopian, comprising all of Africa except its northern fringe plus a little of Arabia; the Oriental, which includes tropical Asia and associated continental islands; the Australian, embracing New Guinea as well as the continent of Australia; and the Neotropical, which includes all of South America and extends northward to embrace the tropical parts of Mexico. The boa constrictor ranges slightly into the Nearctic region (North America above the tropics); the Indian python ranges northward to the borders of the corresponding Palaearctic region of the Old World.

The meeting of the Oriental and Australian regions has puzzled zoogeographers for a long time. Lines of demarcation have been drawn through the East Indies along various courses. The most famous of these is Wallace's Line, which runs between Borneo and Celebes and just east of Java. Darlington and others consider such a sharp separation impossible because the faunas of the two regions widely overlap. The solution approved by Darlington sets up a broad transition zone reaching from Wallace's Line to another line passing just west of New Guinea and northwest of Australia.

HABITATS

The habitat, or biotope, of an animal is the type of country in which it lives: forest or savanna, mountain or plain, desert or well-watered region, and so on. Habitat and distribution are often expressed in much the same terms, as when it is said that the habitat of a snake is the "rain forest of Africa," its distribution the "rain forests of the Congo and adjacent countries."

World maps of rainfall and vegetation show reasonably definite zones based on moisture and temperature. The first of these zones, inhabited by the Boidae, straddles the Equator and is characterized by warm, heavy rains, which produce the equatorial rain forests. The next zone to the north has less rainfall and more noticeable rainy and dry seasons; it supports tropical savanna and grassland. The third zone, barely reached by the giant snakes, is one of rapidly decreasing rainfall; it culminates in the Sonora, the Sahara, the Arabian, and the Persian deserts. A similar succession can be distinguished south of the Equator, though less clearly.

The first two of these zones make up the tropics, the most familiar limits of which are those imaginary lines known as the tropics of Cancer and Capricorn. Certain isotherms (70° annual, 70° or 60° January) have been suggested as more scientific demarcations, but these closely approximate the tropics of Cancer and Capricorn.

Elevation has great significance for animal life, because temperature decreases with ascent as well as with progress in a northerly or southerly direction (from the Equator). Changes in vegetation and other elements of the environment accompany rise in temperature. For every sixty-eight miles or so traversed north or south of the Equator, there is a drop of about one degree Fahrenheit; one would have to ascend approximately 300 feet to experience the same reduction. Thus, a python at 5,000 feet in central Africa would contend with average temperatures sixteen degrees lower than another living at low altitudes. Reptiles, being relatively sensitive to thermal changes, are affected even more than mammals and birds.

DISTRIBUTION AND HABITATS OF THE GIANTS

Each of the six giants has its special range and its own preferences in regard to habitat.

Anaconda: This species is found on Trinidad and generally over tropical South America east of the Andes. Thus, it occupies the heart of the Neotropical region. It is one of the three completely tropical giants and stands out among these by having a large proportion of its range south of the Equator. In fact, its range extends over a greater area in the Southern Hemisphere than does that of any of the other giants except the boa constrictor. The Andes and southernmost South America are too cold and dry for it, and most of the lowlands west of the Andes are also too dry.

The anaconda, the only one of the six giants that is truly aquatic, has the most distinct habitat preference. A liking for either sluggish or still waters, rather than clear, swift-flowing rivers and streams, confines it to the lowest average altitudes of any. It is not surprising that swamps are a favorite haunt. There is no specific information about the distance that anacondas wander from water; William Beebe never found one far from water in the jungle of British Guiana.

Climbing seems to be restricted to limited activity on trunks and branches over water where it can bathe in the sun.

Boa constrictor: The boa constrictor, the more handsome of the New World giants, is widely distributed from northern Argentina in the south to Sonora and Tamaulipas in the north. The northernmost place where it has been found in Sonora lies only 150 miles from the Arizona border and slightly beyond the limits of the Neotropical region, in the Nearctic. In Tamaulipas it is found about 40 miles south of the Tropic of Cancer, but in tropical forests. The tropical conditions that prevail far northward on both coasts of Mexico have allowed this species to forge its way north, but it avoids the intervening highlands. The boa constrictor is not found in the Greater Antilles, although it does inhabit Trinidad and a few other islands of the Lesser Antilles.

No other giant has a range that extends beyond the limits of the tropics both on the north and on the south; thus, the boa constrictor surpasses the others in its adaptation to different habitats.

The boa constrictor and the anaconda illustrate a general rule that related species do not occupy the same region unless they have markedly different habitat preferences or habits, or both. Now, the range of the anaconda is totally within that of the boa constrictor, which means that the two might come into severe competition if something did not keep them apart. The significant factor is, undoubtedly, the selection of an aquatic habitat by one and a terrestrial habitat by the other. Among all the giants, the boa constrictor shows the least inclination to enter water, although it may do so occasionally; in contrast, it exhibits the greatest ability to adapt itself to arid conditions. The marked arboreal tendencies of this species would further accentuate the separation.

The boa constrictor thrives in jungle, savanna, and cultivated areas such as cane fields, from sea level to moderate elevations. A few samples of records of altitude suggest that much is to be learned about its vertical distribution: in Costa Rica it ascends to 3,000 feet, in El Salvador to 2,132, whereas in the state of Michoacán, in central Mexico, one was captured at about 2,600 feet.

The most detailed observations of this smaller giant have been made in Mexico. Paul S. Martin found its northeastern limits to be the tropical deciduous forest of southern Tamaulipas. Typically, this forest has trees of medium height. They are widely spaced and rise out of a dense, almost impenetrable understory of lower trees, which are leafless in winter. The altitude is low. On the opposite coast, we presume, it is the higher temperatures (summer maximum of about 110° F. or even higher) that allow penetration beyond the limits of the tropics well into the arid state of Sonora. Here Edward H. Taylor found a boa constrictor five feet aboveground in a tree cactus, another in a dry arroyo, and still another in the mouth of a cave. There is a recording of a specimen taken at an altitude of 1,485 feet near Guirocoba in Sonora. These boas of western Mexico show remarkable adaptability to dry conditions and to surprising altitudes even at northern latitudes.

The Michoacán specimen already mentioned was found coiled in the fork of a bush in a cleared area not far from a palm grove. Near Mazatlán, Sinaloa, a boa was discovered by Thomas H. Lewis and Murray L. Johnson "on a low, brush-covered bank, perforated with iguana holes, bounding a shallow salt-water lagoon." It had just seized one of the lizards living in the holes, but it released its prey and struck repeatedly.

Emmett R. Dunn's unusual study of tropical snakes was based on almost 12,000 specimens of the sixty-nine species known to inhabit the lowlands of Panama. Tabulation of these by frequency of occurrence showed that the boa constrictor approximated a median frequency among the fourteen most abundant species of four regions studied separately. Admittedly, Dunn's results are open to criticism: certain large, easily detected snakes are encountered more often than small ones having secretive habits. In general, however, the boa constrictor may be counted as a reasonably common snake of the lowlands of this country, and probably of other parts of Central America and adjacent South America and Mexico.

African rock python: The African rock python ranges over all of the well-watered parts of the Ethiopian region. It and the boa constrictor have the biggest ranges of any of our six giants; indeed, few snakes of any species can match them in this respect. They are the only two that range beyond the tropics in the Southern Hemisphere, whereas the boa constrictor and the Indian python do so north of the Equator.

I have found for the African species the greatest number of references, technical and otherwise, to habitat preferences. Deserts and other arid regions are not inhabited; there is universal agreement on this. By far the most numerous reports describe this giant as a denizen of savannas, of many kinds and altitudes. No general type of habitat is more widespread in Africa, and some savannas there, being extremely rugged in spots, support patches of low but rank vegetation of the kinds that afford excellent cover for large reptiles. The African rock python also frequents forests, but it greatly prefers clearings in them. In addition, it invades human habitations and cultivated fields.

There are surprisingly few references to the arboreal habits of African rock pythons, although enough of these snakes are encountered while climbing to prove that the species does climb occasionally. Its liking for savannas correlates with its lack of strong arboreal tendencies.

There is constant mention of aquatic habitats—big lakes, swamps, small rivers, and their borders. The African rock python has been met far out from shore and has been repeatedly taken in fish traps. Thus, there can be no doubt that this reptile is thoroughly at home in water. W. Uthmöller has stated that during the rainy season the African rock python leaves the water and wanders far over the land. This brings up the question of migration and makes us wonder how far individuals go and whether they ever set up permanent residence at some distance from water.

The several records dealing with altitude agree well enough. Charles R. S. Pitman has stated that the African rock python can be found as high as 7,500 feet in Uganda. Extensive studies, chiefly by French workers, in the high country of the great lakes, extending from the borders of Uganda southward, indicate ascent to at least 5,900; as the 4,000-foot level is approached, the records grow more numerous and no doubt the pythons themselves do. We may conclude that this reptile is certainly found at points lying between 6,000 and 7,000 feet, and possibly a little higher. Distance from the Equator is not relevant because the highlands in question lie, for the most part, within five degrees of this line; no part of them is farther north or south than ten degrees.

Indian python: The Indian python ranges from the valley of the

Indus River, in Pakistan, eastward (south of the Tibetan plateau) across northern India, Burma, and southern China to the South China Sea. To the southeast, it reaches Borneo, Java, Sumbawa, and Celebes, but apparently is not found on Sumatra or the Malay Peninsula. Thus, it ranges widely over the Oriental region.

In northern India and adjacent areas it seems to surpass the limits of the tropics by attaining considerable altitudes in the mountains. The hiatus in its southeastern distribution is a puzzle. Conceivably, man took it to the East Indies and inadvertently allowed it to become feral only on certain islands.

The Indian python ascends to elevations comparable to those reached by the African rock python. Frank Wall put the limit at 6,000 feet, and another report states that it is fairly common up to 5,500 feet in southern India. I published records for 1,000 and 1,500 feet in Fukien and Yunnan provinces of China.

In 1921 Wall gave a detailed account of the haunts of the Indian python, and this can scarcely be improved upon. I summarize his main points: For the most part, this species frequents jungles and may be found in tracts of dense forest as well as in the sparse growth of rocky hill slopes. In country devoid of forests, it inhabits rivers and bodies of still water. (Presumably, Wall means the borders of such bodies rather than the water itself, but, in any case, the water would be entered constantly.) This species is so fond of water that it might be considered semi-aquatic, and Wall reports seeing one individual remain submerged for half an hour and another keep its head under water for fifteen minutes. The Indian python also has strong arboreal tendencies.

Reticulate python: This giant of Asia ranges throughout the peninsula of southeastern Asia (the Indochinese Peninsula) and southward through the islands of the Oriental region and those of the transition zone between the Oriental and Australian regions. It is found in the Philippine Islands, but not on New Guinea.

There has been contention over the haunts of the reticulate python. Wall's statement that it frequents only the "densest jungle" has been denied by more than one other authority. Stanley S. Flower, Malcolm Smith, and Felix Kopstein have described it as living near human habitations, the first two showing that it may be common even in the ·middle of large cities. Smith used to catch small individuals every year in his compound, which was within 100 yards of Bangkok's main thoroughfare.

Another contention is over aquatic tendencies. Some reports have the reticulate python living only near water, whereas others describe it in situations that can hardly be considered aquatic; the answer must be that the reticulate python thrives in both situations. Like the Indian python, it is a good climber, and it has even been reported as living chiefly in trees. We would like to know just how the habitat preferences of these two competitors differ.

The reticulate python is chiefly an inhabitant of tropical lowlands, although it has been found at 4,000 feet in Java. The limits of its range do not extend beyond the tropics.

Amethystine python: The amethystine python has a range that conforms little to any of the zoogeographic regions, but cuts across two of them. It inhabits the northern Australian region from Queensland (subspecies *kinghorni*) northward through New Guinea and adjacent islands, and across the eastern part of the transition zone to the southern Philippine archipelago (Mindanao), in the Oriental region. It also reaches the Solomon Islands, but not Celebes. This giant comes near being an island species.

The amethystine python is strictly tropical. It has been credited with living in trees in the East Indies, and an Australian python took refuge in a tree when discovered. It also has aquatic tendencies. Eric Worrell's excellent account of a hunt indicates that it has a preference for wild, rugged country, but other reports show that it is also found near human habitations and may even raid fowl yards.

The Beatrice and Johnstone rivers form a junction (2,500 feet, altitude) in the bottom of the Johnstone River gorge of the Atherton Tableland, in northeastern Queensland. This tableland lies at the base of Cape York Peninsula and attains a maximum altitude of 5,438 feet.

The hunt described by Worrell started early one morning after a party of nine hardy men had scrambled for 2,000 feet down the wild, precipitous sides of the Johnstone River gorge to the junction of the two rivers, where a series of rapids, a great number of huge boulders, flat expanses of rock, and impenetrable jungle create a wild scene. Much of the remaining part of the day was spent searching in the vicinity of the junction and up the Beatrice River. Thirteen pythons were caught, all of them sighted as they lay on rock or in grass along the stream, but no mention is made of any of them taking to water to escape. The success of these hunters suggests but does not prove that riverbanks are a preferred habitat of these snakes.

Meeting the World

Senses

THE SNAKE's way of perceiving the outside world differs radically from ours. Snakes have two sense organs entirely lacking in man—facial pits and Jacobson's organ. They all but lack ability to perceive sound transmitted through the air, but they readily perceive sound carried by solid matter and they lean heavily on odor. Snakes do not have the sense of taste, and they use vision only to a limited degree.

VISION

I shall begin with vision, not only because an unblinking lid, the transparent eye cap or "spectacle," makes the snake's eye unusual among those of land vertebrates but because it has a unique organization and an astonishing history. Both literally and figuratively, there is nothing like it for the student of comparative anatomy. Any eye is such a complex structure that even the briefest account of it would take pages of print; a few broad generalizations, then, will have to serve. Those who would pursue the matter further are referred to the monograph by Gordon L. Walls, which, like the snake's eye, is unique; its 689 pages are so lucidly written and clearly illustrated that the lay reader can enjoy and understand all but the highly technical sections.

The snake's eye, to begin with, differs as much from the eye of all its relatives (other reptiles and birds) as does the eye of mammals from that of amphibians (frogs, including toads, and salamanders). Lizards, close cousins of snakes, have "normal" eyes, the snakes having lost certain parts that we would expect to have been passed on to them from their lizard ancestors: scleral cartilage and ossicles, ciliary processes, annular pad, and iris muscles. Even without knowing just what all these are, or the purposes they serve, we wonder how an organ that has been deprived of so much is able to function. The answer is simple: substitutes were developed to such an extent that the snake's eye is chiefly a bundle of substitutes. For instance, Walls states this about the ophidian retina: "The snakes alone have rung as many changes upon their visual-cell patterns as have all the other vertebrates put together."

The serious researcher ordinarily feels obliged to offer an explanation for the origin of so aberrant a structure, and Walls has not failed us. He believes that the early snakes lived underground and there came near to extinction. During this precarious period they nearly lost the eyes through degeneration, but finally recovered by means of an astounding evolutionary revival. All those substitutes were necessary to restore the organs to usefulness for an aboveground, daylight life. The same theory nicely accounts for the loss of movable eyelids, limbs, and ear elements. Just what survives in the ophidian eye, and how does it work? The retina of vertebrates has either or both of two types of cells, the rods and the cones. The former are dim-light receptors, the latter bright-light receptors. Primitive snakes, including the boas and pythons, have both types of cells. The more advanced groups, such as the huge family of ordinary snakes (Colubridae), typically have only cones, though some have become secondarily nocturnal and have developed special rods from cones. This fits Walls's evolutionary theory and is part of that great adaptability described above.

The iris is responsible for controlling the size of the pupil, the opening through which light is admitted to the retina. Regulation of the size of this opening is all-important in the working of eyes; the amount of light admitted must be enough to stimulate but should not dazzle or injure. A pupil that is always round has limitations in its ability to shut out light; it cannot close completely. In contrast, one that, though round when expanded, closes to a slit like the cat's pupil can shut out the light more effectively. An animal with a highly sensitive retina must either stay out of bright light or develop a pupil that shuts down to a slit. Some snakes have such a pupil.

The cones are important for color vision. The ability of snakes to perceive color has not been studied very extensively, but what little has been done suggests that they have color vision, chiefly at the red end of the spectrum. The significance of such an ability in snakes (if, indeed, they have it) is evident when we recall that the vast majority of mammals are color-blind (that is, have achromatic vision); man and the apes happen to be notable exceptions. The cones of birds and most reptiles have oil droplets (one to a cone) that promote acuity of color vision, but the snake eye lacks these; diurnal species have a yellowish lens serving the same purpose. Another substitute!

The ability to focus the eyes on objects at various distances is technically known as accommodation. We human beings accomplish this by releasing lateral tension on the lens, thus causing its shape to change through inherent elasticity. Birds and most reptiles, excluding water snakes, get the same result solely by bringing direct pressure on the lens, thus altering the curvature of its anterior surface. The snakes developed a method like that of the amphibians: the firm lens is itself moved forward or backward, an act that has the same effect as changing the shape of the lens.

Embryological studies have shown that the eye cap of the snake is formed of fused lids, the lower accounting for the greater part. Some lizards have lower lids with "windows" in them, convenient for keeping out particles such as sand grains. In the snake this arrangement is carried to its extreme, a permanently protected, unblinking eye, which promotes convenience in going from air to water and back.

There is a general belief that, in the course of evolution, the eyes of vertebrate groups have tended to shift from the lateral position, as in the rabbit, to one that allows the lines of vision to lie parallel, as in man. Actually, within each of three vertebrate groups (fishes, birds, and mammals), a complete series of positions can be found. The only generalization is that the predators tend to have forward-vision eyes, better for pursuit, whereas the hunted tend to retain the laterally placed eyes, better for detection of prey approaching from any direction.

The dividend of the forward position is binocular vision: overlapping of the two visual fields. This seems to have been developed even at the expense of the greater width of the single-eye field. In animals of prey, the acuity gained by overlapping is of value in pursuit and capture.

As snakes are predatory animals, it is not surprising to find in them a preponderance of wide binocular fields. The range given by Walls is from 20° to 46° overlap. About half of his nineteen species have 38° or more. The overlap in man is 140°; in the domestic cat it is a little less, but the cat has a total visual field of 287° compared with 180° in man, nearly 360° in the horse, and complete periscopy (360°) in some rodents. For thirteen of the same nineteen species of snakes, one eye's range of vision is from 146° to 168°. A single human eye sees through 150°, a cat's through 200°. None of the giant snakes is included in Walls's study. The only related datum given for one of them is the angle between the optic axes of the Indian python, which is 137°. This same angle in the seven other species listed (none of them boas or pythons) ranges from 110° to 165°. (The optic axis is a line through the centers of the curvature of lens and cornea; it would run through a point in the approximate center of vision of, let us say, a human eye looking straight forward.)

Man is able to increase his field of vision considerably by rotating his eyes. The snake's eye is capable of only limited rotation.

Experiments and observation indicate that the eye is not especially important to snakes, which are shortsighted. They are prone to rely on the sense of smell, used in two ways, rather than sight. Yet the motion of objects coming within their field of vision plays a definite role, especially for the initiation of feeding and courtship reactions.

HEARING

Snakes lack an external ear, ear opening, tympanum (eardrum), tympanic cavity, and Eustachian tube. One of the bones that transmit vibrations to the vertebrate eardrum is, in the snake, connected to the quadrate, the hinge bone of the lower jaw. It seems likely that the mere act of swallowing would produce a loud noise in the snake's head. This unusual arrangement hardly appears to be set up for transmission of air-borne sound waves. Indeed, experiments indicate that the snake is indifferent to sounds as we ordinarily think of them.

This does not mean that vibrations carried through the ground or any other solid material in close contact with the snake are not quickly sensed, for they certainly are. Air waves strong enough to cause solids to vibrate would, of course, be indirectly perceived long before the shortsighted eyes give notice. With virtually all of its body applied to the ground, a snake may well become conscious of the step of any nearby heavy animal. For the giant snake lurking by trail or water hole, awareness of approaching mammals would be important.

HEAT-SENSITIVE LABIAL PITS

Now we come to a sense organ we lack entirely and must use our imagination to comprehend. Some 5 per cent of living snakes have

39

heat-sensitive organs in their heads known as facial pits. The pits can be readily divided into two types: those found in the pit vipers (a subfamily of the Viperidae) and those of the Boidae. The pits of the pit vipers are by far the more complex in respect to structure, yet anything but complex in other aspects: there is always one on each side of the head, and every one has the same basic organization. The pits of the pythons and boas, known specifically as labial pits, are, in contrast, depressions in the scales that border the mouth and vary greatly in number and structure. In a single snake they will range from large, deep, conspicuous hollows occupying almost entire scales to tiny ones that are mere dots in a big scale. Nearly all pythons, as currently classified, have pits.

Labial pits are useful to us in distinguishing one species of giant python from another. For example, the African rock python and the Indian python have a deep pit in each of the first two of the upper-lip scales (on either side), whereas the reticulate python and the amethystine python have such a pit in each of the first four of these scales. The number and distribution of the pits in the lower-lip scales are too variable and complex to consider, no two of the four species just mentioned being alike in lower-lip pit pattern. Labial pits may even vary in number from individual to individual of the same species.

The boa constrictor and the anaconda, like many other boas, are readily distinguished from our four giant pythons by the absence of (labial) pits.

Among the many pit vipers are the rattlesnakes, the water moccasin, and the copperhead—that is, all of the highly venomous snakes of the United States except the coral snakes. The pit is a deep cavity having inner and outer chambers. These are separated by a thin membrane richly supplied with nerves from the ophthalmic and supramaxillary branches of the fifth cranial nerve. The nerve tips of the membrane connect with large sensory cells. Even for anyone who does not understand the full significance of these names, they suggest that the pit is some sort of a sense organ. In spite of the relative simplicity of the labial pits of the pythons and boas (the membrane and inner chamber are entirely lacking), the nerve supply is like that of the pit vipers. The difference would lead the anatomist to the conclusion that these two types of pits with similar function have separate developmental histories: they are analogous though not homologous.

Here we have the kind of a situation which fascinates the student of evolution: two unrelated groups of snakes with sense organs very different in structure yet similar in service to their possessors. The snake is unconcerned about how pits evolved as long as they work; let the student of evolution worry about the problem. Actually, students worried for a century or more about both form and function, but it took the special techniques of the twentieth century to solve the problem. G. S. West and W. Gardner Lynn made the basic anatomical studies. Several years elapsed after Lynn's report, published in 1931, before experimental work proved that the pits are heat-sensitive organs, or, more technically, thermal receptors.

The more elaborate experiments have been carried on with the pit-viper type of pit. Working with the actual nerves, T. H. Bullock and Raymond B. Cowles found that these showed marked sensitivity to radiant heat reaching the membrane of the pit. For example, heat from a human hand held at a distance of about one foot elicited a response. Thus we see that the pit could make the pit viper aware of "warm-blooded" prey or enemies at a considerable distance. In earlier experiments, G. K. Noble and A. Schmidt, using light bulbs of different temperatures, had arrived at the same general conclusion with a simpler technique; both boas and pit vipers were the subjects of their experiments. The pits of the boas and pythons call for experimental work of the kind performed by Bullock and Cowles.

When taking care of Sylvia, I noticed that her breath was expelled backward over the top of her head. This would be advantageous to an animal that depends partly on warm prey for food:

air blown straight forward would interfere with detection of slight heat radiation.

JACOBSON'S ORGAN AND CHEMORECEPTION

The other important type of sensory reception peculiar to snakes has no ordinary name because man does not possess its counterpart. We smell with our noses and taste with our tongues. The snake's nostrils work much as ours do, but in its tongue it has only the sense of touch. Yet its tongue serves another use—that of stimulating a special sense organ in the roof of the mouth called Jacobson's organ.

We run into trouble because Jacobson's organ, being reached through the roof of the mouth, strongly suggests an organ of taste. Embryological studies indicate, however, that the sense aroused by stimulation of this organ is probably smell rather than taste.

A way of simplifying the whole matter is to put the human senses of smell and taste in the same category with the snake's senses of smell and perception via Jacobson's organ, calling the whole category chemoreception. Thus, chemoreception in snakes operates via either the nose or mouth. Chemoreception is based on a chemical reaction brought about at the surface of a moist receptor by solid, though often minute, particles; it contrasts sharply with sight, hearing, and touch.

Chemoreception is vastly more important to the snake than it is to us, a fact in part accountable for the proneness of these reptiles to tongue all objects, which is merely "chemoreceiving" (if I may coin a term) by transporting minute particles to Jacobson's organ. Recent experiments by Cowles and R. L. Phelan indicate that odor, as we think of it, may have much more significance for snakes than is usually believed, former research having shown how effectively snakes may trail prey by use of the tongue. Cowles and Phelan show that rattlesnakes are highly sensitive to odor, which serves as an alerting mechanism warning of impending danger. These experimenters think that even the faintest odors, arriving from a distance, arouse the snake, which then investigates further by means of its tongue and Jacobson's organ.

With reticulate and other species of pythons, Gustav Lederer performed many experiments designed to test their ability to (1) find a dead rabbit concealed at the end of a scent trail made with the rabbit and (2) find a perforated box having a rabbit concealed in it. His snakes apparently were able to sense the presence of the boxed rabbit by odor and to locate the buried rabbit with tongue and Jacobson's organ. The results strongly suggest that chemoreception is also important to pythons. Many variable factors enter into the picture, however, and final proof will come only with the use of elaborate physiological apparatus.

SENSE OF TOUCH; SUMMARY

The sense of touch is also fairly well developed in snakes. The skin is reasonably sensitive, and the tongue, as has been noted, undoubtedly is used as an organ of touch as well as an accessory in chemoreception.

Placing relative values on the types of perception in snakes is partly guesswork. But we can say with assurance that chemoreception is the most important, ordinary hearing the least. When we pity them for dependence on the chemical senses, we must recall that our sight is a part-time sense all but useless at night, whereas their chemoreception works well throughout the twenty-four hours and is somewhat improved by conditions prevailing at night. It is not surprising that snakes emerged from their subterranean period with chief reliance on senses that are independent of light.

Strength and Constriction

✷

THE QUESTION of strength first brings to mind the totality of an animal's power in dealing with prey or enemies; how well does the animal overpower an intended meal or defend itself against a ferocious enemy? The scientist is apt to break the problem down into its components and test, let us say, a given number of isolated muscle fibers. This will allow animals of different sizes to be compared with some accuracy. For example, it has been demonstrated that the muscle of the huge jumping leg of one kind of grasshopper is strong enough to snap its tendon; proportionately, it is ten times as strong as a human muscle. As far as I know, the isolated muscle of a giant snake has not been tested, but almost certainly such a muscle has nothing like the power of the grasshopper's; otherwise a constricting python or boa could literally pull itself apart.

Anyone might expect a snake to exhibit strength by biting; a lion crushes large bones, and other animals will bite off a hand or a foot. Nearly all snakes, in contrast, bite without applying appreciable pressure and quickly let go; it is next to impossible to experience the full strength of a snake's jaws. If, however, a snake can be persuaded to retain its grip and apply maximum pressure, the jaws do have astonishing power.

I was once handling a small snake that knew no fear of man because it had been hatched and reared in captivity. Suddenly decid-

African Rock Python. Different shades of light brown are blended in the ground color, whereas the markings are made up of blended shades of dark brown. Speckling is evident on the sides. The entire animal is iridescent. (Photograph by Isabelle Hunt Conant)

Ball Python (*Python regius*). This is a common species of western Africa. The average length is about 3 feet. (Courtesy Staten Island Zoo. Photograph by Carl F. Kauffeld)

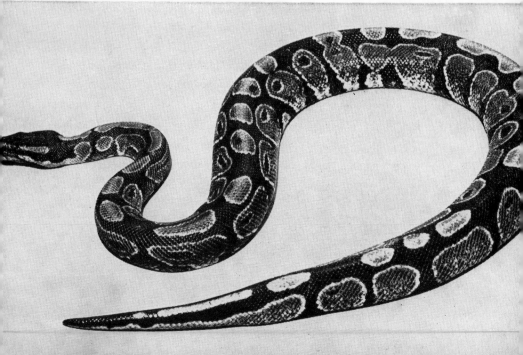

Reticulate Python. This gigantic female is 28½ feet long, 37½ inches in girth, and has an estimated weight of more than 320 pounds. Various shades of brown and yellow are blended with black in the pattern of this snake. The entire animal is iridescent. (Courtesy Highland Park Zoo, Pittsburgh. Photograph by William B. Allen, Jr.)

Reticulate Python. Highland Park Zoo giant in a cage tree. (Courtesy Highland Park Zoo. Photograph by William B. Allen, Jr.)

ing that my finger was edible (no doubt I had the odor of a mouse on my hand), it clamped down. My effort to get free only stimulated it to bite harder; the force exerted was far beyond what I had imagined, and getting it off without injuring the jaws—it was a highly prized pet—proved to be a task. My finger came through a lot the worse for wear. I should hate to have a large, friendly python mistake my arm for a tender morsel!

An interesting point here is that a boa or a python uses no such jaw strength in ordinary swallowing; pressure is exerted only if violent struggling of the victim makes it necessary. Sylvia, when small, started to swallow my son's big toe; the skin was barely penetrated, so delicately did she work. The boy luckily knew enough to call me rather than to put up resistance, and I managed to extract the toe almost undamaged.

The great snakes are commonly alleged to show their strength by butting. The blow of the head has been compared with that of a prize fighter's fist, and Kipling's Kaa could batter down walls. This is sheer foolishness; the snout of a snake is not only soft and tender but easily injured. Recent experiments by Walker Van Riper have shown that the strike of even a rattlesnake is slow; the head of a striking rattlesnake moves at the rate of but eight feet a second (about five and a half miles an hour). The python strikes no faster, if as fast, and the force of its blow would be no greater than that of any other object of similar size and weight moving at the same rate. If one sixth or one seventh of the front end of a 200-pound snake were projected forward at the rate of five or six miles an hour, the impact would be roughly similar to that of a trotting 30-pound dog bumping into a man. Such a bump would certainly be felt and might conceivably cause a loss of balance in a man unprepared for it, but the chance of injury by the impact itself would be negligible.

HANDLING GIANT SNAKES

Before coming to the crux of this matter by dealing in detail with the power exhibited in constriction, I shall give a brief account of the snakes' ability to resist being stretched out or pulled from a hole. Is there anyone who has not seen a picture of a dozen zoo keepers stretching out a python to be photographed or force-fed?

It is a rare human being who can struggle with a giant snake and retain enough objectivity to give a literal account later. R. M. Isemonger, who began handling snakes when he was a small boy, relates how he tried to pull an African rock python from a crevice in some big rocks. The snake, about 17 feet long, got three feet of head and neck into the hole and easily continued its retreat in spite of all Isemonger's efforts. He recruited help in the form of a 195-pound, six-foot-two friend and tried again. This time, in approximately the same position, the python resisted a combined pull of 350 pounds and escaped again. What more need be said?

It is clear that a 25-foot giant could easily defeat the combined effort of twelve men to get and keep all the kinks out of it. Conversely, it would be entirely unable to resist the total effort of so many men to hold it out *almost* straight. To stage a fair contest between man and giant snake would be nearly impossible because of the discrepancy in shape. I believe that a big professional wrestler could defend himself against a 20-foot python bent on constriction if the snake could be prevented from lacerating with its scores of teeth, all needle sharp and slanted toward the throat. But no python will ever be persuaded to enter such a contest with heart, to say nothing about the willingness of wrestlers.

The average white-collar worker, with his poor physical condition, would have little chance in such a contest because the sheer weight of the snake would bear him down and thus lose for him the help of gravity in pushing the many coils of the adversary down and off. More than one competent observer has expressed the conviction that a 12-foot boa or python, when yet untamed, is about all that even a man in good physical condition should tackle single-handed. Obviously, this should not be done unless the jaws are avoided in some way.

POWER OF CONSTRICTION

It would seem that constriction could be measured with an instrument concealed in a dummy scented to arouse the appetite of a big snake. As no one has ever performed such an experiment, we must draw on casual observations of snakes dealing with large prey. It is widely believed that a constricting giant "breaks every bone in the body" of a victim, but this is certainly fallacious. The questions are whether any bones are broken and whether failure to break bones is evidence of weak pressure. There is a fair amount of information that will help us to answer the first question, and I feel sure that failure to break bones is not evidence of weak power of constriction; it all depends on how the bones lie in relation to the pressure applied by the coils.

A constrictor that throws a series of neat coils about the body of an animal, so that one coil is against another, will apply even pressure from all directions. Such pressure could no more be expected to break bones than that of a wide elastic cloth wound around and around the animal. Death of the prey will result from suffocation and interference with circulation even if little or no pressure is applied. Just as in the case of the use of the jaws, the snake would not exert its entire strength. At the minimum, all it has to do is hold its ground once the coils have closed snugly about the animal; contraction of the prey's chest with each spasmodic effort to breathe will give the snake all the opportunity it needs. If several coils have been used, the friction of one against the other may make unnecessary the exertion of any pressure whatsoever.

The evidence against bone breaking far outweighs but by no

means negates the evidence for it. In evaluating reports, two points must be kept in mind: there is a strong tendency for any observer to "see" what he firmly hopes or expects to see; and any animal caught in the wilds might well break a few bones in violent efforts to escape before any coils have been thrown around it. Observations of animals in captivity are the best, because under such controlled conditions the violence of the pre-constriction struggle can be determined.

A report from India by P. Mash describes the killing of a 4-foot monitor (*Varanus monitor*) by an Indian python 8.5 feet long. Bones of the lizard were distinctly heard to crack during the long contest; the victim did not die for seventy-five minutes and was not swallowed for some time after death. Considering the shape of this giant lizard, it is not surprising that its ribs were broken. Charles R. S. Pitman's secondhand story of a circus performer having bones broken in eighty-four places is incredible, and his description of a gazelle whose bones were broken by an African rock python can be discounted because the event took place in the wilds. In spite of citing these two cases, Pitman is not really a believer. He remarks: "Bone-breaking force is unnecessary, and incidentally few snakes are capable of it."

Belief in bone breaking can be carried beyond reason. In the East Indies, L. Coomans de Ruiter heard of human python victims whose skulls were broken along with the other bones. Imagine the force required to crack a skull, even if our heads were large enough for a coil to take effect.

A. Sokolowsky writes of an event that took place in Stellingen, Germany, many years ago. A large captive reticulate python disgorged a female ibex whose neck was "broken" and other major joints disarticulated. The reasonable explanation is that the python had shaped the goat for convenient swallowing, and an observer of the act has stated as much. This story is clearly not evidence for the *breaking* of bones; all damage could have been done by stretching, and, as discussed later, there is additional evidence that snakes sometimes manipulate prey to shape it for easier swallowing.

Gustav Lederer, who has had experience with captive boas and pythons for three decades, presents the most convincing evidence against bone breaking. He failed to find a single broken bone in three piglets, three rabbits, and two rats killed, but not swallowed, by his giant snakes.

It is reasonable to conclude that bones are not ordinarily broken by the act of constriction, although under special conditions or in certain kinds of animals they may be. The matter calls for further investigation by observers with open minds and some knowledge of anatomy. When all is said and done, we can glean little information about giant-snake strength from bone breaking.

FLEXIBILITY OF THE VERTEBRAL COLUMN

Just how does the snake's body combine strength with flexibility? The basic unit is the vertebra, whose seven points of articulation (at each end) join it firmly with those of an adjacent vertebra. So effective is this articulation that only about 25 degrees of movement from side to side is allowed, and appreciably less up and down. The union between two vertebrae is not only firm but has little play. The giant constrictors (together with snakes in general) have extreme flexibility thanks to a great number of joints, as many as 350 (excluding those of the tail) in some cases. Each joint contributes its 25 degrees of movement, the result being that combination of firmness and flexibility already mentioned.

A convincing test can be made with a snake and a chain whose links are tightly joined. Bend both snake and chain and compare the results. The former will bend double more readily. Another interesting test can be made by twisting a dead snake (a living one may object) and then a length of chain with as many links in it as the snake has vertebrae. (A snake has one vertebra for every elongated, crosswise scale, or "plate," of the continuous series that covers the belly.) A twist of the tail will cause almost the entire snake to turn simultaneously. I have never seen a chain with links tight enough to turn as the snake does. The analogy breaks down somewhat because the chain's links are not bound together at all; however, the great difference in performance of snake and chain emphasizes the fact that the vertebrae *are* firmly held together.

Intelligence

✳

THE ACCURATE MEASUREMENT of intelligence is difficult even in mammals, with their quick and obvious responses. The apparent lack, or at least delay, of reactions in many reptiles and their dead-pan faces make them even more frustrating subjects; physiological apparatus comparable to the lie detector must often be used. In my opinion, reptiles are much more intelligent than we now realize; the next few decades should see a revolution in our concept of their ability to modify behavior as a result of learning.

The snake is an especially baffling subject, due in part to the form of its body, its unusual feeding habits, and the difficulty in finding a suitable stimulus. It is patent that instinct plays an important role in its activity, and preoccupation with this fact has kept the student from focusing on the significance of the snake's learning ability in coping with a new situation.

In spite of the current popularity of trial-and-error learning experiments, snakes have rarely been subjected to maze running. One set of experiments was a failure. Another yielded a typical learning curve in a "T" maze, in which the sense of touch was more important than vision, the snakes largely feeling their way. Running a large python through a maze would, indeed, be exciting work.

A more subjective consideration of snake intelligence allows several approaches, and these I shall take up after citing the observations of Raymond L. Ditmars and Grace Olive Wiley. The former, after a long life of work with snakes and some actual experiments, concluded that the king cobra was the most intelligent species he had observed. Grace Olive Wiley, a fanatic on venomous snakes as pets, convinced herself that this species was more easily tamed than any other she had worked with. Various species of rattlers tenderly cared for by her manifested recognition in many ways. Some would, for instance, rattle at the approach of anyone else.

It is interesting that Ditmars and Wiley, using entirely different methods—one never taking risks, the other blandly confident that all snakes would love her—independently arrived at the same conclusion about the king cobra. Ditmars had the safe way. Only dedicated persons who literally love animals and feel that they are almost human can, with the aid of infinite patience, safely get the results that Wiley did. Finally, after several decades of handling dangerous snakes, she was killed by a cobra, which she too obligingly demonstrated only after being persistently urged to do so by a visitor who had come thousands of miles; the snake had not yet been sufficiently tamed.

The first of the subjective approaches considers snakes in relation to man. Many fanciers in addition to Wiley have felt certain that their pets recognized them as individuals, and keepers have had similar opinions about their charges. The historic example is a report by Charles Darwin that the keeper in the London zoo credited the rattlesnake and the python with this ability. Darwin was obviously using these terms in a generic sense.

That snakes in general, including our giants, readily become tame is well known. Both Sylvia and Blue Boy (a captive reticulate python) are illustrations of this. There is no need to enumerate more cases, but I cannot refrain from repeating Robert Mertens's account of four amethystine pythons, two of them about 16 feet long. Though captured only a few days before they were observed by Mertens, these snakes seemed unconcerned when released from their bags and could safely be returned to them without caution; it was not even necessary to tie the bags if the openings were tucked under the snakes. Though temperament differs from individual to individual, I hazard the statement that any hatchling or newborn giant snake can be tamed by daily gentle handling. This change involves learning of a sort.

H. Hediger, in his fascinating book on the effects of captivity, relates how an African rock python retreated, through shyness, to its water basin, where it remained for weeks on end. When the basin was drained and part of it got very hot, the giant refused to leave, and consequently got badly burned. Although strong reaction to captivity, rather than lack of intelligence, is probably responsible for this type of behavior, it is worth mentioning for the benefit of keepers and fanciers. Such results will be the experience of all who fail to take extraordinary precautions in protecting their charges.

In the chapter on Feeding Habits, I discuss at length the capture of multiple prey. Certainly the snake's ability to cope with more than one food item at a time can be regarded as a sign of intelligence —as also can their shaping of bulky prey for easier swallowing. When hungry, Lederer's reticulate pythons became restless in the evening, often crawling about the cage, repeatedly extending the tongue. P. Chalmers Mitchell and R. I. Pocock long ago reported restlessness correlated with hunger in giant snakes; also, that the movement of persons in the passageway behind the cages was noticed. Laurence M. Klauber remarks on the attentiveness of rattlesnakes at the approach of a keeper, the rearing up and facing the door, the ability to recognize the regular attendant as well as to distinguish a feeding forceps from a cleaning implement. Such behavior appears to be modified to suit a special occasion and therefore should be considered the result of learning.

A more complex aspect of the snakes in relation to food is the eating of foreign objects. Several zoo pythons have swallowed their blankets, as popular writers like to relate. There are, too, many records of snakes being tricked by nest eggs; I once found a wooden egg in the stomach of a rat snake caught near a chicken house in Arkansas. Keepers learn to be duly careful about putting their hands near hungry snakes after handling rats, mice, or birds.

These examples suggest low intelligence and seem to be contradictory to my general thesis. The natural interest in such errors causes them to be unreasonably emphasized; who would bother to recall the countless times that captives do not devour scented objects or, after tonguing a hand, decide against seizing it? There certainly are degrees of hunger; starving human beings eat things they know have no nourishment in them.

Lederer, using the scientific method to study this problem of deception, secured puzzling results of considerable interest. Two hundred and fifty trials with various python species resulted in only one actual seizure of a model prey. Even replicas of rats and rabbits made of wool, cotton, and other substances, and scented with freshly killed animals, failed to elicit the seizure reflex in hungry reticulate, Indian, and African rock pythons. As movement by prey is known to be important for recognition of it, the models were moved in front of the snakes, and they still did not seize them.

Next we shall consider whether snakes can tell one end of the prey from the other and, if so, how. In many cases it may make little difference, though in others swallowing the wrong way presents great difficulties and may even be impossible. E. E. Brown determined how 200 items had been swallowed in nature by the common water snake (*Natrix sipedon*), and he found that 80 per cent had gone down headfirst and nearly all of the rest tailfirst. He found that the young snakes were more careful than their elders to take the prey headfirst, a discovery contrary to what might be expected: experience should teach the older snakes to seize the head first. Here the relative size of prey to predator is very significant; the young individuals might have been unable to swallow tailfirst many of the (relatively large) food items, whereas the large snakes could easily get the smaller fishes down either way.

Lederer had under his care a young Indian python that nearly always tried to swallow prey tailfirst, and a reticulate python about 11 feet long which occasionally swallowed guinea pigs this way. He also writes of a half-grown boa (*Corallus hortulanus*) that sometimes seized its prey in the middle of the body and bent it double; an extra squeeze was consequently required to prepare it for swallowing. The ages of these snakes and the fact that they were living as captives (if not also born as such) may be factors; at any rate, the cases are too few for valid conclusions. According to Lederer, O. Heinroth believes that the direction of the hair growth on mammals gives the snake its cue for headfirst swallowing. This is a theory that could readily be tested.

It has been pointed out by D. F. Munro that young racers (*Coluber constrictor*) usually subdue their prey in a manner unlike that of adults. It is possible that the adult learns its more effective method from experience. Be that as it may, the giant snakes from the start of life resort to one method: constriction.

It is possible to catch a giant snake by getting it to swallow large bait placed in a pen of stakes set just close enough together to allow the predator to enter; it cannot escape with a great lump in its belly. Were the snake highly intelligent, perhaps it would either comprehend the danger and curb its appetite or, having made the mistake, escape by disgorging the prey. As far as I can determine, no python or boa has ever demonstrated such foresight or realized that its freedom could be gained by the simple act of vomiting. As fright will sometimes cause a snake surprised in the act of eating to disgorge its prey, why should being trapped fail to do the same!

It is highly probable that snakes vary considerably in degree of intelligence from group to group, and even from species to species within a group. The rating of the king cobra as especially intelligent is a case in point. There are marked differences among mammals (even when man is excepted) and among birds, so we should expect to find a comparable situation among snakes.

Locomotion

As a snake glides over rough ground it appears to defy some
natural law. Though this apparently effortless motion has always
fascinated man, he acquired an understanding of snake locomotion
only a few decades ago. A largely fruitless study made by E. Home
in the early 1800's may be taken as the beginning of the scientific
approach, and the lapse of time between this work and the recent
successful efforts is some indication of the difficulty involved. The
mere determination and naming of the various types of locomotion
have given a great deal of trouble.

One type, common to all snakes, is used more than the others
combined. This is lateral, or horizontal, undulatory progression,
aptly named so as to refute a widespread belief that the undulations
of a crawling snake are vertical like waves of water. Actually, the
entire body of an undulating snake stays against the ground.

After this universal type of movement come two that might be
called specialized; one is used by heavy-bodied snakes when not
hurrying, the other by a limited number of species for progressing
over sand or other shifty ground.

The first of these, rectilinear (or "caterpillar") locomotion, is
characteristic of our six giants, all of them being heavy-bodied and
not easily hurried. A snake using this type moves forward at a
uniform rate, the body held straight.

The other method, highly developed in certain desert snakes and the most perplexing of all, is known as "sidewinding." The sidewinder, advancing at an angle to the expected direction, loops along. In reality, it is progressing with minimum backward thrust; ordinarily it moves over a surface that offers little resistance. To a slight degree, this movement contradicts the statement that the crawling snake has no vertical undulations; the sidewinder raises the body slightly upward by sections, moves these forward, and puts them down again. It goes without saying that our six giants, in view of the type of country they prefer, have little use for sidewinding. A 25-foot python sidewinding would be a sight to behold.

A few principles involved in the two types of progression important to giant snakes are worth considering. First, for lateral undulatory locomotion, the body must be thrown into one or more curves and a point at the back of each curve pushed against projections of the ground. If a snake is put on a piece of oiled glass, it cannot advance because there is nothing to resist the push; a row of pegs attached to the glass will enable it to crawl with no difficulty and, at the same time, demonstrate its dependence on pivot points. When put on sand, the snake will show this dependence more clearly. If the resistance of the sand increased, the speed of the snake would do so too.

Study of the rectilinear, or straight-line, type of progression brings up several points of anatomy. At a distance the snake seems to glide along, but close inspection reveals rearward waves of movement of the long scales that lie across the belly. These waves are made by muscles attached to the skin. As a snake has a pair of ribs for each of the crosswise scales, early observers reasonably assumed that the ribs were moving the scales, the snake literally walking on its ribs. It took some careful experimentation to dispel this false assumption.

One clever method of detection is described by H. W. Lissmann. He attached lead disks to the tips of the crosswise scales and to the crest of the back of a boa constrictor about 23 inches long. As the snake crawled, Lissmann X-rayed it from above. The photographs showed that the disks attached to the scales shifted their position relative to the tips of the ribs, while the ribs did not move relative to the bones of the back. The ribs act as almost stationary anchors for the muscles that move the crosswise scales backward and forward in waves. Two opposing muscles extend from each rib to the belly skin; one slopes backward from the rear surface of the rib, the other forward from its lower end. Successive contractions of groups of such muscles will produce the waves. Rectilinear progression requires no lever action of bones, a characteristic that apparently distinguishes the snake as a unique type among vertebrate animals.

Just as the numerous ribs once suggested feet, so the overlapping scales across the belly bring to mind the action of a ratchet. Many accounts explain that the slightly raised edges of these scales, or "plates," catch on projections and thus prevent slipping. Believing that friction of the belly with the ground is sufficient, I tested Sylvia on linoleum, which, being smooth, is free of projections. When weighing but 22 pounds she was able to give an even forward pull of 4 pounds, evidence that catching on projections by means of the scales is entirely unnecessary. Moreover, the giant snakes have such short crosswise ventral scales that much of the belly on either side of them is in contact with the ground. I am convinced that the scale edges take no such direct part in rectilinear crawling in these or in any other snakes. If they did, they would become frayed in wild individuals, a condition I have looked for in vain.

So persistently do the giant snakes depend on rectilinear or very slow undulatory locomotion that at least one experienced snake man reported he had never seen one accelerate. I have been fortunate enough to observe Sylvia on at least one occasion break into a "run," or the equivalent; in an obvious effort to increase her speed, she momentarily threw her body into rapid undulations. Lissmann implies that his boa constrictor could do the same, and Charles M.

Bogert states that a small Cuban species of boa (*Tropidophis melanurus*) is even capable of sidewinding; any sidewinding snake can, of course, progress by simple undulating.

Snakes leave tracks when they crawl over sand, on ground with a soft surface, or through dust; an animal with its weight so evenly distributed would not be expected to do so under other conditions. Henry C. Raven has given a graphic description of the trail left by a python in a jungle in Borneo; among the signs were a crushed piece of dead wood and moss scraped off a tree. He probably saw the track of a huge reticulate python that, having just swallowed a large animal, found it difficult to drag an overloaded belly through the jungle. Ordinarily, a python would not leave such signs, for no foot-long section of it could weigh more than a few pounds, a small part of the weight on a human foot.

The form of track obviously reveals the type of progression and even offers a clue to the speed. A straight track would hardly be that of a snake in a big rush. Only a sidewinding snake leaves a discontinuous track, a series of staggered but parallel impressions, straight except for a J-shaped tip made by the head at one end. The direction of the undulating individual can readily be determined from the pile of sand at the *rear* of each curve. For rectilinear locomotion, the direction can be worked out only when there are small depressions in the ground. As the scales drag sand or dirt into these only on the side first reached, close examination will reveal the direction of travel.

OVERLAND SPEED

The spinner of yarns about snakes should abhor the stop watch as much as the teller of tales about fish fears the tape measure. Careful measurements have proved beyond question that man is faster than the snake. This at once dispels the dread of being overtaken by any snake; a rapid walk will leave behind the vast majority of them.

Exceedingly few snakes ever pursue man, but even the speediest can crawl at the rate of only seven or eight miles an hour, which is about a third of the maximum speed for the fastest man. Snakes also have low endurance, due in part to a type of heart and circulation that prevents prolonged strenuous muscular activity. No one seems to have tested carefully the ability of the swift snakes to maintain their speed, but certainly it is not comparable to that of man or horse.

Our six giants are among the slowest of snakes of moderate or great size because they depend so largely on rectilinear, or straight-line, locomotion. J. Stevenson-Hamilton estimated the rate of crawl of an African rock python in the open as one mile an hour, whereas Sylvia's crawl was incredibly slow: in three five-minute periods she covered only twenty-six feet nine inches, twenty-six feet, and twenty-five feet eleven inches. At that rate, it would take her seventeen hours to crawl a mile! She was not hurried, however, and could probably move much faster in a straight line, possibly at the rate of one mile an hour.

G. E. Shaw, E. O. Shebbeare, and P. E. Barker have stated that a half-grown Indian python, caught unawares, "outdistanced" them on a river bed. This sounds like gross exaggeration, but it does fall in line with my observation that Sylvia, though she rarely did so, could make rapid undulations; surely the python of the river bed was moving by undulations. A species tested by Walter Mosauer in his classic experiments was the rosy boa (*Lichanura roseofusca*), one of the two members of the Boidae found in the United States. In the tests, this reptile, which grows to be only two or three feet long, prowled at a rate of almost one tenth of a mile an hour and exhibited a top speed of 0.224 miles an hour.

SWIMMING AND CLIMBING

Swimming is natural to a snake for several reasons: the body is buoyant and makes extensive contact with the water, which the polished scales readily shed; submersion of the head causes no discomfort, because of the watertight eye caps and an ability to suspend breathing for long periods of time; the normal undulations of crawling are typical swimming movements. All our six giants are adept swimmers with some degree of liking for water.

Three generalizations can be made about climbing: snakes in general have some ability to climb, although many show little desire to do so; some habitually climbing snakes have a body shape or scale structure that enables them to climb readily. Many tree snakes are so slender and light that it is all but impossible for them to fall through foliage; even leaves will sustain them. Other arboreal species are not slender and yet they can go up the vertical trunk of a tall, rough-barked tree by literally crawling upward with the help of ridges, one along either side of the belly. The ridges catch on the projections of the bark to give ample support.

Pictures of snakes wrapped around a tree like a ribbon around a Maypole are misleading; occasionally such a position may be taken, but usually only when the trunk is very small in comparison with the snake. William Beebe has illustrated a method by which a tropical snake (*Leptophis*) climbed a bamboo stem. It threw S-shaped coils around one half the circumference of the bamboo and maintained a grip by exerting pressure on opposite sides of the stem. Incidentally, a snake can "walk a rope" by draping sections of its body alternately on the sides, an arboreal application of horizontal undulatory progress.

The giant snakes, though lacking structural advantages such as belly ridges, readily climb trees and crawl among branches that will support them. But resting on light foliage and ascending straight trunks are, obviously, kinds of arboreal activities they must forgo. On the island of Hainan, I released a 9-foot Indian python at a large banyan tree. It climbed with agility and rested on the small leafed limbs at the very top; to recover it, I had to shoot the limbs off.

The ability of the giant snakes to get about in the three environments of the tropical forest—the aquatic, the terrestrial, and the arboreal—leaves no refuge for their unfortunate prey.

Activity

THIS CHAPTER treats primarily of the "diel" activity of the giants. "Diel" is a simple, convenient word to use instead of "daily," which is ambiguous, because it may either include or exclude night. The diel activity of an animal is that of day and night taken as a unit of twenty-four consecutive hours. The diel cycle is divided into day, night, dawn, and dusk.

Man, with his good vision but relatively poor sense of smell, is admirably suited to daylight living, and he may well wonder why any creatures ever became nocturnal. The immediate ancestors of the vertebrates, the chordates, were bright-light animals. The early fishes developed the first rods (dim-light receptors) and extended their sphere by venturing into the safer, though relatively lightless, depths. The first land animals, being without carnivorous enemies, were able to enjoy light and sunshine to the fullest extent. But competition increased as they multiplied, and some took up nocturnal activity to escape predators. Mammals, for the most part, became either nocturnal or crepuscular (active at dusk). Owls and some other birds are night prowlers.

The early reptiles were strictly diurnal, but many of the groups now living have become nocturnal or at least partly so. The snake's eye is unique as an organ that apparently underwent degeneration and adaptation resulting in a condition like that of an eye suited to nocturnal existence. This is the type found in the pythons and boas, which are in turn primitive snakes. As noted in the chapter on Senses, the giant snakes have both dim-light and bright-light receptors. The primitive pure-cone eye was useless at night but gave great acuity of vision during the day. On the other hand, the rod-rich retina provides low visual acuity at night and yet is not entirely useless in the daytime.

Snakes, like all creatures that depend so much on the absorption of heat in order to maintain a tolerable body temperature, are prone to sun themselves, even if they prowl at night. Yet they must avoid excessive dry heat. For this reason, rattlesnakes, because of their preference for hot, arid regions, are forced to avoid many of the daylight hours and so resort to crepuscular and nocturnal activity.

The giant snakes, thanks to their dependence on a humid environment, do not encounter the problem of excessive dry heat. Still, on the basis of the observations reported in the later discussion of individual species, we must conclude that they are active chiefly at night. It is perhaps also worth noting that the big snakes in zoos are usually fed at night. This is partly for practical reasons: the absence of visitors is an advantage.

No treatment of the diel activity of snakes would be complete without reference to sleep, a subject that comes to mind especially in regard to a creature lacking movable, opaque eyelids. It may help to recall that some human beings sleep with their eyes open, and that the technician who constantly looks through his microscope with one eye has little difficulty disregarding the image that reaches the retina through the other. The sleeping snake must react in much the same way.

A snake in deep repose differs from an active one both in the position of its eyeballs and in the shape of its pupils. The two eyeballs may be shifted to place the pupils at their lowest position, or one eyeball may be lifted rather than lowered. This change of position seems to vary from species to species. The pupil contracts to the greatest degree when the snake goes to sleep. If such a snake is awakened by a light, the pupil will dilate, if but slightly, which, of course, is an effect opposite to that usually produced by increase of light. This dilation is a normal reaction to awakening and takes place in spite of the increased light.

CHARACTERISTICS OF THE SIX GIANTS

The foregoing discussion prepares us for the consideration of the diel activity of the six giants one by one. I shall also consider here what little is known about their tendency to congregate.

Anaconda: Detailed information on the anaconda is lacking, though it has been included in a list of nocturnal snakes. William Beebe found an anaconda on a moonlit beach of British Guiana, and he implies that others were met under the same conditions. He adds that "it is difficult to distinguish anacondas when they lie motionless, for they rest so flatly on the sand that they scarcely cast a shadow, and when they move, it is so silently and in so straight a line that the ear and eye give little warning." Apparently he is here referring to moon shadows.

Rolf Blomberg writes of encountering an anaconda sunning itself on a trunk over the Caguán River, a tributary of the Caquetá, in Colombia, and William Beebe shot one from a branch over water (presumably while it was sunning). Few such accounts are detailed enough for the reader to be sure just what the anaconda was up to; the mere fact that it was discovered in daylight may not be evidence of diurnality; it might have been aroused from sleep. Neither this nor any of the other giants is sufficiently nocturnal to refuse food during the day.

Evidence of the congregation—or, to use a technical term, aggregation—of anacondas comes from the northern part of the range: eleven individuals were seen together on the bank near the mouth of the Caucayá River; a "mass" of them in a pool was reported from the region south of the mouth of the Amazon; the date of the latter was June 21. There is no word concerning what had brought the anacondas together.

Boa constrictor: Again we have Beebe to thank for the best detailed report: "Most of our specimens were taken at night, as they crawled along the trails or crept over low branches." Beebe, incidentally, adds that 80 per cent of his specimens were collected during the height of the rainy season. The capture of a Mexican iguana by a boa constrictor (referred to on page 79) occurred when the sun was shining; however, in Sonora, Edward H. Taylor found a boa constrictor crawling at night. This species has been listed along with the anaconda as nocturnal.

African rock python: There is abundant general and circumstantial evidence of the daytime activity of this African giant, but little or no information on what it does at night. Many reports come from hunters, who are abroad by day rather than by night. The swallowing of large objects often requires so much time that accounts of pythons so engaged in the daytime can be misleading. Nearly all feeding by night escapes notice. J. Stevenson-Hamilton states that this snake is most active during the cool conditions of morning and evening, though it captures prey at all times. Charles R. S. Pitman claims that "although diurnal in certain respects the python is more lively at night," and that "during the hot weather" it lies in water, "often wholly submerged, throughout the heat of the day."

Indian python: Frank Wall's long account of the Indian python considers at some length its diel round. "In spite of its cat-like pupil the python is very much on the alert during the day-time, and very frequently when encountered in its native haunts is found in the act of swallowing some animal captured in broad daylight. On the other hand, it is frequently on the move at night, for on many occasions, where it has entered a poultry run, its depredations have been committed under cover of darkness." Surprisingly few subsequent observations throw additional light on this subject.

Reports of aggregation are more persistent for this than for any of the other five giants. In 1939 Shaw, Shebbeare, and Barker stated (of northern Bengal and Sikkim): "From October to December, in the plain forests of our area, it is not unusual to come across several Pythons together, up to seven or eight but more often four or five. Dent, who saw a number of these collections, pointed out that they usually consist of one large female and a number of males of 12 ft. or less." Wall wrote of six individuals from 10 to 12 feet long which were dragged from a cavity in the bank of a stream. He also refers vaguely to two somewhat similar discoveries, one in the Himalayas.

A much more recent record from Assam recounts briefly how a group of five fully grown pythons was discovered, and a sixth about sixty yards away. Finally, there are records of five found together in the Darjeeling foothills, four of them measuring from 12 to 17 feet, and four others discovered just within Nepal, opposite Darjeeling Terai. The five were seen on December 24, the smaller group in February. What part the sexual drive plays in this aggregating cannot be estimated until a great deal more is known about hibernation and courtship in the Indian python.

Reticulate python: In general, this python has been described as both diurnal (sunning) and nocturnal. There is little to distinguish it from the preceding species in diel activity, but we should note the observations by Stanley S. Flower and Malcolm Smith on its proneness to live in close proximity to human habitations (in Bangkok). Flower's account tells how the reticulate python hides by day in "some hole or crevice in building, timber-stack, or bank," emerging at night to feed on the numerous domestic animals.

Gustav Lederer notes that hungry reticulate pythons become restless in the evening; his experimental subjects, dealt with in the chapter on Senses, usually would not search for concealed prey in the morning, a good indication that hunger is at its ebb then.

Amethystine python: There is good evidence of the nocturnality of the amethystine python: Arthur Loveridge reports a night raid on a fowl yard by one and discovery of another extended on a trail during hours of darkness. This giant has also been characterized as very sun shy. It is just possible that part of the docility of the captives seen by Robert Mertens (pages 52–3) was due to light shyness. That they did not escape from the bags tucked under them (rather than securely tied) could have been due to docility, light shyness, or both.

Eric Worrell's account of hunting this species along the Beatrice River in Queensland gives definite information on its diurnality. First, he saw depressions made in the grass where individuals had lain in the morning sun. Then the hunt was abandoned for a time because the gorge had become too hot. Later in the afternoon the hunters found a python lying on a rock—then several more coiled inconspicuously where they could enjoy the warm afternoon sun.

In conclusion, I shall briefly deal with a few instances of puzzling behavior on the part of captive pythons.

As these snakes are not given to fighting even when living under crowded conditions, Lederer was at a loss to explain a short but violent battle, which began so suddenly that he was unable to stop it. When twenty-one male and fourteen female reticulate pythons were caged together, a large male started the melee by seizing another, which promptly retaliated but, missing his mark, bit yet a third. Removal of a badly wounded male, one of the two that had started the fracas, brought a return of calm, but not until one male had suffered seventeen big wounds, to which he succumbed, and fourteen other participants had received wounds of some sort.

Lederer also describes a fight between two formerly friendly males, one of which died of his wounds; in this case, sexually active females might have given the stimulus. This last remark, however, is not to be interpreted as meaning that males commonly fight over females.

Indian pythons under the observation of Carl Stemmler-Morath often went through a period of restlessness which could not be correlated with seasonal or sexual activity, and did not alter their relationship with keepers. The giants would crawl aimlessly about the cage for hours with their heads held high. When they pushed against the glass front, they frequently fell to one side.

Shedding

LET US IMAGINE that human beings regularly shed their skins as snakes do. What vast ceremonial importance would have been attached to the shedding by early man. And how advertisers of today would capitalize on it! What a picture: television, radio, and the press crammed with descriptions of special salves and ointments; sentimental parents proudly displaying handsomely mounted sheds of Junior and Grandpa's farewell molt, cast when he passed on at the age of ninety-five; whole storerooms filled with sheds of those Orientals who believe in taking to the grave old hair, fingernail parings, and similar products of the human body.

Man has been tremendously impressed even by the shedding of the snake. Reverence for the serpent possibly reflected a conviction that shedding was rejuvenation, even an indication of immortality.

Although nearly all higher land animals (land vertebrates) shed, few of them do such a complete job. In birds and mammals the process is a gradual or continuous one and may be almost imperceptible, as in man. Our lack of a hairy coat no doubt makes the process relatively simple for us; the molting bird or mammal is often conspicuous and, at least in the case of the bird, emotionally disturbed.

Periodic complete shedding is all but universal in reptiles and amphibians; some turtles retain the old horny shields of the shell until they are worn off by use. In a great many reptiles with limbs,

68

the old skin does not come off at once and in a single piece simply because the shape of the body causes the delicate old skin to be cast off in sections. The plain shape of the snake and its lack of movable eyelids make the process a simple, complete one, and allow the skin to come off whole, including the covering of the eyes and the spurs.*

The so-called scale of the snake is not a separate part like the scale of a fish. The skin of a snake is folded, a condition revealed by the shed; what appears to be a separate scale is actually a relatively thick part of the skin set off more or less completely by a fold. Such a part may tear loose along its edges, leaving the casual observer to mistake it for an entity like the scale of a fish. To the embryologist, fish and reptile scales are fundamentally different because the former is derived from a deeper layer of the skin.

In the process of shedding only the dead, keratinized outer layer of the true skin peels off to reveal a completely formed new covering. The deeper cells of this fresh skin will be gradually pushed toward the surface, becoming keratinized (like those of our fingernails) as they approach it. By the time they reach it, they will be fully keratinized and without life or color. Thus the cycle is completed. The act of shedding is also known as ecdysis, desquamation, and exuviation.

The shed's fragility and lack of color are further indications of its superficial nature; the pigment cells, which give the living snake a color pattern, lie in the deep, growing part of the skin. The strength of snake hide is due largely to its collagen fibers, an element entirely lacking in the shed. The cells of the shed, in spite of being dead and devoid of color, do reflect their early history enough to show faintly the pattern of the living skin. When a shed is held against the light, this pattern is clearly visible. Presumably, the more pigment a cell contains, the darker it is when keratinized.

* That the covering of the spurs is shed was kindly determined for me by Charles E. Shaw, Curator of Reptiles, San Diego Zoological Gardens, San Diego, California.

What about the advantages or disadvantages of this cataclysmic method of renewing the outer covering of the body? Does the snake pay a price for this efficiency? Some days before shedding, it becomes irritable, lacks an appetite, loses some contrast in color pattern (if it has one), and suffers a change in general hue. In correlation with this modification of color, the eye gets a cloudy or bluish look that is very noticeable. Most likely, sight is somewhat impaired, and the irritability indicates a state of mild discomfort, possibly a feeling of insecurity. No one knows the magnitude of the disadvantage of this pre-shedding condition, but we may guess that it is appreciable. The eyes clear a few days before the skin is actually cast off; presumably sight is then fully restored.

Loss of appetite before shedding is probably advantageous. To an animal capable of fasting for months, if not years, a week or so without appetite means little. A big, heavy lump in a snake about to shed would have two disadvantages: moving about might tear the loosened outer layer, the future shed, and make shedding more difficult, and certainly the snake would have trouble peeling the shed back over the lump.

It is commonly stated that shedding is necessary to reptile growth because, as in some insects, the body, rigidly encased in the part to be shed, cannot increase in size until the casing is cast off. This is a fallacy; the shed of a snake does not mechanically prevent expansion. Reptile growth is basically like that of other higher animals, not like that of invertebrates.

FREQUENCY OF SHEDDING

That a connection between growth and shedding does exist is strongly suggested by the correlation of growth with frequency of shedding. Young, rapidly growing snakes shed more frequently than do older individuals that have nearly or entirely finished their growth. (It is not known whether aged snakes stop growing entirely or just grow very slowly.) Further evidence of the close connection between the shedding cycle and growth is shown by the fact that the same chemical agents, or hormones, that control growth also control the shedding cycle and process.

Our knowledge of the frequency of shedding is definitely limited, especially for snakes living in nature. Data on young rattlesnakes are available because a segment is added to the rattle every time the skin is shed, and young rattlers often retain their complete rattles. The most complete record of shedding frequency, given by Klauber, is based on 670 sheddings of thirty-two individual rattlers, all two or more years old, kept in the San Diego Zoo under exceptionally favorable conditions. Various species of rattlers were involved. The average number of sheddings per year was 2.3, and the greatest for any snake in a single year was 6; but no individual averaged more than 3.9 times per year. Observations by Henry S. Fitch have shown that a northern Pacific rattlesnake, in Madera County, California, shed three times in its first full active season of about seven months, and twice in the second.

A captive snake kept warm throughout the year would inevitably shed more frequently than one living in the wilds of a region with a temperate climate, where hibernation for several months would interrupt the normal sequence. The warmer a snake is kept, the more often it sheds. A difference of ten degrees Fahrenheit is enough roughly to double the rate.

Removal of either the thyroid or the pituitary gland also increases the rate. These glands of internal secretion produce hormones, which are of vast importance to the entire internal economy of all higher animals, not just to their rate of growth and molt. A single gland may secrete several hormones, and one hormone may have varied effects on the animal or plant producing it. Surprisingly few of us realize the importance of hormones and how many of them there are. The study of endocrinology has developed with incredible rapidity during the last few decades.

As our giant snakes live where hibernation is brief or unnecessary, their frequency of shedding in zoos might well approximate that in nature. Because such large snakes cannot be kept in any great numbers, observations on their shedding are limited. The few records available indicate that the rate is not unusual as snakes go, though somewhat higher than the quoted rate of rattlers.

In 1921, Frank Wall compiled data for the Indian python and stated that it sheds five or six times annually. But he did not take age into consideration. Sylvia shed nine times from the beginning of her second to near the end of her third year. Another Indian python, about 8 feet long, also shed nine times in fifteen months; still another of approximately equal length shed eleven times in one year.

A shedding event in the life of Sylvia when she was four years old may be taken as typical for her species. Her eyes became cloudy on September 29, were almost clear on October 5, were entirely clear the next day, and she cast off her skin on October 9. Laurence M. Klauber gives the average time between the onset of cloudiness and the clearing of the eyes as 8.1 days, that between clearing and shedding as 3.7. His data, based on twenty-one sheddings of nine different subspecies of rattlesnakes, agree well with the data on Sylvia.

Another shedding record is given by Charles E. Shaw, his subject being a prize reticulate python kept nearly eighteen years in the San Diego Zoo. Blue Boy was secured in Borneo and grew from about 14 to 18 feet in length during his sojourn in San Diego. He shed on the average of every fifty-five days, the intervals varying from twenty-three to one hundred days. If stretched out end to end, his 115 sheds would be about a third of a mile long—a lot of skin to leave behind. Blue Boy was both lazy and docile, a happy combination of traits, and he refused to get his old skin off by himself. He enjoyed being helped and would co-operate by arching his long back. It is not hard to calculate that a python 25 feet long and thirty years old would have shed three fifths of a mile of skin, or almost twice as much as Blue Boy shed.

Shedding

Gustav Lederer's study of many captive reticulate pythons indicated that the young shed from five to nine times a year; the adults from three to seven, usually five times; individuals of intermediate age from four to seven, usually five or six times.

THE PROCESS OF SHEDDING

It is often stated that the old skin of the giant snakes "normally" comes off in pieces. In spite of Blue Boy's piecemeal shedding, there is no evidence to substantiate this. Sylvia often shed her old skin in one piece, and many other captive giant snakes have been known to do so. Perhaps the sheer weight of big snakes makes shedding in pieces relatively normal, if it is permissible thus to qualify this word.

Ordinarily a snake gets its skin free from its lips and head by rubbing them against a rough object. Its skin is next worked off its body inside out. The snake may crawl through or against anything available, or even rub one part of its body against another. Movements of its scales, especially those of its belly, are of substantial help, these movements being similar to those used in the "caterpillar" type of locomotion (slow crawling in a straight line). I recently watched an anaconda in the Brookfield Zoo, near Chicago, shedding under water; it pressed the part of its belly at which separation was taking place against the smooth bottom of the tank. Curator Robert Snedigar informed me that such underwater shedding is entirely normal.

As the skin is moved toward the tail, it bunches up; this facilitates matters by causing the skin to catch on all objects very close to the body. If the snake moves too rapidly and tears the skin, the ragged edge will not turn back readily, and the remaining skin may stay on for days.

Shedding may be accomplished in a matter of minutes under the best of conditions, in days under the worst. When the individual is

73

lucky and crawls slowly through a pile of brush, let us say, the skin may come off at once, the snake literally crawling out of it in one slow, continuous act.

Keepers have often noticed that a snake will soak itself in water a short time before shedding. This indicates an association of shedding with moisture, but the exact nature of the association has never been clarified. Some experiments have suggested, though not proved, a great increase of water loss through the skin of a snake preparing to shed. If this does take place, it is easy to see why a captive enjoys a bath before shedding. However, no experienced keeper would go so far as to say that a healthy snake cannot shed properly without soaking. It is likely that the amount of water lost through the skin varies considerably from species to species (see chapter on Use of Water).

Fuel

✹

Boa Constrictors. These infants were born in the Staten Island Zoo on March 31, 1940, and averaged 20 inches in length. There were 17 in this unusually small brood (Colombian female). The light areas on the back are grayish brown, the dark ones shaded blackish brown. On and near the tail the dark areas are many times wider than the light ones and are in part tan. On the sides the colors are much less sharply separated and more irregularly distributed. (Courtesy Staten Island Zoo. Photograph by Carl F. Kauffeld)

Habitat of Amethystine Python. Scene on the Beatrice River, Atherton Tableland, Australia, fifty yards downstream from the site where the individual shown in the following photograph was discovered. (Photograph by Henry L. Hirschhorn)

Amethystine Python. This individual, about 13 feet long, was photographed in life where it was discovered, southeast of Millaa-Millaa, Atherton Tableland, northeastern Queensland, on August 15, 1959. The ground color is yellowish brown, whereas the markings are purplish brown. Iridescence is evident over the entire animal. (Photograph by Henry L. Hirschhorn)

Head of Amethystine Python from Queensland. (Photograph by William Hosmer)

What They Eat—
and How Much

THERE IS LITTLE SPECIALIZATION of diet in the giant snakes. The young eat a great variety of small creatures, and the large adults seem to subsist on a basically similar assortment, but one that includes many additional items and, of course, bigger animals.

The technical difficulties of collecting and preserving adult giant snakes prevent the accumulation of scientific data on food. The available information consists largely of casual field records, made by laymen, based on feats of swallowing. Accounts and photographs often depict a python or boa with incredibly distended midriff, or a butchered giant lying by a victim crudely cut from it. Records of this kind tell little about the average meal, which is probably of moderate size. Snakes that gorge themselves are all but immobilized for hours and are therefore readily discovered.

Only the largest vertebrates are immune to attacks by the hungry python or boa of gigantic dimensions. Almost any not too formidable creature weighing less than 125 pounds is a potential victim, horns, armor, and spines notwithstanding. Hundreds of species of mammals, birds, and fishes, not to mention numerous kinds of reptiles, if not amphibians, fall victim to these giants. Perhaps it is only man himself who rivals the giant snakes in richness of diet. (The reader who has noticed that *Homo sapiens* is not included among the victims discussed is referred to the chapter on Attacks on Man.)

A problem that vexes many herpetologists is whether snakes eat fruits and berries. Although there are various circumstances under which such items might be found in a snake's stomach as secondary food (that is, food first eaten by a victim of the snake), a few of the accounts of direct consumption of fruit are beyond controversy. For example, S. Mookerjee reported the discovery of four mangoes in the esophagus of an Indian python. Tooth marks were visible on the mangoes, which were infested with insect larvae, an indication that they were not fresh. Walter Rose and Fred R. Irvine give additional records, one involving the African rock python and tomatoes. A plausible explanation is that the vegetable matter happens, when putrid or otherwise, to have an odor much like that of the animal prey, and is mistaken for such. More farfetched is the assumption that the fruit or berry acquired the odor of a mammal by growing at the mouth of a burrow or through some other chance contact.

The data on snakes as vegetarians will simply have to be kept until we have enough to permit better evaluation. An experimental approach might be used, and it would be helpful to know what the ophidian digestive juices make out of such food. For the present, it is better to continue to describe snakes as carnivorous.

FOOD PREFERENCES OF THE SPECIES

I shall now take up the six species of giant snakes to discuss what is known about their preferences for food.

Anaconda: Ludolf Wehekind's recent consideration of this snake's food includes only one specific record: a 6-foot caiman devoured by an anaconda 25 feet long. The animals on his general list are deer, peccaries, large rodents (agoutis, lappes, and pacas), and turtles, a surprising assortment for so aquatic a species. The ducks, other fowl, sheep, and dogs mentioned by him presumably are also prey of anacondas living in a wild state.

William Beebe, in *Jungle Days*, one of his books for laymen, writes of finding in British Guiana a basha in the stomach of an anaconda. This torpedo-lined fish, also known as the red-bellied drum, is a sciaenid that grows to be 2 feet long and is itself carnivorous. In this same country, Beebe dissected from the stomachs of three anacondas twenty-seven fishes, "including sharp-spined catfish and four species of armored catfish." (Catfishes of many species, great and small, abound in British Guiana.) Fishes contrast sharply with the animals included by Wehekind and suggest a diet by no means confined to endotherms ("warm-blooded" creatures). The relatively small aquatic creatures that most likely form a large part of the anaconda's diet would not be detected by the casual observer or the sportsman.

Boa constrictor: According to Wehekind, this boa eats large lizards (ameivas and tegus), birds, opossums, mongooses, and such rodents as rats, squirrels, agoutis, and pacas. Henroosts are raided, and ducks are eaten whenever they are found. Wehekind states that in 1894 an ocelot weighing between 30 and 40 pounds was taken from the stomach of a 10-foot boa constrictor. He does not include dogs, which boas relish.

Confirmation of the liking for lizards is found in a recent record of a boa constrictor "about five or six feet long" which had seized a large iguanid lizard (*Ctenosaura*). This took place in the state of Sinaloa, Mexico.

The most specific information is given by Beebe, who dissected three British Guiana boas and found these stomach contents: two lizards (an ameiva and a race runner, *Cnemidophorus*) in one; an ameiva and a pregnant spiny rat in another; an ant bird, a spiny rat, and an ameiva tail in the third. The tail is evidence that the snake was cheated of a full meal by the lizard's trick of dropping that appendage in a crisis. Three young rabbits were taken from a boa in northwestern Mexico, and Bert Tschambers gives evidence of the eating of a prehensile-tailed porcupine by a boa of Central America. Details of this incident will be found in the chapter on Digestion.

African rock python: There are more records on the feeding of this giant than on any of the other five. The explanation probably lies in the popularity of Africa as the happy hunting ground of sportsman and scientist alike. A contributing factor, no doubt, is the African rock python's habit of eating antelopes in relatively open places during daylight hours, making discovery easy. On the other hand, it is unlikely that we have a true conception of the normal feeding habits; antelopes, especially large ones, are reported too often. Most observers, moreover, would be concerned only with finding evidence of meals of unusual size.

For practical rather than scientific purposes, I shall divide the quarry into three categories: antelopes and other large mammals; domestic animals; and miscellaneous, mostly small, creatures. According to the records at least, only the first category is important; the antelopes reported far outnumber the surprisingly few other items, which include jackals, pigs, baboons, and other monkeys. One observer has listed antelopes of no fewer than nine types: duiker, oribi, steinbok, kob, reedbuck, impala, gazelle, bushbuck, and situtunga. Apparently any small species, or the young of large ones, will satisfy the python's appetite, provided, of course, that the horns are not too formidable.

Domestic animals, which constitute the next category, have not been properly emphasized. Charles R. S. Pitman remarks on the fondness of this snake for dogs, and sheep, goats, and barnyard fowl have also been recorded as victims. However, python-antelope encounters have more appeal for observers than those between pythons and domestic animals. Nevertheless, it is likely that domestic animals form a larger part of the diet, as they are more easily caught and overpowered.

The miscellaneous, relatively small prey includes birds—among them the crested crane and the Egyptian goose—dassies, hares, ground squirrels, rats, and porcupines. Pitman states that pythons are "not averse" to taking frogs and toads, but he does not give the source of this information, which, perhaps, should be confirmed. The most interesting aspect of this third category is that young pythons are involved.

Arthur Loveridge has furnished us with the most significant data on what young and medium-sized rock pythons eat in eastern Africa. He found the remains of a bird in a young individual, and a fowl was disgorged by one of medium length (8 feet 2 inches). The most pertinent data reported by him were based on the observations of J. P. Ionides, who twice saw a python eating a bird, once a dove, the other time a drongo; although the predators' lengths are not recorded, it is unlikely that they were large. Ionides knows of four occasions on which young pythons were caught in fish traps, a strong indication of fish-eating habits. He also found one slightly over 4 feet long near a dead ground squirrel (*Xerus*) it apparently had just killed and was about to eat.

Indian python: In his book on the snakes of Ceylon, Frank Wall devoted seven pages to the food and the feeding habits of this snake. His data, taken together with many brief reports, show that deer of several species (muntjac or barking deer, hog deer, chital, chevrotain, and sambur fawn), leopards, jackals, langur monkeys, and porcupines make up the known victims of large size. Domestic goats are included, and, among birds, pigeons, peacocks, pheasants, ducks, and other fowl. Wall records the discovery of two or three toads in one python, and R. W. Keays states that in the rainy season they live almost exclusively on fishes and rats; the basis of this information is not given. Data on the food of the young are scanty. A wood pigeon was taken from a small individual found on Ceylon, and I dissected a rat from a very little python collected in southwestern China.

Pangolin scales voided by captive Indian and reticulate pythons in the Ross Allen Reptile Institute, Silver Springs, Florida, were considered secondary food. However, I should guess that it is just as likely for a python to devour a pangolin whole as for the ordinary prey of this giant to swallow the scales of a pangolin after killing it for food. These scales form a smooth surface that would present no difficulty to a large python.

As mammals, especially hoofed ones, that attract explorer and sportsman are relatively scarce in tropical Asia, we have a somewhat more reliable picture of the Indian python's appetite than the one painted above for its African cousin. The difference is not great, and some of the same distortions appear in both. It is highly probable that domestic animals are even more important to the Asiatic giant, which can live far from human habitation only in the most remote parts of its range.

Reticulate python: This is the only giant snake for which the published reports emphasize the eating of domestic animals. In 1899, Stanley S. Flower published his astounding account of how this species lives in the busiest parts of Bangkok and "makes an easy living, devouring fowls, ducks, cats, dogs, and, it is said, pigs." His report was confirmed at a much later date; it seems that nothing short of covering every square inch of ground with concrete and asphalt will drive this reptile from cities and their environs. In country districts of thickly settled areas, the food habits would hardly change. Lim Boo Liat has given the result of dissecting seven individuals brought to the Institute for Medical Research at Kuala Lumpur, Federation of Malaya. Three had empty stomachs, one had eaten a wood rat (*Rattus jalorensis*), and each of the others had ingested a domestic animal (a duck, a fowl, and a young pig).

Such wild animals as pigs and deer are likewise eaten. There is a scarcity of reliable scientific records on other kinds of wild prey, however. Wall wrote a full account of this snake in 1926, but included only a third of a page on its food and feeding habits. This is in sharp contrast to his seven pages on the Indian python.

Tortoise alveolar ridges voided by a large individual at the Ross Allen Reptile Institute were considered secondary contents because the python refused to eat tortoises.

Amethystine python: Kangaroos and wallabies are popularly considered to be the chief food of this snake, just as antelopes are thought to be highly important in the diet of the African rock python. Any discovery of a large python devouring a kangaroo or a wallaby receives wide notice. No doubt, in Australia large marsupials are regularly eaten, though it is likely that a good variety of other creatures forms the greater part of the diet, especially throughout the insular part of the range. An amethystine python was caught killing a hen, and another was surprised while raiding a fowl yard in which it had already killed a bird. Both of these incidents occurred in Queensland. A cuscus (a marsupial) was found in the stomach of an individual on Ceram. Less is known about the feeding habits of this giant than about those of the others, yet in all likelihood it has an appetite for at least as many types of prey as any of them.

SIZE OF PREY

How big an animal can a giant snake swallow? This popular question is less important to the scientist than it is to the layman. Scientists, not content with a mere extreme, want to investigate the full implications of the capacity for large meals. For instance, Francis G. Benedict's elaborate researches showed that his 17-foot, 70-pound reticulate python, by eating a 20-pound pig, easily supplied itself with 400 times its daily energy need. We can use this statement as a measure for the feats of swallowing that I shall presently describe, and marvel at the ability of a giant snake to stoke the furnace so effectively. That such an animal can thrive on three or four good meals a year is not surprising.

Even a large python or anaconda has to strain when devouring a mammal weighing 100 pounds. In actual experiments with and observations on captives, three experienced snake men have come to much the same conclusion. Raymond L. Ditmars fed an 80-

pound pig to a 20-foot "python"; J. Hagenbeck got a gigantic reticulate python to eat an 84-pound goat; and Gustav Lederer topped both when his 24-footer ate first a pig weighing 120 pounds and later an Indian *Langohrziege*—a donkey (?)—just 15 pounds lighter. Two days after eating the pig, the snake was so swollen that Lederer feared it had been injured. A 130-pound impala recorded by Rose and considered by James A. Oliver to be the maximum even surpasses these extreme performances.

No authority to my knowledge has expressed a belief that a creature heavier than 150 pounds could be swallowed by even the largest python or anaconda, though two or three have stated that this figure is probably the ceiling. The African rock python that devoured the impala was only 16 feet long, and therefore I should hazard a guess that this species at 25 or 30 feet could pass the 150-pound ceiling.

According to reliable report, a big reticulate python was once surprised while trying to eat a fully grown boar. Thus, it would seem that the huge snake may misjudge the size of a prospective meal and that its eyes sometimes get bigger than its stomach. Wall long ago expressed the conviction that any reluctance to move about freely after a repast of gigantic proportions is not due to a desire to digest in peace and quiet, but to a fear of internal injury from hard and sharp appendages of an outsized prey. He cites the case of the Indian python found dead with numerous porcupine quills sticking out from its belly. He also relates the case of another Indian python, which refused to move until pestered. Soon two logical reasons for its reluctance appeared: the 7- or 8-inch horns of a hog deer. A snake in such a situation certainly would run great risk of damage if it crawled about much.

Detailed study might well show that meals weighing in the neighborhood of 100 pounds are rare exceptions, their apparent frequency being a delusion based on the amount of notice they receive.

How well the giant snake uses the food it consumes so readily depends on the rate of growth and other, less obvious factors. Sylvia, while still young and growing rapidly, had to eat almost two pounds of rats to add one pound to her weight, whereas Charles E. Shaw's Blue Boy added only about 77 pounds to his weight by eating 1,638 pounds of horsemeat and chickens. Blue Boy was adult when the records were begun, and increased only 4 feet in length during almost eighteen years, whereas Sylvia added 6 feet in two years. It is clear that Blue Boy's (average) 14½-pound meals, given about once every thirty-five days, supplied him with more than the necessary amount of fuel. Being about the size of Benedict's snake, he could have, at least theoretically, subsisted on one 20-pound pig a year.

CAPACITY OF THE BIG SIX

Before any consideration of the six giants species by species, two important points call for clarification. First, by capacity I do not mean the size of the largest single meal a big snake can take in, but the amount of food that can be ingested over a period of time by a snake of known dimensions. Although photographs of giant snakes and their victims are commonly published, and zoo curators and keepers are fond of listing the items consumed, surprisingly few complete records are available. To be rated as complete, a record must include such basic data as identification, dimensions, and weight of the predator as well as of the prey.

Second, it must be kept in mind that a snake is not just an empty bag to be stuffed with food. The powerful pyloric valve that closes the stomach at its lower end marks the point of no further passage; the stomach and esophagus can be crammed at the time of swallowing, but not the intestine. It would be interesting to know whether the stomach is fixed or can be moved posteriorly by the pressure of food. Determination of this would require X-ray photography or observation by fluoroscope.

Anaconda: One of these snakes from French Guiana held a "pig" whose estimated weight was 100 pounds. The anaconda was killed and measured as 25 feet 8 inches in length and 18¾ inches in diameter; it weighed an estimated 300 pounds. The pig must have been a peccary.

Boa constrictor: E. Reichert's pet from Guatemala ate 55 white mice between June 24 of one year and December 6 of the following year. During this period it increased in length from 19¾ to 35 inches, in weight from 1⅗ to 14 ounces. Another young boa, identified as *Boa constrictor constrictor*, ate in twenty-six months 104 mice, 22 golden hamsters, 5 guinea pigs, and 5 sparrows. At the beginning, it was 24½ inches long and weighed 5¼ ounces; at the end, the weight had increased to 4⅗ pounds.

African rock python: It is probable that this python can at least match any other giant of equal length in swallowing capacity. Unfortunately, none of the following records is complete, but all are, nonetheless, impressive. Pitman gives two astonishing cases: a fully grown Thomson's gazelle with horns intact was devoured in one and a half hours by an African rock python only 11 feet 9 inches long; a situtunga weighing approximately 60 pounds was ingested by one only 13 feet in length. Loveridge took a bushbuck doe in milk from an individual 14 feet 4 inches long and 1½ feet in diameter. With such thickness it is little wonder that the reptile could overpower the bushbuck. The American Museum of Natural History received a 16-foot specimen that held an antelope 1 foot 7 inches high at the shoulders and 3 feet 5 inches long. Oliver quotes the record of a reedbuck weighing about 60 pounds found in a python 16 feet 1 inch long. I have already referred to the 130-pound impala that, according to Rose, was swallowed by a python only 16 feet in length.

A young captive individual kept by A. Woerle ate, in two years and a few days, 109 mice, 24 golden hamsters, 2 guinea pigs, and 14 sparrows. At the beginning of the two years, it was 2 feet 3½ inches long and weighed 7 ounces; at the end, its weight had in-

creased to 4⅘ pounds. Another captive juvenile African rock python, 6 feet long, consumed in twenty-nine meals 92 rats, 6 sparrows, and 1 pigeon; there is no statement in regard to growth. An
adult of this species will consume 7 fully grown Belgian hares at a
meal.

Indian python: Wall described a most interesting feat of swallowing. An individual "over" 6 feet long was found in southern Burma
with its head beneath a rock; an enormously distended midriff had
prevented it from entering a retreat. The lump turned out to be
a mouse deer (chevrotain) in an advanced stage of pregnancy. Another interesting case is that of an 18-foot Indian python that had
devoured a leopard measuring 4 feet 2 inches in length from the
snout to the end of the body. Oliver quotes three records for this
species: a three-year-old barking deer (horns missing) by a python
13½ feet long; an adult hog deer with antlers 7 or 8 inches long by
a snake 15 feet in length; a barking deer with horns nearly a foot
long by a snake 18 feet long.

Sylvia ate 123 laboratory rats (61 pounds) during her second
year and nearly all of her third, adding 34½ pounds to her own
weight. An old record from Paris gives an Indian python credit
for consuming about 29 pounds of food during the first six months
of life. This surpasses Sylvia's consumption, but may be reasonably
explained by the fact that Sylvia's diet was rationed; when her appetite was good, she was not given all she would eat, for fear of
damage to her. Another individual (size not given) ate, in five
years, 36 rabbits, 7 guinea pigs, 18 rats, 3 doves, and 1 hen.

Reticulate python: By far the most widely publicized data on
the swallowing ability of giant snakes are those taken from
Hagenbeck. His 25-foot reticulate python devoured a 71-pound
ibex (deprived of horns) several days after swallowing two goats,
one weighing 28 pounds, the other 39 pounds. This made a total of
138 pounds of mammals. The flash set off by a photographer
caused the python to throw up the partly devoured ibex, but
the record is certainly valid. Another accomplishment for a 25-

footer was the swallowing of a roebuck weighing 67 pounds three days after taking in a 17-pound swan. I have already mentioned the enormous meal consumed by Lederer's 24-foot captive reticulate python.

Unsurpassed for elegance of taste is the famous python that was found in the King of Siam's palace; it had eaten a royal Siamese cat, bell and all.

For variety, the food eaten in one day by a big individual takes the prize: one duck, two pigeons, one rabbit, and one guinea pig. Another, about 12 feet long and weighing 46½ pounds, would consume as many as six chickens in one meal. Charles E. Shaw's Blue Boy ate the equivalent of nearly three dressed-out horses, but it took him almost eighteen years. It should be added that weight of the chickens consumed along with the horsemeat is included in this calculation.

Amethystine python: Kangaroos and wallabies would not seem to be ideally shaped for easy swallowing. Many an amethystine python has probably discovered this by firsthand experience. A few decades ago one of these giants, 19½ feet long, was shown to have devoured a kangaroo about 3 feet high and weighing an estimated 50 pounds. Another python, only 12 feet long, is credited with a wallaby as big as a fully grown sheep dog. These events took place, of course, in Australia. I do not know just what prowess this reptile shows in the parts of its range which lie north of Australia. There it would have ample opportunity to demonstrate an extensive appetite without resort to kangaroos and wallabies.

FREQUENCY OF FEEDING

The snake's ability to survive incredible fasts has been mentioned earlier. Lederer tells of a female reticulate python kept in Frankfurt am Main, Germany, that fasted at least nineteen months (about 570 days), resumed regular feeding for a time, and then fasted 415 days before eating again. He relates how a gigantic individual of the same species, also kept in Frankfurt, went 679 days without a meal, but drank frequently during this period. (Incidentally, a Gaboon viper in the Frankfurt aquarium lived two and a half years without nourishment.) The longest period that I have found credited to a boa or python is a little more than four years, allegedly attained by a Madagascar boa in the Paris zoo; though often cited, this record has not been confirmed. There is a record of a python that was not fed for three years. One of Benedict's Indian pythons used in an experiment was kept without food for 149 days and lost only 10 per cent of its weight during the last 110 days. F. W. Fitzsimons recorded a nineteen-month fast for an African rock python. More records could be given, but these are enough. There is no doubt about the ability of snakes to live as long as two and a half years without food. These data are based on individuals kept at normal temperatures; presumably, fasts could be greatly extended through reduction of metabolic rate by chilling, which, if properly instigated, would induce hibernation.

Basically, the life of a snake is cyclic: feeding, digesting, shedding, and hibernating or estivating. Of course, hibernation or estivation takes place only after the feeding-digesting-shedding combination has occurred several times. All of these processes are subject to enormous variation, except, perhaps, shedding. Some snakes feed regularly on small meals and thus merge feeding and digesting, and some neither hibernate nor estivate.

Feeding Habits

FINDING FOOD

THERE IS a persistent and widespread belief that pythons obtain their prey by lurking above jungle trails and dropping on it. Scientific confirmation of such behavior is lacking, although in 1911 W. Forsyth described an actual incident that took place in eastern India involving an Indian python and a deer. The python, using its head, allegedly knocked the deer senseless and then descended to it. This is probably a case of an observer "seeing" what he was sure would happen. Yet this incident cannot be summarily dismissed simply because Forsyth seems to have erred in one detail; it is possible that the deer died of fright and merely appeared to have been propelled by the blow.

In many areas, conditions would make such a method impossible; giant snakes must have other ways of securing food. R. M. Isemonger has, indeed, described another type of lurking behavior. He repeatedly watched an African rock python that lived in some bushes near a pool. On one occasion, when a family of bushbuck approached the site, the giant crawled nearer to the pool. One of the younger mammals came close, was seized by the neck, and was forthwith swallowed. We may assume that this python had only to wait until food arrived on the hoof. But how long might this be? The giant snake's ability to eat large animals and to survive incredible fasts makes the waiting game a winning one.

There are only a few firsthand observations of just how the giant snakes go about hunting for food. In his excellent summary, Laurence M. Klauber concludes that rattlesnakes use two methods: they either lie in wait or actively search by investigating burrows and crevices inhabited by their prey. He believes the first method is predominant. Therefore, we can conjecture that giant snakes also do a lot of waiting for prey.

Concerning the senses used in finding food, suffice it to repeat here that smell, in its broadest meaning, is most heavily relied upon. Sight is of much less importance. Hearing is ruled out by the deafness of snakes, though the giants probably detect the approach of large prey by vibrations transmitted through the ground.

SEIZING PREY

A snake is able to grip its prey securely because of the flexibility of its jaws and the number, sharpness, and shape of its teeth. The backward slope of the teeth is insurance against the escape of a struggling animal; the harder it pulls away, the deeper the teeth sink in. To release a finger seized by a snake's jaws, you have to open them and push the finger farther in until it is freed, and then take it out. The ordinary victim can get away only by leaving some of itself lodged in the escape-proof jaws.

A reticulate python has about one hundred teeth deployed in six rows, four above and two below, plus a few teeth in the front of the upper jaw. In a 14-foot individual, the larger teeth are eleven sixteenths of an inch long.

The adult giant snake must take an especially firm hold on its prey because the victim makes violent, spasmodic efforts to escape. The snake not only must withstand these efforts but, at the same time, must haul itself toward the struggling creature in order to wrap coils around it.

Prey much lighter than its assailant is whirled around on its long axis while the snake coils. This maneuver is advantageous for the reptile because once a victim has lost its balance and orientation (by being revolved), its ability to pull away vanishes. The speed of the giant snake in this act of seizing and wrapping has never been measured, but it probably is not so fast as it appears to be.

There are three fairly common beliefs about how a python or boa deals with its prey: the giant snake twists its tail about some object, such as a trunk or branch of a tree, for support while constricting; it covers the lifeless victim with saliva; it squeezes the prey into a shape right for swallowing.

The origin of the first belief is easy to detect. The snake does not necessarily use all of its great length in wrapping itself about a victim, and the part that is left over may inadvertently twine about a tree. The casual observer could reasonably conclude that the entwined tail was serving a highly useful purpose, but there is little or no supporting evidence for this.

The lubrication-of-prey theory can be even more readily explained. If a snake is alarmed in the act of devouring, the prey may be vomited. As the snake's flow of saliva is copious, the meal, whatever it may be, comes up covered with this secretion. The size and structure of a snake's tongue would not allow it to be used like a paintbrush to apply saliva.

In contrast to these two fallacious beliefs, the theory that the snake squeezes its prey into certain shapes has good support. The fact that a great many large objects are swallowed without any shaping throws doubt on this theory, but there is convincing evidence that prey is sometimes shaped. In an earlier chapter I tell of an ibex that was disgorged with disarticulated joints; in addition, James A. Oliver once watched a small python pull and stretch a bulky chicken until it had a better form.

SWALLOWING PREY

The time required to swallow an animal depends on its size, its shape, and the nature of its surface. If the prey happens to have a suitable shape, it may be equal to the predator in bulk. The best is a snake much chunkier, but shorter, than the predator. If the two are similar in build, the length of the prey introduces problems. Nevertheless, a snake may swallow another of equal proportions; there is a record of such an act, which required five hours for completion. The tail of the victim has to be forced into the esophagus in such a way that it lies in continuous S-shaped curves.

As the diameter of the prey increases and the length diminishes, there is greater difficulty. A spherical object causes much trouble. The nature of the surface is also of great significance. Spines, thick fur, and feathers slow up the process, as do horns and limbs. I have seen the feet of a bird catch like two anchors in the corners of a snake's mouth and bring the swallowing to a dead halt.

Many are the stories of how giant snakes deal with the various types of bony or horny growths on the heads of mammals after the animals have been swallowed. All of these obstructions are dislodged by the dissolution of the skull, and some are disintegrated by the digestive juices; some may actually pierce the body wall of the snake, the wounds eventually healing. The disposition of these growths must depend on the size and nature of the horn or antler; detailed information is not available.

Hours may pass while a giant snake eats one of its prodigious meals, for a great deal of its time is spent in resting and in pausing to breathe through the heavily reinforced glottis, which is periodically forced forward between the prey and the tightly stretched floor of the mouth. Prodigious meals are the exception, and because of this they receive too much notice. Swallowing done on a smaller scale is astonishing enough: a common water snake (*Natrix sipedon*) once devoured a bullfrog in my back yard; the snake weighed eleven and a quarter ounces, the frog three, and the time required was fifteen and a half minutes. This is the equivalent of a big man eating fifty-five pounds of meat at a sitting, or a large giant snake devouring an animal of about this same weight.

I kept records of the time it took my Indian python, Sylvia, to eat rats and guinea pigs; she was fed almost entirely on the former. Ten of her typical rat meals when she was small, and eleven when she was noticeably larger, are tabulated on page 95. The time periods given in the table are those of the actual swallowing, including, in some cases, a momentary pause made by Sylvia to shift the position of the prey or her coils, or both. No time spent in constricting is included because the rats were stunned or dead when given to her. Although inactive rats did not stimulate her as much as live ones would have, occasionally she weakly constricted the dead or stunned ones.

The table shows that Sylvia, though always fed at room temperature (see page 104), swallowed an adult rat in less than three minutes on one occasion, whereas on another she required almost thirteen; the average time was about midway between these extremes. One of the factors that influenced this variation was "warming up"; the first rat took longer than the rats eaten immediately afterward, the reduction in time being appreciable.

I have only two records for Sylvia's consumption of guinea pigs; she required 23 minutes to eat each, one weighing 2¼ pounds, the other 1½ pounds. When she ate the larger, she was 10 feet 7 inches long; the smaller was consumed when she was 2 inches longer and weighed 34 pounds.

Watching Sylvia convinced me that a constrictor uses its body much as a mammal uses limbs; hence the ability to shape prey.

Still better evidence for these snakes' excellent body control is seen in cases of simultaneous seizure of as many as three creatures. A small python once caught a sparrow, captured another without taking its attention off the first, and then pinned a third with its tail. An African rock python is credited with capturing three jackals at the same time and eating one after the other. Gustav

Feeding Habits

TIME REQUIRED BY SYLVIA (INDIAN PYTHON) TO SWALLOW DOMESTIC RATS

(Weights given to nearest whole unit)

TIME		WEIGHT OF RAT	LENGTH OF SYLVIA		WEIGHT OF SYLVIA
Min.	*Sec.*	*Ounces*	*Feet*	*Inches*	*Pounds*
8	20	5	5	10	6
11	45	8	6	1	6
9	23	6	6	5	6
10	0	7	7	0	12
3	0	6	7	0	12
3	15	6	7	1	13
12	30	10	7	4	14
5	0	9	7	4	14
10	0	9	7	5	15
11	30	13	7	5	15
9	7	8	9	11	35
5	25	8	9	11	37
5	12	10	10	0	37
7	44	8	10	0	38
8	20	9	10	1	38
5	22	8	10	1	38
4	20	8	10	1	38
12	50	9	10	2	38
2	40	8	10	2	38
5	25	14	10	2	38
3	34	9	10	2	38

Lederer writes of a powerful reticulate python that seized and constricted a piglet, then, in a few seconds, wrapped the rear part of its body about another, and soon after killed a rabbit by pressing it against the wall of the cage; all were eaten. Lederer also relates that an Indian python took two rabbits almost at once. Thus, three of our giants have been known to handle multiple prey.

Internal Economy

❈

Digestion

An ANIMAL able to take in 400 times its daily energy requirement at one ordinary meal must have interesting digestive processes. The ability to get large objects into the digestive tract without the help of limbs calls for special structure and methods. The skin of the snake is elastic, the bones of the jaws are loosely connected, and the needle-sharp teeth slope toward the throat. Once the prey has been seized, the jaws begin alternating movements that literally draw the object in, or, if it is heavy, pull the snake over it. The elasticity of the skin and of the ligament connecting the two halves of the lower jaw in front allow the mouth to be stretched over the prey.

There is a lower limit to the size of prey, for a relatively small creature—a frog, for example—might simply hop out of the throat of a giant snake trying to make a meal of it. In man, such a difficulty would be eliminated by chewing, but this is something a snake never does.

Another basic difference between the snake and man lies in the use of the tongue. In man, this organ is essential to the manipulation of food and assists in passing it back to the throat. The snake's tongue is sheathed during ingestion and therefore can play no part.

In man, the esophagus itself is able, with the help of gravity, to get mouthfuls of food down. In the snake, as soon as part of the prey has reached the throat, powerful muscles of the body walls help the esophagus push the food on down by means of successive S-shaped waves that start at the head.

The air and food passages are not so well separated in the snake as in man. The snake's nostrils open into the roof of the mouth, which makes breathing with the mouth full impossible. Even in man, there is momentary conflict as food passes a region common to breath and food, but the entire act of swallowing is accomplished in a few seconds and breathing has to be held up only a fraction of this time. The snake may have a big object lodged in its mouth for minutes, possibly hours. Although the snake needs to breathe much less often than man, there are definite limits to its ability to hold the breath. To avoid suffocation, the snake periodically halts deglutition to push its reinforced windpipe far enough forward to allow air to pass.

The esophagus merges into the stomach; folds of the walls of the lower part of the esophagus gradually increase until they reach the stomach, where they are at their maximum. The stomach, a highly elastic sack, ends abruptly at the pyloric valve, a powerful muscle which keeps food from entering the intestine until dissolution has taken place. It is something of a puzzle just how this dissolution is accomplished in a distended bag that cannot churn as human stomachs do.

Absorption takes place in the coiled, but relatively short, small intestine. Beyond this organ, which holds its contents for a surprisingly long time, waste material accumulates and is formed into large balls. These are eventually passed as feces.

Alexander W. Blain and K. N. Campbell's valuable X-ray studies of digestion in a 7-foot boa constrictor, the basis for some of the foregoing, will now be summarized. An adult laboratory rat was fed to the boa; four hours and forty-five minutes later its position was still unchanged in the stomach and large gas pockets had begun to accumulate there. The rat's tail lay in the esophagus, which often holds parts of food items that are too long for the stomach. Twenty-two hours after feeding, the rat's skeleton had begun to lose its density, the skull was being demineralized, and material was collecting in the small intestine; no change in position could be detected. At forty-seven hours, there was noticeable loss of mineral content in most of the rat's bones, though they remained in much the same position. At fifty-two hours, the head bones had practically disappeared. At seventy-five hours, gas pockets of the stomach had vanished, the vertebrae and bones of the head had decomposed, and the contents of the snake's small intestine had greatly increased, though the pyloric valve still held in position the remains of the rat. At ninety-three hours and thirty minutes, only a few remnants of the skeleton were visible in the stomach (and none in the intestine); gas shadows had about disappeared from the entire digestive tract, and much fecal matter had been passed. Digestion of an indigo snake (*Drymarchon corais*) equal in size to the boa was also observed and found to differ in no important respect.

The time that may elapse before the initiation of digestion is suggested by the following incident. A captive grass snake (*Natrix natrix*) in England, about a yard long, ate a fairly large frog and disgorged it still alive ninety minutes later.

DIGESTIVE JUICES

The digestive juices with their enzymes are the agents of digestion. The enzymes are not modified during the process of breaking the food down into the building blocks of growth and repair, the amino acids. Moreover, many different enzymes are required because each is specific in action.

Saliva, the first of the juices to reach the food, differs from the others in an important way: it both prepares the food for easy handling and changes its chemical composition. In most snakes the saliva has the sole function of lubricating the food so that it will pass through the enlarged gape. As the prey is never chewed, the saliva cannot penetrate it. The remarkable exception to this is the venom of poisonous snakes, a highly modified saliva that not only kills the prey but may start the digestion of it even before the jaws have taken hold for swallowing. (Even in man the salivary glands can also be divided into two groups according to their structure and the nature of their secretions.) Once the prey of venomous snakes has been killed and seized, the swallowing process does not differ from that of the other species.

ELIMINATION

The excrement of a snake is made up of two noticeably different parts, one white and chalklike, the other blackish brown and similar in appearance to the dung of many other animals. The white part is largely composed of uric acid, an insoluble product of the kidneys, and may be classed as solid urine. In man the urine is liquid because the human kidneys degrade their waste products into urea, which is readily dissolved in the water that passes through the kidneys. The dark part of the snake's waste product is composed of undigested material from the intestine. Some liquid is also passed along with the mass of solids.

In snakes the receptacle for all waste materials is the cloaca. Most vertebrates—the exceptions being nearly all mammals and some fishes—have a cloaca. Into it enter the reproductive organs of the male during copulation, and through it must pass the eggs and young of the female. The cloaca is literally a catchall. The anus is merely the exit from the cloaca to the exterior.

In general, bones are digested, whereas products of the skin, such as hair and feathers, are not. Bones may occasionally be passed, especially by captive snakes in poor health. Hans Schweizer, for example, relates how a captive anaconda killed and devoured an Indian python on July 5. Nine days later the anaconda passed vertebrae, the jaws with the teeth still in place, and many jaw scales. Further evacuations took place on July 22 and August 10. Numerous scats, or droppings, of the western rattlesnake examined by Henry S. Fitch and H. Twining included hair relatively unchanged, rodent teeth that often fell to pieces when handled, and bird feathers and bills in somewhat disintegrated condition, but identifiable.

An interesting case has been reported of a boa constrictor that evidently devoured a prehensile-tailed porcupine. Short quills were taken from the roof of the boa's mouth. Its excrement contained hair and several claws of the porcupine. It is not surprising that armored catfishes, spiny-finned fishes of various groups, bony-skinned lizards, and crocodilians also fall victim to the giant snakes. The powerful digestive juices handle such protective devices by freeing them from their moorings.

Francis G. Benedict's monumental study of reptile physiology provides us with pertinent data. On January 24 two guinea pigs were fed to an Indian python about 8 feet long. On January 31 and February 13 some liquid was voided. On February 5 whitish excrement (urine) was passed, weighing 1.5 ounces fresh, 1.1 ounces dry. On February 13 excreta of the same kind with a fresh weight of 1.7 ounces appeared. The first dark (intestinal) waste product was voided on February 14; it contained some hair and weighed 5.7 ounces fresh, only 2.0 ounces dry. The next evacuation was of a similar kind and occurred on February 27, the product weighing 1.6 ounces. When, on March 4, the snake was dissected, 0.9 of an ounce of excrement (intestinal) and fourteen of its own teeth were found. (Snakes constantly shed their teeth.) Presumably this python had an empty stomach when it ate the two guinea pigs.

Sylvia had thirty-one eliminations in one year and ate rats forty-eight times at regular intervals during the same period. She was only eighteen months old at the beginning of this period. Later, when she was 10½ feet long and almost three and a half years old, she defecated a mass weighing about 23 ounces wet, 7 ounces dry.

The small part of the excrement which was white weighed 0.7 of an ounce when dried. Usually Sylvia lived at or near ordinary room temperature.

EFFECT OF TEMPERATURE

As explained in the chapter on Temperature, reptiles have no built-in heating mechanism, but take on the approximate temperature of their surroundings. Those kept in confinement absorb or lose heat, as the case may be, until they approximate the temperature of their cages. Experiments by Benedict proved that the giant snakes' rate of digestion increases markedly as the temperature of their bodies is raised.

Selected data from his report will show what great differences may be brought about by changes of only a few degrees. An Indian python about 8 feet long was kept by him at a temperature of 64° F. while it was digesting a rabbit that weighed a pound, which was 8 per cent of the weight of the python. At the end of fifteen days the rabbit was still incompletely digested, even though the snake had been given two days' precautionary relief from the low temperature. In another experiment the same snake was fed a rabbit equal in size to the first, and the temperature set at 71° F. Digestion reached its peak three days and six hours later, and was complete in a week. Yet another experiment was carried on at 82° F. with a rabbit weighing 10 per cent as much as the python. By the end of twenty-two hours, digestion was in rapid progress and continued at the same pace for sixteen hours. It then even increased in rate and came to virtual completion in four or five days. Thus the correlation between the temperature of the Indian python's body and its rate of digestion is clearly demonstrated.

It may be a long time before we know anything about digestion in big snakes living under natural conditions, where their bodies would, presumably, be kept at some relatively constant temperature.

Use of Water

WATER MAKES UP a large part of the bodies of animals, from about half in some insects to 90 per cent or even more in certain other creatures. Man, when adult, is 66 per cent water, whereas the percentage for the Indian python studied by Benedict was 75.

Animals get water into themselves by drinking, by eating "wet" food, by soaking it up through the skin, and by releasing it from dry and fatty foods through chemical action, the product of which is known as "water of metabolism." Snakes, like man, acquire water chiefly by means of the first two methods, though metabolic water may be of importance to some snakes; frogs and salamanders soak it up with great facility and get it in other ways as well.

When a snake drinks, the tongue plays no part, though it is used in testing water for suitability. A thirsty snake submerges much of its head, so that both its mouth and its nostrils are below the surface. Water is drawn in by rhythmic movements of the sides of the head. The mouth is opened slightly with each intake, but it takes close observation to notice this. A thirsty snake will drink steadily for two or three minutes, the sides of its head expanding scores of times. Only shallow water is required, and captives drink most readily in a vessel with little depth. After a long draught, some of the water will quickly run out if the snake is handled roughly or held with the head down.

How often a snake needs to drink, or whether it needs to drink at all, depends largely on humidity, temperature, and food. As snakes live on food that contains a great deal of water, abundant food will provide a good supply. A great many of the mammals devoured by the giant snakes would be, like a lean common house cat, composed of about two-thirds water by weight. Fat animals have relatively less water than thin ones, the old less than the young. Living in moist regions as they do, the giant snakes probably have little desire to drink no matter what food they eat; moreover, they undoubtedly avoid desiccating temperatures by moving from place to place.

All captive snakes seem willing to take advantage of a supply of water, especially before shedding. There is general agreement that a great deal of moisture is lost just prior to shedding, but little agreement on the explanation. Is it due to increased metabolism, or to a need of water to facilitate ecdysis, or to both? One of Benedict's boas increased its rate of metabolism just before shedding.

RETENTION AND LOSS

The acquisition of water is not so difficult as its retention, and the methods by which various animals manage to keep enough water for comfort and safety are numerous as well as complex. As respiration, elimination, and temperature regulation involve loss of water, retention is actually a matter of regulating the amount of water in the body—maintaining a balance between what is taken in and what is lost—not simply keeping water in. A more or less watertight skin is the chief retainer of water. Internal breathing organs such as lungs permit respiration with minimum evaporation. The extraction of water from the excrement and the passing of other waste products without undue loss are extremely important measures in this battle to conserve water. Migrating to more humid places and suspending activity during dry spells are also ways of cutting down loss.

Snakes do not have sweat glands, and their skin is keratinized on the outside, two conditions that prevent excessive loss of water; on the other hand, they presumably evaporate water at a relatively uniform rate and therefore one easy to measure. Many other animals, among them numerous mammals, lack sweat glands. Man, however, is almost a sieve when his are working at full capacity; he can sweat a quart of water per hour.

The most detailed data we have on water loss in snakes have been provided by Benedict, who performed elaborate experiments on reposing snakes—several boa constrictors and an Indian python. Water was lost through the lungs and the skin at the daily rate of 0.08 ounces, or a little more, for every 2.2 pounds of body weight at about 72° F. A rise in temperature increased the rate, which was also higher in a snake preparing to shed. This means that a python weighing 150 pounds would lose roughly three fourths of a cup of water every day, whereas an inactive human being would lose 3.8 times as much. It would take a python fifteen months to lose an amount of water equal to it in weight. The amounts of water lost through the skin and the lungs were treated together because of the mechanical difficulties of separating the two completely.

While studying water relationships of the common water snake (*Natrix sipedon*), David Pettus tested with an osmometer the permeability of a piece of skin, getting only negative results. Water would not pass through it, even at the beginning of the experiment, when the cells were undoubtedly alive; skin is considered to be more permeable dead than alive. Confirmation of this result with skin still in place on a living snake would be most welcome.

In contrast, Benedict was convinced that his giant snakes evaporated a considerable amount of water through the skin. He compared his snakes to wet-bulb thermometers, for he found them to have rectal temperatures somewhat below that of the surroundings, and skin temperatures considerably (nearly four degrees Fahrenheit) below. It is highly probable that snakes differ from species to species in this matter. Charles M. Bogert and Raymond B. Cowles submitted three Floridian species to the drying effects of a chamber with high temperature and low humidity, and found marked differences among them. The technique used was not designed to tell by what route the water escaped, however.

Snakes eliminate waste products without undue loss of moisture. As indicated in the preceding chapter, some water is necessarily lost with the intestinal waste, less through that of the kidneys. Here we come to that controller of the watery internal environment of the body, the kidney. Next to the heart, it is the organ most deeply involved in the regulation of circulation. Recent research has even shown that the human kidney produces an enzyme having profound effect on blood pressure. It receives and processes more than a quarter of the blood that circulates at each contraction cycle of the heart.

As salt is an important and indispensable part of the body fluid of all vertebrate animals, the kidney must maintain the necessary amount in the blood as well as get rid of the metabolic waste product of protein nitrogen. In the ancestral fishes and amphibians, this was disposed of as urea, which is soluble; reptiles, faced with the problem of conserving water, overhauled the earlier method of protein metabolism to replace urea with uric acid, which is not only relatively insoluble but requires only half as much water for a given amount of protein metabolized. Thus, reptiles make a tremendous and necessary saving of water.

DANGER OF DEHYDRATION

Excessive dehydration invariably spells death. For each species there is a limited and remarkably constant amount that can safely be lost, though a related species may tolerate the loss of much more or much less. The lethal amount is usually stated as a percentage of the total weight of the animal; for rats and mice it is

Head of Carpet Python from Queensland. Note the small scales, which sharply contrast with the large scales on the head of the amethystine python. (Photograph by William Hosmer)

Carpet Python. This is the common python of Australia, where it is found in almost all areas sufficiently moist. It is absent along the coast of New South Wales because there the diamond python, a member (subspecies) of the same species, takes its place. The carpet python has often been confused with the amethystine python, which reaches a length about twice that attained by the carpet python. The technical names of the diamond and carpet pythons have also caused much confusion. They have been known as *Morelia argus argus* and *Morelia argus variegata*, respectively, but are currently *Morelia spilotes spilotes* and *Morelia spilotes variegata*. (Photograph by William Hosmer)

33 per cent, for man only 20. Under extreme conditions of dry heat, an exercising man loses water so fast that he succumbs in a matter of hours; his sweating, which effectively cools him, dehydrates him as well and causes a dangerous loss of salt. Rats and mice do not perspire; they, along with nearly all other rodents, lack sweat glands. This is true also, as noted before, of snakes.

The few species studied suggest that snakes are poor losers of moisture and may die even more readily than does man. Although the experiments of Bogert and Cowles did not give exact figures, they indicated considerable variation from species to species and a loss of 9.1 per cent as fatal to one of their three species. This may be surprising when we bear in mind the resistance of snakes to starvation and even thirst. But these experiments subjected the snakes to such a high temperature (about 100° F.) that it is impossible to estimate the part played by dehydration alone.

Every keeper knows that reptiles may be deprived of water for weeks without apparent harm. Clearly, the lack of sweat glands enhances the ability to resist drying out. Until further work is done, no valid conclusions can be drawn about the amount of water a snake can safely lose while living at reasonable temperatures.

Temperature

HUMAN BEINGS readily appreciate the importance of keeping the temperature of their bodies constant. Many are even too conscious of this necessity, using the clinical thermometer at the least hint of a degree or two of "fever." The Eskimo at times maintains a body temperature scores of degrees above that of his frigid world, whereas desert peoples may keep theirs well below that of the overheated air around them. How do man and other animals cope with fluctuations in the temperature of the environment? Research of the last few decades has made great progress toward an understanding of their complex adjustments.

Near the beginning of this century, a physiologist discovered that the temperature of mammals is relatively independent of their surroundings, whereas that of lizards is not. From such observations developed the concept of two types of animals: the "warm-blooded" and the "cold-blooded." In the former category were placed the mammals and birds, in the latter the reptiles, amphibians, fishes, and vast numbers of invertebrates. The cold-blooded animal was defined as one that, being satisfied with various degrees of heat and cold, takes on the temperature of its surroundings; the warm-blooded creature as one that has a built-in heating system and maintains its temperature at a relatively constant level. This theory has persisted because, though not literally correct, it has an element of truth: the mammals and birds do keep their temperature almost constant, and the lower animals, when not free to move about, absorb heat from relatively warm surroundings and lose it to cool ones.

The major advance in the understanding of reptile temperatures has been made by Raymond B. Cowles and Charles M. Bogert, who, some twenty years ago, began investigating lizards and snakes in the field and in the laboratory. It did not take these workers long to decide that the terms "warm-blooded" and "cold-blooded" are best replaced. For "warm-blooded" they use endothermic, and for "cold-blooded," ectothermic. The endothermic animals have elaborate mechanisms for maintaining a preferred temperature by producing heat internally or ridding themselves of an excess amount, whereas the ectothermic animals derive their body heat from external sources; they avoid chilling or overheating by more or less constant activity.

An animal that lacks insulation afforded by fur or feathers and that makes broad contact with the ground constantly loses or absorbs a great deal of heat. A proneness to lie in the sun and an ability to change color introduce additional interrelated and discouragingly complicated factors. Descriptions of the techniques necessary to overcome these and other difficulties would be far too lengthy for this book. Suffice it to say that modern instruments instantaneously record temperatures of the smallest reptiles to a fraction of a degree; slight handling or the briefest delay can bring about an appreciable change.

To birds and most mammals, air, in contrast to the substratum (the surface on which a creature rests), is the important medium in heat loss and gain. The reverse is true of the reptile, especially the snake, every inch of which loses heat to or gains it from the substratum. Some rattlesnakes, for example, succumb in about ten minutes on ground heated to approximately 135° F., whereas only the soles of a man's feet would be affected. Desert-sand temperatures frequently exceed this figure by twenty or more degrees.

Snakes living in hot deserts obviously are in a predicament similar to that of human beings dwelling in areas of heavy automobile traffic; sudden and swift death lurks on all sides.

Snakes have not been studied as much as have the lizards. The latter seem to prefer higher temperatures and have a narrower range of tolerance. Such differences make them easier and more satisfactory subjects.

Studies by Cowles and Bogert of the dependence of the spiny and earless lizards on relatively constant body temperature suggest that its regulation is something of great stability and significance in the evolution of these and other reptiles. It would seem that each reptilian group inherits a degree of tolerance for temperature as part of its unalterable equipment, and members of each group must find a way to live without violating these basic requirements. This is accomplished by incessant activity. During its diel round each individual moves in and out of the sun or the shade, retires to some crevice, or buries itself in the warm substratum. The desert earless lizard even has a blood receptacle in the head which acts as a heater for the body when the head is exposed to the early-morning sun after the lizard has spent a night buried in sand chilled by the air.

More effort should be spent in studying temperature control in the giant snakes before the leather hunters further decimate their populations. The way has been paved by Francis G. Benedict's elaborate researches on the physiology of pythons and boa constrictors. His work, done in the laboratory, was not intended to answer directly some of the problems tackled by Cowles and Bogert, but it does include lengthy accounts of techniques of temperature recordings.

Temperatures taken by mouth, by cloaca, and by skin contact showed little difference between mouth and cloaca, but some between skin and cloaca, the skin being cooler. The snakes were often co-operative, one of them even lying quietly for an hour with the thermometer in its cloaca, where it was read at will. The extensive contact of the giants with their cages and other containers, as well as with the air and even themselves (they were habitually coiled compactly), caused innumerable difficulties. Benedict's snakes were confined, and therefore his conclusions are not wholly applicable to giants living under natural conditions.

The giant snakes would be ideal for the study of the importance of size in temperature regulation, but unfortunately no one has made studies of the reactions of these reptiles to fluctuations in the temperature of their natural surroundings. It is evident that the larger an animal is, the less it is affected by sudden change, because of the greater time required for penetration of lethal heat or for loss of valuable warmth. Yet all the giants live in or adjacent to tropical regions where they are not subject to sudden fluctuations of temperature. The most rigorous climates for ectotherms are not those of the tropics, as common belief would have it, but temperate deserts, where changes from day to night may reach great extremes, not to mention tremendous seasonal fluctuations.

Reproduction
and Growth

�֍

Sex and Mating

✵

ALTHOUGH reproduction in snakes is essentially like that in other higher animals, there are characteristic aspects worthy of special notice here. But before considering actual courtship and mating it will be well to enumerate most of the sexual differences of snakes and describe certain pertinent ones.

Color distinctions are unusual. For instance, only three of thirty-one European and five of seventy-two Chinese species exhibit any; the probable percentage for the world falls between 5 and 10. Color changes correlated with season or time of mating are unknown.

Differences in scale counts, in total size, and in relative size of body and tail commonly occur, though seldom to a conspicuous degree. Gustav Lederer describes the male reticulate python as appreciably smaller and slenderer than the female. All individuals more than 15 feet long seen by him were females. He also estimates that the largest female Indian pythons are 5 or 6 feet longer than the largest males. The tail of the male reticulate python is thicker at the base and relatively longer, a condition found in numerous other snakes as well. R. F. Laurent found remarkably little sexual dimorphism in a small series of African rock pythons, the largest of which was only 7 feet 1 inch long.

The most noteworthy feature of sexual distinction in the giants is the size of the "spurs." These vestigial appendages occur only in the Boidae and some other primitive groups of snakes. The spurs are larger and longer in males of the southern anaconda, the boa constrictor, and the Indian, reticulate, and African rock pythons. In a pair of mature African rock pythons of equal age and about 8⅓ feet long, the male's spurs measured eighteen sixty-fourths of an inch (7 millimeters), those of the female only eleven sixty-fourths of an inch (4½ millimeters). According to Alphonse R. Hoge, the female boa constrictor's limb has no ilium (a bony element), which in the male is by far the largest part of the entire internal structure.

SEX RECOGNITION

In only a few species are males and females known to live together, and it has not been determined how long the unions last in these few. The first step in reproduction for the vast majority of snakes must therefore be the yearly or (rarely) biannual identification of one sex by the other. In this respect none of the types of sexual dimorphism mentioned so far plays a broad and important role among the giants or, for that matter, any other snakes.

Fortunately, the experimental approach has revealed important clues in the matter of sex recognition. G. K. Noble demonstrated a stimulating odor in the skin of garter snakes (*Thamnophis*), whereas F. E. Baumann, working with a European viper, showed the anal gland to be the source of such a stimulus. There is a seasonal variation in the production of these odors. (Anal glands of snakes, present in both sexes, lie in the base of the tail.) As Noble failed to confirm sexual use of anal-gland secretion by garter snakes, marked differences in methods of sex attraction must exist among snakes.

Giant snakes have not been used in experiments on sex recognition, though Lederer's observations of the southern anaconda in captivity convinced him that males were aroused by an odor ema-

nating from a female. He has also seen a captive female Indian python raise her tail and open the cloaca as if to leave a scent for a
male following her. This behavior is much like that of the European
vipers studied by Baumann, who determined that the places where
the cloaca had been opened were highly attractive to the males. As
intimated by Lederer, experimentation with these large animals is
anything but easy.

COURTSHIP

Special movements, some elaborate enough to be called "dances,"
have been observed prior to mating in male snakes of a few species,
and this behavior undoubtedly plays a part in recognition. The difficulty lies in distinguishing antics of this category from those that
arouse the female after recognition has taken place. There is no
way sharply to separate recognition behavior from courtship,
which will be considered next. In lively types the male chases the
female about, or both sexes may dash around together. In some
species the jaws are used, the males even fighting among themselves,
though combat is rare. The males are usually satisfied with jostling
each other to secure the favors of a particular mate.

Male snakes sometimes have sparring contests. In the past these
contests were frequently mistaken for courtship, thanks to the
difficulty of identifying the sexes at a distance. Some old accounts
of extremely vigorous "courtships" have, therefore, to be taken
with a grain of salt.

Courtship has been observed in relatively few species, and there
remain whole families of snakes to be investigated.

Perhaps the most common type of courtship is that indulged in
by water snakes (*Natrix*), garter snakes (*Thamnophis*), and members of related genera. The excited male begins by rubbing his
chin, which has sensory tubercles, along the female's back until
their bodies lie parallel and together, his head near hers. Proper

juxtaposition of the cloacas is facilitated by sensory tubercles of the anal region. Convulsive waves pass forward along the body of the male at the rate of one every few seconds, or more frequently, and his head may nod in a jerky fashion. Finally, his cloacal region, bent in the form of a wedge, is forced under his mate's body. When several excited males are gathered about a single female, the scene is indeed an animated one. In this type of behavior, the males never fight among themselves.

The movements of giant-snake courtship are simple enough. The male rapidly flicks out his tongue while following the female about and attempting to crawl over her; his head may come to rest on her head or neck. Females of both the Indian and reticulate pythons have been seen to open the cloaca during this early stage, presumably to leave a scent. Lederer describes the male reticulate python as moving in a jerky manner and both sexes of the Indian python as sometimes swaying the (elevated) forward part of the bodies.

The incessant waves that course through the body of the male in many courting snakes are absent in the boas and pythons. It is possible that the jerky movements of the giants are the forerunners of the waves.

Though apparently of a subdued type, the courtship of the boas and pythons introduces an interesting element: active use of the spurs of the male in stimulating the female. This has been observed in the anaconda, the boa constrictor, and the Indian and reticulate pythons. The spur is raised until perpendicular to the body and then, in most species, moved rapidly forward and backward. Lederer watched one courting reticulate python that moved each spur backward and forward a few (from "about one to three") times per second, from five to forty movements being followed by a period of rest. In this and other giants, the male presses his cloacal region against the female while scratching her with the spurs, which touch the corresponding region of her body, now above, now on either side of her cloaca. The spurs have been described as making a scratching sound audible at six feet in the boa constrictor, though no longer audible at twenty inches in the Indian python. The spur movement of a blood python seen by R. Marlin Perkins was too slow to produce a sound, but it was continued without interruption for as long as two hours.

The end of courtship comes when the stimulus of the male's spurs induces the female to raise her cloacal region, allowing the two cloacas to come together. This act is accompanied by the wrapping of the tail and the rear end of the male about those of the female.

ORGANS OF REPRODUCTION

In snakes the male organ is remarkable in structure, location, and use. Instead of having a single penis for injection of seminal fluid, the male has two, one on either side. They are housed in the base of the tail, rather than in the body, and take no part in the elimination of urine. At rest each penis is turned outside in, like a glove finger drawn into the palm. After use, a muscle anchored far back in the tail returns the penis to this resting position.

Before being put in use, the penis is forced out and erected largely by pressure of fluids, the inner surface coming to lie on the outside. The organ then may be long or short, single or forked, and is covered with numerous pleats, calyces, flounces, sharp baseward-sloping spines, hooks, or even more complex structures. Each species has its special combination. Spines and hooks could hardly have been developed on an organ not withdrawn in a special manner.

The male fluid flows down a deep groove. It was formerly believed that during copulation the two penes were pressed together, the grooves forming a tube; each organ is still commonly called a hemipenis. Observations on numerous unrelated species have refuted this belief in the simultaneous use of both penes, though recently an African snake has been erroneously described as inserting the two organs at the same time (see Brain, and also Dowling and Savage, in the bibliography).

It might reasonably be asked why an organ with relatively little to do has such a complex structure in addition to being duplicated. Perhaps the lack of limbs puts the sexes at a disadvantage and this is compensated for by male and female organs that fit securely together like lock and key; certainly a spiny penis is not readily dislodged.

Each penis in the giant snakes is forked and spineless, the surface adorned with fleshy structures, some of which suggest the flounces of women's skirts. Yet as snake penes go, these are simple ones.

The female's receptacle for the penis has scarcely been investigated. Students have studied the penis as an aid to classification, which accounts for our superior knowledge of it.

COPULATION

At the end of courtship, when one penis is inserted, the male ceases his aggressive actions. The union is so secure that the male no longer has to maintain his position, and may even be pulled about by his mate.

The chief characteristic of copulation is its great duration. Laurence M. Klauber has expressed the belief that in rattlesnakes a period of from six to twelve hours is normal, unions of less than an hour or two being rare. The maximum given by him is twenty-two and three quarters hours. There is little information on the length of time the giant snakes remain locked, though periods of one hour (two cases) and of thirty-five minutes have been reported for the Indian python, two and a half and three hours for the reticulate python.

There is some evidence that, in snakes, unions lasting only a few minutes are not fruitful. This may be due to the complexity found in both sexes. No one knows how the fluid moves along the groove of the penis, how the sperm make their way into the receptacles and later fertilize the ova. Possibly, much time is required for the passage of the sperm; early removal of the penis might have an adverse influence.

The penis of an Indian python at the time of copulation has been described by Carl Stemmler-Morath as about an inch and five eighths long and "blue violet" in color. In another snake, it changed slowly from "white to red and violet." The noticeable swelling produced in the female by an inserted penis has been remarked more than once.

FREQUENCY AND TIME OF BREEDING

Not all snakes living under natural conditions follow the familiar pattern of breeding once a year. The female prairie rattlesnake of the western United States and the common viper of Europe (*Vipera berus*) produce young every other year in the colder parts of their ranges. This is, obviously, correlated with the shorter period of activity in the more northern climate. Felix Kopstein's data, on the other hand, show that some tropical snakes lay several lots of eggs a year.

The nature of the cycles of the giants when living in their native tropics is not known. Stemmler-Morath's Indian pythons bred annually for several years, whereas Lederer concluded that the captive female reticulate python is not ready to breed every year.

Vague information on the mating season in nature points to a season centering on the months of December, January, and February. Concrete evidence is scarce. R. R. Mole believed that boa constrictors of Trinidad mate from December to March, anacondas in December and January. Specific cases are not cited. Frank Wall long ago named December, January, and February as the mating period of the Indian python in India. As these snakes hibernate in northern India (and Pakistan) at this time, the suggested coincidence with hibernation is odd. Nevertheless, there are persistent reports of winter aggregation in this part of Asia, and such aggregation usually indicates mating activity. Many additional observations are needed to settle this problem, especially the relation of mating to a period of winter reduction of activity, including actual hibernation.

HYBRIDIZATION AND DELAYED FERTILIZATION

A minor yet interesting subject is hybridization. I have no evidence that any of our six giants are able to crossbreed. It would seem possible, however, for several species of snakes not closely related have been known to cross, and a rattlesnake with parents belonging to different genera is on record. The hybridization of subspecies is another matter. Two of the several subspecies of the boa constrictor have crossed: a race of southern South America (*occidentalis*) with the more familiar one (*constrictor*), which is found chiefly in the northern part of the continent. Just as interesting, though negative, is the failure of so experienced a snake breeder as Lederer to induce the two subspecies of the Indian python (*molurus* and *bivittatus*) to cross.

The next special aspect of reproduction is the ability of some female snakes to store living sperm in their reproductive tracts for months or even years, an ability often referred to as delayed fertilization. This, obviously, makes it hard to find out the time required for eggs or young to develop within the female, which I shall call the period of internal development (commonly known as the period of gestation in animals that give birth). This period is readily determined whenever the life of a released sperm is brief. Such is the case in nearly all higher animals; in man it is about forty-eight hours.

In some fifteen species of snakes it has been determined that the sperm remain active for several months or longer. The record periods are four and a half and six years. (C. Leigh reports an Indian python that laid eggs nine, ten, eleven, and thirteen years after mating. The history of the eggs is not given and therefore their fertility has not been established beyond all question.) Just how is this long retention of sperm accomplished? A complete answer is far in the future, though a recent anatomical study by Wade Fox is revealing. He found in a species of garter snake (*Thamnophis*) tiny receptacles near the forward end of the reproductive tract, where fertilization would most likely take place. These were packed with sperm and opened into the oviduct, the chamber in which the eggs develop.

INTERNAL DEVELOPMENT

The period of internal development in a few of the snakes of the United States has been estimated with a reasonable degree of accuracy. For example, Klauber, basing his statements on his own broad experience as well as on the work of others, records some figures for populations of rattlesnakes living in their natural state: the rattlers of southern California, about 153 days; the Pacific rattlesnake, living farther north in the state, approximately 172 days. He gives periods based on rattlers in the San Diego Zoo as ranging from 141 to 295 days. The constant, high temperatures of the zoo cages undoubtedly have their effect. As the rattlers are strictly live-bearing reptiles, their period of internal development would be comparable to that in the boa constrictor and the anaconda, which use the same method.

The four remaining giants, being egg layers, would be expected to have abbreviated periods of internal development, for much growth takes place in the egg (the pre-hatching period). When Indian python eggs are laid, they contain embryos from about one to three inches long, and clearly have a relatively brief period of internal development; hatchlings are approximately twenty-four inches in length. An embryo three and three sixteenths inches long has been found in a newly laid egg of a reticulate python; hatchlings are about twenty-seven inches long. W. A. Forbes dissected an eleven-inch embryo from an Indian python egg that had been incubated forty-three days. P. L. Sclater records an embryo of equal length taken from an African rock python egg after eighty-one days of brooding; another of the same clutch measured only six inches after fifteen days (see next chapter).

Some very helpful data have been given by Stemmler-Morath, who, in 1950, bred a female Indian python hatched in his zoo during 1945. Because of her extreme youth, there is little chance that such an individual could have been fertilized at an earlier date. Various males copulated with her from April 22 through May 9, 1950, and she laid fertile eggs on June 28. There are many records of zoo matings and subsequent laying, but few of these exclude the possibility of error if used as a basis for calculation of the period of internal development. Leigh made an interesting report on two young virgin females, one of which mated on April 4, the other a few days before; one laid eggs on June 4, the other on June 30. Unfortunately, it was not shown whether the eggs were fertile, and we cannot categorically state that the male was involved until we have positive information on the relation of copulation to fertility in reptiles. It is well known that domestic fowl lay (infertile eggs) without having copulated. Wild birds lay infertile eggs in limited numbers, but the relationship between this phenomenon and mating has not been properly investigated.

An extensive study of tropical snakes made by Kopstein gives some information on the period of internal development in several egg-laying species of Java. Being fully aware of the difficulties caused by sperm retention in the female, Kopstein gives his results with reservation. The development in the species concerned required from thirty-six days to a few months, though a period of more than seventy days was exceptional. The ability of many tropical snakes to lay several times a year suggests rapid internal development.

The final and by far the most significant aspect of snake reproduction is the varied ways in which the young are developed. In mammals and birds the story is simple enough: mammals, with few exceptions, give birth, whereas birds lay eggs. We are apt to think of these methods as the two "normal" ways of reproducing. When we go down the scale, we find a variety of methods among the reptiles, amphibians, fishes, and fish kin. As snakes and lizards well illustrate this variety, I shall confine the discussion to them. Two important statements must be made first. Reptiles were the first of the higher animals to develop an egg making possible a wholly terrestrial life cycle, and thus new vistas in methods of reproduction were opened.

Textbooks often make the mistake of stating that all snakes reproduce by means of eggs though, in certain species, the eggs are retained to be hatched inside the female; in these species, the young appear to be "born." Such retention actually does occur in some snakes, so the statement cannot be thrown out bag and baggage. In a few species with extremely short incubation periods, eggs may even be laid by one female and the young produced directly by another that could not manage to deposit them in time. Research is constantly discovering lizards and snakes with a placenta, species that have a method of reproduction much like that of mammals.

A placenta is an outgrowth of an embryo dovetailed with part of the maternal growth chamber to serve chiefly as the passageway for the material of nutrition or respiration or both. Now, a single type of placenta may involve one or even two of the three or four embryonic outgrowths. In mammals, with very few exceptions, it is formed in but one way, whereas in lizards and snakes at least three types are already known. Descriptions of these various reptilian types would call for the use of many technical terms. Suffice it to add that the outgrowths or so-called embryonic membranes involved in the placenta formation of reptiles are the yolk sac, the allantois, and the chorion. The allantois is basically an organ of respiration.

Laying, Brooding, Hatching, and Birth

THIS CHAPTER deals with the remaining aspects of reproduction including brooding and certain theoretical considerations that revolve about it. There will be some duplication because of the impossibility of precisely separating brooding from the general behavior of the female before, during, and after laying.

BEHAVIOR OF WILD FEMALES

As virtually all of the available information on the female before and during brooding originates with studies on captives, I shall put together here what little is known about females living under natural conditions. In his book devoted almost entirely to the African rock python, F. W. Fitzsimons, listing places chosen by it for nests, gives two categories: (1) cavities and hollows associated with trees, dense underbrush, and boulders and holes abandoned by aardvarks and anteaters; (2) surface sites such as tufts of long, rank grass, rushes bordering streams, sugar cane, and dead leaves in dense scrub. J. W. Lester states that the nests are "frequently" found in termite nests and hollow logs. Charles R. S. Pitman records an abandoned heap of about fifty newly laid eggs discovered at the end of January in a shaded patch of long grass fringing the shore and forest of Damba Island, and his account of another nest will be given later on in this chapter. It would seem that this python lays almost anywhere on or just under the ground.

Data on nests of the reticulate python are scarce. Two found on Sumatra have been recorded; one in a hollow log, the other in a hole under bamboo roots. When encountered, a female amethystine python of Australia was coiled around nineteen eggs in a hollowed-out section of staghorn at the base of a tree. It is not clear why things as conspicuous as python nests are seldom found.

BEHAVIOR OF CAPTIVE FEMALES

Resigning ourselves to the fate of knowing little or nothing about the reproductive behavior of wild females, let us consider captives, beginning with the Indian python. Carl Stemmler-Morath has given some details of its actions while bearing eggs and preparing to lay them. The gravid parent refuses food for weeks before her time and exhibits peculiar behavior, such as lying on her back or side, or perhaps putting merely her rear part in one of these unusual positions. (A snake normally lies on the back or side only when injured or feigning death.) One of these positions may be taken several times during the few weeks before laying. In one instance the female coiled to form a circle and revolved on her long axis for a quarter of an hour, her body often contracting as if from great pain. At times the cloaca may be tongued and still other probable signs of discomfort are exhibited. The belly finally becomes noticeably enlarged. A short time before actual laying, a site is selected and the female stays in it, soon making a depression in the available material. Exact details of this last process are not given by Stemmler-Morath.

Gustav Lederer's large reticulate python took her final pre-brooding meal on December 20 and became extremely restless on

January 23, when she crawled around excitedly and hissed if approached. She was obviously attracted to the area warmed by the artificial heating, and she settled there on January 24. Her first egg was found the next morning, but the last of her fifty-seven was not deposited until February 21; only thirty-two of the lot were brooded.

LAYING

The actual laying of Lederer's snake was carefully observed. An egg was slowly forced toward the cloaca; the tail was raised somewhat and moved repeatedly sidewise, whereupon the egg appeared. From ten to twenty seconds were required to get it out. The laying of one or two eggs was followed by from five to twenty-five minutes' rest. One egg was deposited in Lederer's hand; apparently, at this stage the female was not vicious. When the first twenty-three eggs had been laid, the female encircled them to assume the usual brooding position. She left the eggs for a period of two or more hours on February 1, 2, 4, and 6, but remained with them, so far as could be determined, from February 7 to March 1. After this, her guarding was sporadic until, on March 19, she deserted her charge, which had spoiled and developed a bad odor. (Lederer is convinced that pythons recognize their eggs by odor.)

While brooding, this python noticed every movement of an intruder, as I have already stated. Lederer failed to find any appreciable increase in body temperature, although his effort was much less elaborate than Francis G. Benedict's researches; it is doubtful, however, that Lederer would have failed to detect a marked increase.

Let us return now to Stemmler-Morath's report, for it gives far more information on the Indian python than does any other. He was able to breed a female for several successive years, and he has recorded, in chronological order, the behavior for each year. I have extracted the more interesting facts, and record them here without indication of time sequence or female involved. (He includes a few data not based on the series of broodings by his one female, but these, as they are quite consistent with the other data, do not need to be pointed out.)

In nearly every case reported by Stemmler-Morath as well as by others, laying at least began at night. It is interesting to speculate on just how a captive knows night from day if lights are kept on in a building, as they sometimes are. Perhaps reduced lighting and lack of disturbance would have their effects.

One clutch, however, was deposited entirely during the day. The female lay coiled, her head by her cloaca, and tongued each of the twenty-five eggs as it appeared. The process required seven hours and forty-five minutes. The eggs did not develop. (Decades ago, Frank Wall stated that it took a particular Indian python seven hours to lay sixteen eggs.) A minor point, scarcely worth mentioning, is that the female's spurs stay erect as the eggs pass out. This is hardly surprising when we think of the tension that must be caused by the egg, and the small size of the female spur.

Perhaps the most significant aspects of brooding are the reactions of the female to the egg mass itself, to the brooding site, and to any intruder. Stemmler-Morath gives information on all of these. In 1948 the eggs were removed about the time of laying, but the female brooded the empty space from April 25 to June 14. Quivers ran through her body all the time, indicating that she stayed in the same physiological state maintained when brooding normally.

Most remarkable of all was the experience with a brooding female in 1949. She began laying on May 10 and showed great fortitude, refusing to be disturbed by photographic lights and the taking of two kinds of photographs. Quivers began to run through her in a few hours. Eggs that seemed to be bad were taken from her, and on May 28 the rest were removed, but nine good ones were returned. She remained calm during all this disturbance, continuing to brood. On June 15 three efforts to displace her were fruitless; each time, she was turned on her back by means of a board shoved under her, but she persistently resumed her initial position without sign of anger. Two days later she resisted dislocation in the same way, but did show a little temper by weakly biting at her disturber. When blocked by a board, she crawled into her water basin, but was back brooding by the end of an hour. When, on June 28, other pythons in her cage fed, she left the site to go for food, but she was driven away and she returned to the brooding site; later, she ate two dead cats presumably given to her at the nest site, though Stemmler-Morath does not actually say as much. By July 5 her brooding drive had ceased. (A brooding Indian python reported by Lederer left her charge to eat and returned to resume her vigil.)

I shall now give an account of brooding pythons, gleaned from various sources and largely supplementary to the special cases just dealt with.

Laying usually takes place at night. The eggs, extruded one at a time, may be enveloped by the female as they appear, or she may wait until all are laid before surrounding them to form the characteristic conical pile, the eggs within, her head at the top. She ordinarily manages to keep them completely covered, and she is alert to the presence of any intruder, at least following one with her eyes. (Lederer's reticulate python would not leave her eggs if a human being was in sight; he made vain efforts to surprise her in the act of leaving.) The female may show temper when approached and will return to her charge after being forced to leave. Accounts differ concerning how often and for what purposes she leaves, and she may even remain constantly on guard for weeks on end. Some go to their tubs (probably both to drink and to bathe) about once in twenty-four hours, or leave to eat an occasional meal, or to shed (as one did, on the side of the cage opposite her eggs).

LAYING SEASON AND PRE-HATCHING
PERIOD

The laying season and the duration of the pre-hatching period in the natural state are subjects that we know little about and can well treat together. High temperature speeds up development; most details based on captives are not worth notice and will be omitted. I shall take up the species one by one.

African rock python: On June 2 a wild 14-foot female of Natal was found with eggs about ready for deposition. P. L. Sclater's famous captive, reported in 1862, laid on the night of January 12, whereas the female studied by Benedict in the National Zoological Park, Washington, did not lay until the night of April 5. It is obvious that the laying season of this species cannot be determined with any accuracy from these data.

Lederer states that eggs of this species kept at temperatures from 77° to 93° F., but not brooded, required almost one hundred days of incubation.

Indian python: Wall long ago wrote that, in India, eggs are laid by this species in March, April, May, and June, though he cites the killing on August 2, on Ceylon, of a female containing large eggs; it is possible that their stage of development was misunderstood or that the season on Ceylon, which is so tropical, differs from that elsewhere. Judging by five cases of captive females, the pre-hatching period lasts from fifty-seven or fifty-eight to sixty-six days. This remarkable agreement is possibly due to the fact that zoo curators keep their charges at about the same temperature.

Reticulate python: As also pointed out by Wall, the very little that is known concerning the laying season of the reticulate python suggests a prolonged one; the dates that we have, involving captives, extend from April through October. The pre-hatching period was about eighty days in two cases, from fifty-five to sixty in one, none of them based on females living in nature.

133

HATCHING

On the premaxillary bone of the hatchling there is a structure known as the egg tooth. It projects from the snout and is used by the hatchling to make slits in the shell, thus facilitating escape. This process has been found in many live-bearing species, though in these it is not well developed and does not help the embryo to escape from the birth membrane. The egg tooth is always shed in a few hours or, at most, a day or two after hatching. Lederer observed in the Indian and African rock pythons that the shells often shrink a few days before the eggs hatch. He describes a hatchling of the former as escaping three days after it had made a slit slightly more than an inch and a half long. He also states that in some cases several slits are made. As snake hatchlings in general do not leave the shell for many hours after making the first slit, this three-day period is not surprising. The egg tooth of the African rock python is big enough to show up clearly in a photograph without enlargement.

THE EGG

Every one of us is so familiar with ordinary hen eggs that we think of them as "normal." Next to this type in familiarity are the colored eggs of birds. The snake's egg differs from these in important ways. Its somewhat elastic shell resembles parchment a little and is therefore not brittle; in shape the egg is elongated with the ends alike; pigment is never present, though the shell usually becomes soiled. The highly porous shell allows water to pass either way. The newly laid, firm egg may at first increase in size, and it acquires dents during the late stages of development. Pattern and asymmetrical shape would be useless in an egg that is more or less concealed and not required to fit into a small, elevated nest; a snake's egg is in no danger of falling or rolling. Shape varies widely, some especially long eggs having a greater diameter three, or even three and a half, times that of the lesser, at least when laid (swelling necessarily adds relative length to the lesser dimension).

There is much more information on the number of eggs laid by pythons than on the eggs themselves. As might be expected, those of the Indian python have been described more often and more completely than any others, whereas eggs of the amethystine python have been reported only once (a clutch of nineteen). For the African rock python, Lederer gives the two diameters of one egg as 4 and 2.36 inches and the weight as 6 ounces. Two smaller ones measured only 3.23 and 3.31 inches in the longer diameter, 2.52 and 2.44 in the shorter one. Together they weighed 11 ounces. Eggs of this species adhere if they come in contact immediately after laying.

According to Lederer, the newly laid eggs of the reticulate python are white, soft, shiny, and sticky. They adhere to one another until drying has reduced their stickiness too much, and in a few minutes they lose their shininess as the shell takes on a parchment-like quality. The eggs of the clutch examined by Lederer varied somewhat in size, form, and weight; measurements of three were made just after laying: 4.17 × 2.56 inches, 3.35 × 3.03 inches, 3.23 × 2.99 inches. The weights were 7 ounces for the first and 12.74 ounces for the other two together. Felix Kopstein measured eggs from two small clutches (fourteen and sixteen eggs) laid by small (about 10 feet and 11½ feet) females of Java and showed that whereas the eggs of a clutch were reasonably uniform in size, there was a marked difference between the clutches: four (newly laid) eggs of the larger female had greater diameters ranging from 3.54 to 3.66 inches and lesser diameters from 2.28 to 2.44 inches; six (brooded) eggs from the other clutch had greater diameters ranging from 4.15 to 4.47 inches.

Summarizing the abundant information on the variation in size and weight of the eggs of the Indian python is anything but easy. Wall gave a good account in 1921. Twenty-two eggs from two sources ranged in length of greater diameter from 3.35 to 4.17

inches and from 2.13 to 2.52 inches in the lesser. Sixteen of the twenty-two were taken from a large female and no embryo was found in two, suggesting at least partial infertility of the clutch. Wall recorded weights of three eggs from three sources as 5, 5.5, and 6.25 ounces. Lederer published a table of measurements and weights based on some seventy-six eggs, apparently from five clutches, though measurements and weights of only five individual eggs are given. These five also show relative uniformity in size and weight, the extremes for the greater diameter being 2.95 and 4 inches, 2.32 to 2.6 inches for the lesser. Four of these five eggs have about the same weight (from 5 to 5.32 ounces), whereas the fifth and noticeably the largest in size weighs 6.8 ounces. The seventy-one eggs of the three whole clutches included in the table do not appreciably alter the extremes based on the five, except that the lowest measurement for the shorter diameter is 2 rather than 2.32 inches.

Stemmler-Morath gives the weights of several Indian python eggs, and his figures for the most part run substantially higher than those of Lederer. The former's lightest egg weighed 4.6 ounces, his next was 7 ounces, and the rest ranged from 8 to 10.7 ounces. All but the 7-ounce egg were newly laid when weighed, and that one was only twelve days old. A clutch of thirty-eight eggs, laid on April 16, weighed together 13 pounds on June 3. This gives an average weight of 5.5 ounces per egg, a value not so far above the figures of Lederer.

Newly laid eggs of the Indian python stick together, though Lederer writes of a clutch of them that failed to do so.

SIZE OF CLUTCHES

Although no worker has ever undertaken the technically difficult task of recording the weights and measurements of a python egg from laying to hatching, every casual observer has been willing to count the eggs in a clutch. These numerous counts, besides telling us what to expect of the six giants, are of value in confirming or weakening these two hypotheses: females of large species lay more eggs at a time than do those of small ones; and the older females of a given species lay more eggs than do the younger. The second is generally conceded to be valid for reptiles in general.

The same propositions apply, of course, to live-bearing species, and these bring up the additional question of the relative ability of live-bearers as opposed to egg layers. It should be pointed out again that, because of growth after sexual maturity, the older snakes are usually the larger ones. Keeping these problems in mind makes the subject of number of eggs and young more interesting, raising it to the scientific, rather than merely the factual, level.

Considering the snakes of the world as a unit, the range in the number of young that may be produced in a single clutch or brood is surprising. A great many species average less than ten, whereas a few on occasion may lay or give birth to as many as one hundred, though their average is always a much lower figure. The big producers, those occasionally responsible for more than fifty at a time, seem to crop up in many far-flung regions, among a varied assortment of sizes and systematic groups. Perhaps the average for the majority of the species of the world lies between eight and fifteen, but, admittedly, this is a rough guess. Let us see what the giants do.

Boa constrictor: Remarkably little information on this common boa is available. The number of young produced per birth ranges from 21 to 64, with 15 as a possible lower limit. The low record is based on a somewhat abnormal birth: Earl E. Hoover's captive Central American female, only 3 feet 11 inches long, produced four young and eleven apparently premature "eggs." The event took place on July 19, the parent having been in captivity since the preceding May.

Anaconda: The number of young produced at a time by this giant ranges only from 28 to 42. Records are too scarce to allow correlation of number of young with size of parent.

African rock python: Fitzsimons long ago correlated the size of these pythons with the number of eggs produced. I have amplified his results with additional records, and the confirmation is striking except in the case of the largest specimen of all, a giant from central Africa that held only 26 eggs. It is, of course, possible that this individual was either senile or sick or both.

CORRELATION OF LENGTH OF AFRICAN ROCK PYTHONS WITH EGG COUNTS

FEET	NUMBER OF EGGS
8.33	23
11.00	23
11.75	31
12.50	29
13.00	38
13.25	44
about 14.00	about 20
14.50	40
14.50	49
14.50	54
15.00	51
15.00	62
15.25	58
16.00	57
16.00	55 or 65
17.00	69
about 21.00	about 100
24.50	26

I have records of two more, one (whose *skin* measured 20 feet) with 34, the other with about 50 eggs. From all these data we derive an average of 46 eggs per clutch, a figure far below the maximum.

Indian python: It is difficult to determine with accuracy the number of eggs laid by this species because the early records are so confused. Wall, in his 1921 detailed study, gives the range as from 8 to 107, but fails to name the sources of his information. Eight suggests an abnormally low number, whereas 107 is extremely high, though Benedict quotes a record of a clutch of about 100, and Stemmler-Morath records one of only 11, the first batch of a female just matured. In addition, there are available counts of sixteen clutches that give a range of from 15 to 54 eggs per clutch, though only two exceed 38 and the average is but 29. Correlation between size of female and number of eggs probably is not close. I cannot determine the length of the females responsible for the largest clutches (107 and approximately 100 eggs), and the biggest among those remaining laid only about 30 eggs. However, the next largest was responsible for the clutch of 54. This species, it should be recalled, is the smallest of the gigantic pythons.

Reticulate python: Data on this Asiatic giant show that it, too, may just surpass the 100 mark, though usually falling far short.

CORRELATION OF LENGTH OF RETICULATE PYTHONS WITH EGG COUNTS

FEET	NUMBER OF EGGS
10.00	15
10.00	16
11.50	14
13.50	34
18.00	about 50
about 18.00	33
20.50	57
23.00 to 26.00	103
about 26.00	96

This table clearly shows that the larger females usually lay the greater number of eggs. If we add a clutch of 59 recorded for a female of undetermined length, the average per clutch proves to be 48. Lederer (1944) gives most of these records in a table.

Amethystine python: The only clutch that I have found mentioned in the literature is one with 19 eggs.

It is highly probable that, as a group, the gigantic snakes support the thesis that big snakes produce the greatest number of offspring per birth or laying, though it is also likely that a few species of unrelated groups match the giants. This discussion has been confined to the size of single clutches because, as already pointed out, information on the breeding of snakes more than once a year is so meager.

Among reptiles, the turtles produce the most eggs at a laying (between 200 and 300), and the species that attain the highest numbers are gigantic marine turtles. Some turtles lay more than once a year; the record is seven times, and this was achieved by one of the kinds that lay big clutches. Lizards come last, with clutches even smaller than those of snakes, and there are no species that can produce even 50 young at a time, let alone 100. Recently a species of lizard (*Anolis*) has been found to lay an egg every two weeks during a long breeding season, and it is possible that many of its relatives do likewise. Crocodiles and alligators, with barely more than a score of living species, have perhaps the largest clutches on an average, though the comparison is hardly valid because of the few species making up the group. The maximum per clutch approaches, but does not reach, 100. The four reptile groups may, then, be rated in this descending order: turtles, crocodiles and alligators, snakes, lizards.

BROODING AND INCUBATION

The distinction between merely remaining with eggs (brooding) and actually raising their temperature by transmitting to them internally generated body heat (incubating) must be kept constantly

Diamond Python. (Photograph by William Hosmer)

Constriction on a small scale. This western milk snake, a species
found in the United States, constricts, yet it is not classified as one
of the constrictors. It is about 17 inches long; its victim, a skink, is
just over half a foot. The habit of constricting the prey is widespread
among snakes. As an animal's strength increases much less rapidly
than its weight, the constricting power of this milk snake is relatively
greater than that of a python. (Courtesy Walker Van Riper, Denver
Museum of Natural History)

Skeleton of Reticulate Python. This individual, allegedly a 26-footer, proved to be slightly less than 23 feet long. This is about the extent to which the giants "shrink" when the tape is finally applied. (Courtesy The American Museum of Natural History)

in mind while reading the rest of this chapter. Relatively few of
the hundreds of egg-laying snakes brood and only the Indian python is definitely known to incubate.

Brooding is simpler, as it requires no profound physiological
change in the parent. Though the habit occurs in some thirty species of five major groups of snakes (Boidae, elapids, sea snakes,
colubrids, and vipers), it is much less widespread in snakes than in
lizards. The comparatively recent discovery (1931) of brooding by
both parents of the Indian cobra suggests that it may occur more
frequently among snakes than we realize. Two snakes in which
brooding is well established are our mud snake (*Farancia abacura*)
and the Asiatic pit viper (*Trimeresurus monticola*). The former is
the only snake of the United States in which brooding has been
repeatedly described. G. K. Noble and E. R. Mason observed
brooding lizards shift their eggs and attack a wide variety of small
animals that approached the nests, but no one has investigated the
advantages of the instinct for snakes.

Present knowledge indicates that brooding is prevalent only
among pythons, six of twenty species being brooders: the green python of the New Guinea region, the blood python of the Malay
Peninsula, Borneo, and Sumatra, and our four giants. It is highly
probable that several other kinds have the habit. The regal python
of Africa is a puzzle; it has been credited with laying as well as
with giving birth. If the instinct is developed in such primitive
snakes as the pythons, why is it not of general occurrence? There
may be a correlation with size; concealing batches of large eggs
would be difficult, and a big snake makes an effective protector.

The great scarcity of descriptions of pythons brooding in nature
stands in strong contrast to the number of accounts, some thirty
since 1840, based on zoo or laboratory behavior. Pitman has given
us a moderately good account of an African rock python's activities in Uganda. The nest was in a cleared area six or eight feet
across, at the top of a small, steep hill covered with long grass and
elephant "grass." The python coiled about the eggs in such a way

that they could not be seen. Her head was at the summit of the mass, and she watched intruders but did not seem to object to them. Only once during six weeks were the eggs seen to be unguarded, though no continuous vigil was kept. Her eggs formed a mass approximately a foot high and twelve by eighteen inches across.

Regulation of egg temperature not only prevents lethal chilling but shortens a highly critical period of life by speeding up development. Three primitive methods of temperature control are practiced by this or that group of reptiles, one of them even by a few birds: exposing the nests to the direct heat of the sun, placing the eggs in vegetation warmed by heat of decomposition, and transferring to the eggs solar heat absorbed by a basking parent. Many reptiles, especially turtles, deposit eggs in sunny places. Making nests in rotting vegetation is a habit of wide but sporadic occurrence among reptiles; jungle fowl (Megapodiidae) of the Australian–East Indian region hatch their eggs in this way. Heat transference by basking parents of both sexes has been ascribed to the rat snake (*Elaphe obsoleta*).

As incubation is theoretically impossible in ectotherms, physiologists have long been interested in the brooding python. Does she become endothermic while incubating? If so, a timely study of her physiology might promote a better understanding of "warm-bloodedness." The evolutionary implications are obvious. Incidentally, we are tempted to speculate on the differences between incubation in small and in large animals. The latter have a distinct advantage in that they lose heat much more slowly; raising the temperature and keeping it up is vastly easier for them. Both brooding and incubation seem to be of greater value to the giants than to their small relatives.

The study of brooding and incubation in pythons is almost as old as modern zoology itself. But Benedict's review of incubation and his own research, published in 1932, enable us to divide the history into two parts—before Benedict's work began and after. Three important investigations antedated his.

Between 6 and 9:30 A.M. on May 6, 1841, a 10-foot Indian python laid fifteen eggs in the Jardin des Plantes, Paris. Achille Valenciennes repeatedly recorded temperatures of the air in the cage and
under a cloth covering the snake. The temperature between the
coils was also taken and was always found to be well above both
air temperatures. In those days reptile houses apparently were not
well warmed; this snake lived in a cage kept in the upper sixties
(F.). Even under the cover the air was only about five or six degrees warmer. At the beginning the snake's coils were very warm,
a few degrees over 100° F. (maximum 106.7° F.). This fact alone
suggests absorption of heat; such a figure is near the lethal point
for snakes. Later her temperature dropped to the low nineties. With
allowances made for the crude facilities and ignorance of the importance of substratum temperatures, the results of this initial investigation are astonishingly good. The cool surroundings subjected the female to a severe test of her ability to maintain her own
high temperature.

On the night of January 12, 1862, a 21-foot African rock python
laid about one hundred eggs in the London Zoological Gardens and
coiled about them. Using mercury thermometers made for the purpose, P. L. Sclater took temperatures not only of the female and of
the air in the cage but of a disinterested male in the same cage. The
cage was kept slightly cooler (58.6°–66° F.) than the one in Paris.
The temperature between the female's coils fluctuated 14.4 degrees
(81.6°–96° F.). Though the male's readings varied less, they were
roughly midway between those of the female and the air. The in-
stability of the female's temperature and this incredible rise in that
of the male throw grave doubt on Sclater's results. Moreover, on
April 4 the eggs stank, only a few of them proving to be fertile.
Evidently substratum temperatures were being transmitted to both
snakes; the female's coiled position and probable selection of the
warmest place for nesting would have allowed her to absorb the
greater amount of heat. The male, of course, would not have
rested tightly coiled, and could have absorbed heat or lost it.

On the night of June 5, 1881, an Indian python approximately 12 feet long laid about twenty eggs in the London Zoological Gardens and (without eating) incubated them forty-three days. W. A. Forbes studied her and also a male kept under similar conditions but in a separate compartment. With "self-regulating thermometers of the newest pattern," he recorded temperatures taken in the air, in the cage gravel, on the surface of the pythons (each was covered with a cloth), and between the coils of both. If we consider that the substratum temperature is the important one, Forbes's results compare moderately well with the subsequent ones of Benedict, the chief difference being that the former's were somewhat lower (averages for the coils of the female and for the gravel, 89° F. and 84° F.; maximum for the gravel, 90.6° F.). The air of Forbes's compartments ranged from 72.3° F. to 87.1° F. The temperatures of the male were also high (86° F. average between the coils), but with the gravel kept so warm he would have absorbed much heat from it and could have acquired more through digestion (he ate once). Most of the eggs decayed, though embryos developed in one or two.

Benedict reported on an African rock python about 14 feet long that incubated some twenty apparently infertile eggs (which eventually putrefied) in the National Zoological Park, Washington, from April 5, the day they were laid, to June 3, 1931. Hundreds of readings were made with the best instruments, his account filling thirteen pages of text (including many tables) and supplying seven pages of photographs. Temperatures were taken in the cage gravel around the snake, under her, between her coils, between her and the eggs, at her surface, and in the air at varying distances from her. Benedict's results, no doubt reflecting improved technology, show remarkable uniformity: average for the coils, low nineties; for the gravel, high eighties; for the air, slightly lower than for the gravel. At most, a few degrees Fahrenheit can be attributed to body heat produced without muscular activity (tension of the coils). Benedict gives her increase as "of an order of 3° or 4° C." It is debatable whether he presented evidence of appreciable heat production (excluding that due to muscular activity); in so warm an environment the degree necessary for incubation would scarcely have been detected.

G. K. Noble studied a Sumatran blood python 5½ feet long that laid and brooded sixteen eggs in the New York Zoological Park during January 1934. None of the eggs proved to be "alive" and yet none decayed. He failed to detect any rise in temperature in the female, concluding that "in all probability" there was none.

During the night of April 15, 1946, an Indian python in the Basel Zoological Garden laid thirty-five eggs and incubated them until their removal on June 3, when some were found to be fertile. One or more times a day Stemmler-Morath recorded room and coil temperatures, and these show marked agreement with those of Valenciennes. The chief differences are that the Basel cage was kept a few degrees Fahrenheit warmer (slightly above "room temperature") and the female's coils remained almost constantly in the high eighties (lowest, 86° F.), getting above ninety only six times (the four highest readings at the beginning of the incubation period) and never reaching 101° F.

Muscular contractions course through the bodies of some incubating pythons. Noticing these, Stemmler-Morath made frequent recordings of their rate. The number per minute ranged from none (three cases) to thirty-seven (one case); twenty-four recordings gave the rate as twenty or more per minute, twenty as ten or less. Seventy-one consecutive observations were the basis of these data. Quivers may begin even before the completion of laying and continue to the end of incubation. Stemmler-Morath's attempt to correlate their rate with temperature failed. This is not surprising, as his female lived under relatively uniform conditions; he did not raise or lower the cage temperature. At a loss for a better explanation, he suggested that the quivers served to ventilate the eggs.

A photograph of a brooding African rock python was published in *Animal Kingdom* (May–June 1960), the accompanying note explaining that an Indian python was coiled about her eggs in a nearby compartment. Dr. Herndon G. Dowling, Curator of Reptiles of the New York Zoological Society, made a study of these two pythons and has generously given me data from his as yet unpublished report. He has also discussed the whole problem of incubation with me and emphasized the shortcomings of previous investigators, chief among them being neglect of substratum temperatures.

When Dr. Dowling kept his African rock python at relatively warm environmental temperatures (substratum to about 81° F.), the snake's coils stayed from 2.5 to 4 degrees Fahrenheit warmer, results roughly comparable to those of Benedict. However, when the temperature of the substratum was lowered, that of the python dropped correspondingly. No quivers coursed through her body.

In sharp contrast, the Indian python kept her temperature within one degree of 90° F. from April 24 to May 17 even though the temperature of her surroundings (judged by the substratum) was reduced at times to 78° F., at others raised to 90.5° F. Thus, the experimental approach clearly demonstrated the ability of this Indian python to maintain a temperature well above that of her environment. An important fact established by this investigation is that the incubating female's temperature is relatively independent of that of the air.* This fact may go a long way in explaining some of the puzzling results of former investigations. Moreover, Dr. Dowling detected a correlation between the frequency of quivers and the temperature of the substratum. When the difference between snake and substratum temperatures was ten degrees Fahrenheit, the rate ranged from twenty-eight to thirty per minute; when the difference was less than five degrees, the rate was only seven per minute. The conclusion is that the muscular contractions assist in the maintenance of heat. As two other Indian pythons treated

---

* The correlation of air, snake, and substratum temperatures must vary with the method of cage heating. This problem is too complex to consider here.

earlier in this chapter maintained an elevated temperature without quivering, we assume that contractions are by no means the only source of heat.

It would be interesting to know how important incubation is to the development of Indian python eggs; Lederer hatched eggs of the reticulate and African rock pythons, both non-incubators, without aid of the parent.

Growth, Maturity, and Length

THERE ARE TWO TYPES of growth in the higher animals: (1) determinate growth, which is most rapid during early life, slows down as maturity is reached, and ceases soon after this crucial stage; (2) indeterminate growth, which sharply decreases in rate about the time of maturity, but continues indefinitely, if ever so slowly. The second type may be intermittent, as when it is interrupted by hibernation. Mammals and birds, with few exceptions, exhibit determinate growth. Reptiles, as well as fishes and amphibians, demonstrate indeterminate growth.

It is somewhat presumptive to make such a flat generalization about reptiles; investigation of growth in them has just begun. The pitfalls are many. Some captives do not grow at what seems to be a normal rate, and even marked individuals allowed to live under natural conditions may be affected by necessary handling at regular intervals. Giant snakes living in the wilds have not been studied.

MEASUREMENT

Detailed investigation of growth includes measurement of change in dimensions of any organ or other part of the body. But for ordinary purposes, determination of weight and length of the whole animal will suffice, and even this can be troublesome enough in snakes. The weighing of a snake of moderate size calls for good spring scales, a bag, and some precaution in making allowance for heavy stomach contents; gigantic individuals require large balance scales and handling that is often harmful to them. The investigator's dream is scales built into the cage of the giant.

Taking the measurement of living snakes is extremely difficult, and the longer the snake, the greater the difficulty. It is a rare captive that will stretch out against a wall the way Sylvia does and thus facilitate accuracy. The handling and measuring of the ferocious giant is hazardous, especially when it is valuable and the chance of injury is great. After much experience, James A. Oliver frankly states that he knows of no "really practical method for accurately measuring" any snake longer than 15 feet. He suggests three methods: (1) laying as best you can a string or soft wire along the back; (2) straightening the body and tail out by main force and taking the measurement at the moment of greatest relaxation (of the snake!); (3) persuading it to crawl down a trough. Oliver once used two of these methods on a giant and obtained measurements of 18 and 20 feet. This is about the exactness that can be expected, and one expert's results are as good as another's.

GROWTH BEFORE AND AFTER MATURITY

Though meager and based on captives, studies of giant snakes do give us grounds for tentative broad comparisons. First, the growth of the giants is essentially like that of snakes in general: the rapid increase in length which precedes sexual maturity is greatly reduced after it, and the subsequent growth may continue for a large part, if not all, of the remainder of its life. The giant snake merely starts out bigger and adds more absolute length per unit of time.

If there is a difference, it lies in the change after maturity; at least some individual giants may end up with a length between three and four times the length at maturity. Many other (probably nearly all) snakes at maturity are already more than half their final length. Laurence M. Klauber put length at maturity at two thirds the ultimate length for some rattlesnakes, and Charles C. Carpenter's data on Michigan garter and ribbon snakes (*Thamnophis*) show that the smallest gravid females are more than half as long as the biggest adults. Felix Kopstein states that "when the snake reaches its maturity it has already reached about its maximal length," but goes on to cite the reticulate python as an exception, with maximum length approximately three times that at maturity. It is hard to understand how he concluded that most snakes do not grow appreciably after attaining maturity; he was working with species of Java, so perhaps some tropical snakes are unusual in this respect. Certain individual giants recorded later did fail to show a reasonable difference after maturity, but it is impossible to know whether this is due to captive conditions. Additional records of slow growth have been omitted.

It is possible to make a few generalizations about the six giants themselves. There seems to be a rough correlation between the initial and ultimate lengths, starting with the smallest (boa constrictor) and ending with the largest (anaconda). Data on the former are scanty, but there can be little doubt that the latter is sometimes born at a length greater than that of any of the others, thereby lending support to the belief that the anaconda does, indeed, attain the greatest length. For four of the six (the anaconda and the amethystine python cannot be included for lack of data) there is also a correlation between size at maturity and maximum length, the boa constrictor being the smallest and the Indian python the next in size at the former stage.

Let us speculate a little on the maximum size of the anaconda. If, in a certain part of the range, it starts life 1 foot longer than do any of the other (relatively large) giants, and reaches maturity at, let us guess, 18 inches longer than the others, a quadrupling of the maturity length would result in a maximum of (nearly) 40 feet.

When it comes to rate of early growth, the Indian python leads with a figure of about 3 feet 6 inches per year for the first two years, more or less. The African rock python, a close second, is followed in turn by the reticulate python. There are few data on the boa constrictor, those for the anaconda are unconvincing, and there is nothing at all on the amethystine python. It seems likely that the Indian python comes out ahead because records of its growth have been made more carefully and frequently; it responds exceptionally well to captivity and does not reach proportions that make it hard to keep.

I cannot make sense out of the figures for post-maturity growth; at best the annual increase appears to be a matter of inches rather than feet. Until better records have been kept over longer periods of time and much more is known about the maximum dimensions, it will be wise to refrain from drawing conclusions.

It is often stated that the largest snakes require five years to attain maturity, but this apparently is an overestimation. The best way to determine the correct figure (in captives) is by direct observation of pairs isolated from birth, a method that produced surprising results: maturing of a male Indian python in less than two years, his mate in less than three; data on the boa constrictor about match this.

Another approach is to estimate from the rate of growth and the smallest size at maturity. Results from this approach amply confirm the direct observations: about three years are required, there being a possible slight difference between males and females in the time required. Only the amethystine python and the anaconda must be excluded for lack or paucity of data.

The following information on snakes varying greatly in size (but all with less than a 10-foot maximum) shows, when considered with the foregoing, that there is probably no correlation between the length of a snake and the time required for it to mature. Oliver, in his summary of the habits of the snakes of the United States, could supply data on the maturing period for only three species in addition to the rattlers, which I shall consider separately. These three were much alike: lined snake (*Tropidoclonion*), one year and nine months; red-bellied snake (*Storeria*), two years; cottonmouth (*Agkistrodon*), two years. Klauber investigated the rattlesnakes carefully himself and also summarized what others have found. He concluded that in the southern species, which are rapidly growing types, females mate at the age of two and a half and bear the first young when they are three. Other herpetologists have ascertained that in the northern United States the prairie rattlesnake may not give first birth until it is four or even five years old, and that the young may be born every other year, rather than annually. Carpenter's study showed that female common garter and ribbon snakes of Michigan mature at about the age of two.

MAXIMUM LENGTH

Oversized monsters are never brought home either alive or preserved, and field measurements are obviously open to doubt because of the universal tendency to exaggerate dimensions. Measurements of skins are of little value; every snake hide is noticeably longer than its carcass and intentional stretching presents no difficulty to the unscrupulous explorer.

In spite of all the pitfalls, there is a certain amount of agreement on some of the giants. The anaconda proves to be the fly in the ointment, but the reason for this is not clear; the relatively wild conditions still found in tropical South America might be responsible.

There are three levels on which to treat the subject. The first is the strictly scientific, which demands concrete proof and therefore may err on the conservative side by waiting for evidence in the flesh. This approach rejects virtually all field measurements. The next level attempts to weigh varied evidence and come to a balanced, sensible conclusion; field measurements by experienced explorers are not rejected, and even reports of a less scientific nature are duly evaluated. The third level leans on a belief that a lot of smoke means some fire. The argument against this last approach is comparable to that which rejects stories about hoop snakes, about snakes that break themselves into many pieces and join up again, or even of ghosts that chase people out of graveyards; the mere piling up of testimony does not prove, to the scientific mind, the existence of hoop snakes, joint snakes, or ghosts.

Oliver has recently used the second-level approach with the largest snakes, and has come to these conclusions: the anaconda reaches a length of at least 37 feet, the reticulate python 33, the African rock python 25, the amethystine python at least 22, the Indian python 20, and the boa constrictor 18½.

Bernard Heuvelmans also treats of the largest snakes, but on the third level, and is chiefly concerned with the anaconda. He reasons that as anacondas 30 feet long are often found, some might be 38, and occasional "monstrous freaks" over 50. He rejects dimensions of 70 feet and more. His thirteenth chapter includes many exciting accounts of huge serpents with prodigious strength, but these seem to be given to complete his picture, not to be believed.

Detailed information on record lengths of the giants is given in the section that follows.

GROWTH OF THE SIX GIANTS

Discussion of the giants one by one will include, as far as possible, data on these aspects of growth: size at which life is started and at which sexual maturity is reached; time required to reach maturity; rate of growth both before and after this crucial stage; and maximum length, with confirmation or amplification of Oliver's figures. Definite information on the growth of senile individuals is lacking.

Anaconda: At birth, this species varies considerably in size. A brood of twenty-eight born at Brookfield Zoo, near Chicago, ranged in length from 22 to 33½ inches and averaged 29 inches. Lawrence E. Griffin gives measurements of nineteen young anacondas, presumably members of a brood, from "South America"; the extreme measurements of these fall between the lower limit of the Brookfield brood and its average. Raymond L. Ditmars had two broods that averaged 27 inches. R. R. Mole and F. W. Urich give approximately 20 inches as the average length of a brood of thirty from the region of the Orinoco estuaries. William Beebe reports 26 inches and 2.4 ounces (this snake must have been emaciated) for the length and the weight of a young anaconda from British Guiana. In contrast, Ditmars recorded the average length of seventy-two young of a 19-foot female as 38 inches, and four young were born in London at a length of 35 or 36 inches and a weight of from 14 to 16 ounces. Beebe had a 3-foot anaconda that weighed only 9.8 ounces. A difference between subspecies might explain the great range in size.

I have little information on the anaconda's rate of growth. Hans Schweizer had one that increased from 19½ inches to 5 feet 3 inches in five years, and J. J. Quelch records a growth of from less than 4 feet to nearly 10 in about six years. It is very unlikely that either of these anacondas was growing at a normal rate.

In 1948, Afrânio do Amaral, the noted Brazilian herpetologist, wrote a technical paper on the giant snakes. He concluded that the anaconda's maximum length is 12 or 13 (perhaps 14) meters, which would approximate from 39 to 42 feet (14 meters is slightly less than 46 feet). Thus, his estimate lies between Oliver's suggestion of at least 37 feet and the 50-foot "monstrous freaks" intimated by Heuvelmans.

The most convincing recent measurement of an anaconda was made in eastern Colombia by Roberto Lamon, a petroleum geologist of the Richmond Oil Company, and reported in 1944 by Emmett R. Dunn. However, as a field measurement, it is open to question. Oliver's 37½ feet is partly based on this report and can be accepted as probable. However, many herpetologists remain skeptical and would prefer a tentative maximum of about 30 feet.

It is possible that especially large anacondas will prove to belong to subspecies limited to a small area. In snakes difference in size is a common characteristic of subspecies.

Boa constrictor: A Colombian female's brood of seventeen boa constrictors born in the Staten Island Zoo averaged 20 inches. This birth length seems to be typical. When some thirteen records of newly and recently born individuals are collated, little or no correlation between length and distribution can be detected. The range is from 14 to 25 inches; the former figure is based on a somewhat unusual birth of four by a Central American female (see chapter on Laying, Brooding, Hatching, and Birth), the latter on a "normal" newly born individual. However, as so many of the records are not certainly based on newborn snakes, these data must be taken tentatively; final conclusions will have to await the measurements of broods from definite localities.

Alphonse R. Hoge's measurements of several very young specimens from Brazil suggest that at birth the female is slightly larger than the male.

I have surprisingly little information on the size and age at maturity. Carl Kauffeld has written to me of sexual activity in February 1943 of young born in March 1940. One female, collected on an island off the coast of Nicaragua, was gravid and measured 4 feet 8 inches from *snout to vent* (her tail should be between 6 and 7 inches long). The female from Central America which gave birth to four was only 3 feet 11 inches long.

What data there are on growth indicate considerable variation in rate; unfortunately, no one has kept complete records of one individual, whereas many have been made for a very short period of time. The results are too varied to allow generalization.

The Central American brood of four increased at a remarkably uniform rate: one year after birth (14 to 14½ inches), they were from 27½ to 28½ inches long. An individual from Guatemala grew from 20 inches (1.6 ounces) to 35 inches (14 ounces) in eighteen months; another small one from 14 to 26 inches in four and a half months; yet another from 14 to 23½ inches in two months.

GROWTH OF INDIVIDUAL BOA CONSTRICTORS

SEX	PERIOD		INITIAL AND FINAL LENGTHS			
	Years	*Months*	*Feet*	*Inches*	*Feet*	*Inches*
male	2	0	1	8	6	7
female	2	0	1	8	8	10 (approx.)
?	3	0	2	4	4	11
?	2	0	2	1	5	2
(same snake)	1	1	5	2	5	5
male (*imperator*)	2	6	2	0	5	7
?	0	7	3	0	3	11
(same snake)	3	1	3	11	5	11 (approx.)

The last snake listed in the table weighed as follows: when 3 feet long, 12.3 ounces; when 3 feet 11 inches long, 26.4 ounces; when about 5 feet 11 inches long, 70.4 ounces.

The accepted record length for the boa constrictor is unusual in that it is based on a field measurement (by a scientist) that appreciably raises the formerly accepted maximum. This field measurement was made by Colin F. Pittendrigh, who encountered the big snake one morning in a swampy area of the Central Range of Trinidad. It was coiled up in the hollow end of a tree trunk, from which it had to be extracted by means of poles. After it was shot, Pittendrigh determined its length in the flesh as 18½ feet. This is the kind of field observation which cannot be lightly discredited. Robert Mertens heard of an El Salvador boa constrictor slightly longer (about 6 meters), but questioned the validity of the report. It is probable that, as with the anaconda, the various subspecies of this widely distributed snake will prove to have noticeably different maximum lengths; if this is so, the presence of exceptionally large boa constrictors in northern South America and adjacent territory would have a logical explanation; individuals of two subspecies apparently attain gigantic dimensions.

African rock python: The average length of a brood of less than forty hatchlings of the African giant is given by G. S. Cansdale as 28 inches. This is a little greater than the size of a lot seen in a tree by Charles R. S. Pitman ("nearly 2 feet"). Several other records confirm the hatching size as from 22 ½ to 28 inches. A. Woerle puts the length of one individual at 27 ½ inches, weight 7.3 ounces.

Stanley S. Flower records two individuals that were caught near empty eggshells in February 1929 and hand-reared in London. They were first seen to mate in December 1934, and the female laid eggs the following January, when she measured between 8 and 9 feet. This indicates sexual maturity in about five years and ten months, at a length of 8 or 9 feet. There is another record of egg laying by two females, one 11 feet, the other 11 feet 9 inches. Gustav Lederer confirms, by his own observation, the age of maturity of both sexes at five years.

There are a few data on early growth of captives: one from about 30 inches to 12 feet in six years, another from 21 to 34 inches in four and a half months. Increase in weight is shown in two reports. The first records an increase from 35.3 to 59.4 pounds in approximately twenty months; the latter weight was taken when the python was a little more than 12 feet long. (The exact length was not determined until two months after the final weighing.) The second report shows an increase from 7 ounces to 4.8 pounds in two years; the initial length was 27 ½ inches.

My only record of growth after maturity shows an increment of 1 meter (slightly over 3 feet) in four years; the individual measured 11 ½ feet at first.

Twenty-five feet is a generally accepted maximum length for the African rock python. Arthur Loveridge, who is as well qualified as anyone to pronounce a judgment, stated: "I am quite prepared to believe that this python may attain a length of 30 feet. I have measured a freshly removed skin that was exactly 30, though in the flesh such a monster would probably not be very much over 25 feet. This reptile had been speared by natives on the bank of the Ngeri Ngeri River near Morogoro [in Tanganyika]. . . . The two largest living pythons which I have kept in captivity measured 14 and 12 feet respectively; the weight of the latter when brought to me was exactly 30 pounds."

In 1932 Charles Béart measured an African rock python that was fully 32 feet long (9.81 meters). It was sighted in a hedge of bougainvillaea surrounding a school in Bingerville, Ivory Coast Republic, and shot by Mrs. Béart. Many people saw the corpse. Mr. Béart kindly sent me the details in a letter dated December 25, 1958. Thus, Loveridge's expectations seem to be realized, and we may, with some assurance, raise Oliver's maximum (25 feet).

Indian python: According to Frank Wall, hatchlings from eggs acquired in Travancore averaged 29 inches. In contrast to this stands the often cited Paris record, from the middle of the nineteenth century, of a brood of eight hatchlings which averaged only 19¾ inches. C. Leigh reported two broods of hatchlings, one with an average length of 21 inches and a weight of 3.5 ounces, the other 24 inches and 4 ounces. Calcutta hatchlings, as reported by Wall, averaged about 24 inches in length. W. Wunder noted extreme hatchling lengths of a brood of thirty as 23½ and 27½ inches.

Wall's record of a Nagpur museum male that mated successfully at a length of 5 feet 8 inches remains unmatched; the next male in size to do as much was 8 feet 8 inches long (Lederer). The smallest female to produce fertile eggs is the one that mated with the Nagpur male; she was only 8 feet 6 inches at the time. Confirmation of maturity at this length is found in a gravid female but 2 inches longer killed on Ceylon. One of Lederer's males (both of which were *molurus molurus*) copulated when it was only 8 feet 2 inches, but the result of this activity was not determined. As might be predicted, the female matures at a size somewhat larger than that at which the male does. Females of 10, 11, and 12 feet have also been shown to be sexually mature.

In 1936 Leigh stated that the female of a mated captive pair laid fertile eggs at the age of less than three years (July 22, 1933, to June 3, 1936), and that the male was less than two years old (hatched June 26, 1934—date of mating not given). Eleven years after, he published a note saying that two females hatched at about the same time (late July 1933) laid eggs in June 1938, but it was not proved whether these were fertile; mating had taken place about April 1, 1938.

There are several records of growth, and these indicate that individuals respond differently to captivity. On the assumption that the snakes involved were growing normally, I have selected a few cases of rapid increment. One of the best is the old Paris record. In twenty months eight hatchlings grew from an average length of 19¾ inches to one of 6 feet 7 inches, a fourfold increase. Wall mentions a brood that lengthened 11 inches in four months.

Records of individuals are impressive. One of the eight Paris hatchlings showed especially rapid development, reaching a length of 7 feet 8 inches in the twenty months. Richard G. Paine wrote me that two Indian pythons, hatched at the Hershey, Pennsylvania, zoo but later sent to the National Zoological Park, in Washington, measured 12 feet and weighed 56 pounds when a little over three years old.

Sylvia's growth, given in the table on page 160, is exceptionally complete and accurate because of her docility. Unfortunately, her length as a hatchling was not determined, though she was but a few months old when first measured.

Her girth was 7 inches in February 1947 and increased to 12 during the next year; after that, it changed little or not at all (last taken in 1949).

Almost nothing is known about the growth of this species in

GROWTH OF SYLVIA

DATE	LENGTH (Feet and Inches)		WEIGHT (Pounds and Ounces)	
Feb. 10, 1946	3	5.5		
Apr. 7	3	11.5		
July 25	4	6		
Sept. 6	4	11		
Oct. 13	5	1		
Nov. 23	5	5	4	7
Jan. 6, 1947	5	9.5	5	8
Feb. 2	6	0.5	6	6
Mar. 2	6	4	7	13
Apr. 1	6	7	7	12
May 2	6	9	11	8
June 1	7	1	12	10
July 2	7	5	15	9
July 31	7	8	16	3
Aug. 28	7	11.5	18	14
Sept. 29	8	4.5	20	13
Oct. 30	8	7	21	14
Nov. 30	8	10	25	
Dec. 31	8	11.5	26	12
Jan. 31, 1948	9	3.5	28	
Feb. 29	9	6.5	31	
Mar. 30	9	10	31	8
Apr. 29	9	11.5	38	
May 31	10	2.5	38	
June 30	10	5	36	
Dec. 31	10	6	41	
Aug. 1, 1949	10	7	33	8
Sept. 19, 1951	10	9	34	
Oct. 3, 1956	12 (almost)		56	8
Jan. 22, 1960	13		70	

later life. Wall quotes a record of one that increased from 12 to about 15 feet in two years. The table shows how slowly Sylvia lengthened after she matured (presumably in the fall of 1947; she was never given the opportunity to breed). Her growth was roughly matched by two individuals reported by Flower: one from about 4 feet to about 12 in ten years, the other from 6 feet 6 inches to 13 feet in twelve years, eight months, twenty days.

In 1921 Wall devoted a page and a half of his book on Ceylonese snakes to the question of the greatest length attained by this species, stating that individuals 18 feet long are "not very uncommon"; he concluded that "there is little doubt that it exceeds 20 feet." Since then, no valid evidence of specimens more than 20 feet long has appeared, and we can accept Oliver's maximum of 20. This snake is, nevertheless, often credited with a much greater length, and Wall pointed out that it is relatively thick. An Indian python killed in Assam was 19 feet long and weighed 200 pounds; S. V. O. Somanader records an Indian python of Ceylon equal to this in both length and weight.

Reticulate python: Several old records of hatchlings are brought together by Lederer. A female from Borneo, between 23 and 26 feet long, laid 96 eggs within three days. Thirty-two of the young that hatched measured from 21½ to 29½ inches. A female of the same length and from the same island laid 103 eggs; the young measured from 24 to 30 inches. One hatchling of a brood of 59 eggs measured 24 inches and weighed slightly more than 4 ounces.

The only available information on the size and age at which males mature is given by Lederer, who had one that was sexually active when 9 or 10 feet long and probably five or six years old. Also recorded are three females that were sexually mature at about 10 feet, and a fourth that was at this stage at 11½ feet; these females either laid eggs or were gravid.

We are indebted to the same authority for the greatest amount of information on the growth of the reticulate python, as this table and the paragraph following it will show.

161

GROWTH OF CAPTIVE RETICULATE PYTHONS

DATE		LENGTH		
		(Feet and Inches)		
		Male	Male	Female
May 2, 1925		2 6	2 7	3 0
Jan. 1, 1926		3 3	3 11	4 3
Jan. 1, 1927		4 11	5 11	6 7
Jan. 1, 1928		7 4	7 11	8 6
Jan. 1, 1929		8 6	8 10	10 2
Jan. 1, 1930		9 10	10 2	11 10
Nov. 27				12 2
Jan. 1, 1931		10 10	10 6	
Jan. 1, 1932		11 7		
Jan. 1, 1933		11 10		
Mar. 21			11 7	
Mar. 17, 1939		11 11		

One of his females showed relatively little change in later life: from 17 feet 3 inches to 21 feet 1 inch in thirteen years. Another female (21 feet 9 inches in 1932) increased only 6 inches during the following four years and five months.

One member of a brood kept in London grew from less than 2 feet to 6 feet 6 inches in eighteen months; none of the other six survivals of the brood attained a length of more than 5 feet 6 inches in this same time. A female kept in Hong Kong lengthened from 4 feet 6 inches in August 1950 to 12 feet 1 inch and reached a weight of 46 pounds 8 ounces by June 1953; the average rate of growth was thus about 2 feet 8 inches per year, but it decreased with age. Three individuals in London, the one given last a female, showed the following increase: from 11 to 21 feet in eleven years, when growth apparently ceased; from 19 to 24 feet in fourteen years; from about 10 to "about 18 or 20" feet in seventeen years.

On August 10, 1949, a 22-foot individual from Siam was re-

ceived in Pittsburgh; by February 1953 it was 27 feet long, and
28½ feet by 1957. Its weight in February 1953 was 295 pounds,
in 1957 at least 320. Charles E. Shaw's Blue Boy, in San Diego,
went from 14 feet (103 pounds) to 18 feet (about 180 pounds) in
slightly less than eighteen years. A small individual in San Diego
grew from a little more than 3 feet in August 1950 to 7 feet by
1954.

In the 1840's Gabriel Bibron found the rate of growth to be
2¼ feet annually during the first four years of life.

Wall's 1926 account of the reticulate python gives its maximum
length as "nearly, if not actually, 30 feet," and Oliver states that it
rarely exceeds 30, but sets the maximum at 33 feet. This last is
based on the measurement of a python from Celebes described to
Henry C. Raven by a civil engineer he met there. The giant had
been killed by local men, dragged into camp, measured (with a sur-
veying tape), and photographed there. Somewhat less reliable records of individuals between 30 and 33 feet are in print, and reticulate pythons 25 feet long, or somewhat longer, have been placed
on exhibit. For example, the largest snake ever displayed in the National Zoological Park was a reticulate python that measured 25
feet and weighed 305 pounds. It was briefly on view in Washington in 1942 and may now be seen in the United States National
Museum. An encouraging fact is the lack of highly exaggerated
stories comparable to those about the anaconda.

Amethystine python: Hatchlings are reported by David R.
McPhee to measure from about 18 to 24 inches. A captive once
grew from 10 to 13½ feet in twenty months. This is a good rate
for post-maturity growth, if, indeed, the individual was mature at
the beginning of the twenty months.

A dead specimen of this python 23 feet 8 inches long was taped
in the flesh by S. Dean, and ample evidence exists that a length of
20 feet is reached. I see no reason to alter Oliver's conclusion that
the amethystine python reaches a length of at least 22 feet. A
gigantic specimen measured by Louis Robichaux is variously re-

ported at 25 and 28 feet long, but it would be well to await confirmation of such dimensions.

GIANT SNAKES OF AGES PAST

With so much information abroad on the gigantic reptiles of ages gone by, the question of the greatest size *ever* attained by snakes comes to mind. Are the living ones a mere remnant of a glorious past when colossal snakes roamed the earth? The answer is definite. Snakes, in contrast to so many other reptiles, are in a flourishing state today; they were the last group of reptiles to develop in profusion, coming into their own during the Tertiary period, along with the mammals; the Age of Reptiles had just closed.

Unfortunately, snakes do not fossilize well and have not left remains that appreciably help the student of classification; their family tree is still adorned with question marks rather than branches. Yet it is possible to make a statement about the maximum size of those that did leave a fossil record, for size can be roughly calculated from vertebrae alone, and sufficient numbers of these have been found. It is good skulls—which are the parts that are indispensable for the determiner of relationships—that are excessively rare.

Evidence on maximum size of fossil snakes comes from two widely separated parts of the world, both at present having climates completely inhospitable to giant snakes as we know them. Patagonia had a mild climate and luxuriant vegetation when it was inhabited by the giant *Madtsoia bai*, sixty or more millions of years ago (in the Eocene epoch). This snake probably grew to be more than 30 feet long—"around ten meters," George Gaylord Simpson, its describer, guesses. The other giant, *Gigantophis garstini*, found in Egypt, also lived during the Eocene. Its maximum length has been estimated as high as 60 feet, but there is no clear evidence that it noticeably exceeded *Madtsoia* in size; about twice as many vertebrae (forty-five, most of them with ribs, of a presumed three hundred) of *Madtsoia bai* are available. Simpson called it the most satisfactory of fossil boas and pythons, a statement that shows at what tremendous disadvantages the paleontologist must work. (A jaw fragment of *Gigantophis* has been found, but no skull part of *Madtsoia*.) The Eocene snakes, like those of today, included both large and small species, the latter greatly predominating. As the earliest known snakes lived in the Cretaceous, a period separated from the Eocene only by the Paleocene epoch, it is patent that, early in their evolution, the snakes quickly tried out all sizes and found smaller dimensions most advantageous.

It is sometimes alleged that an enormous viper lived in South America during a more recent geological period, but the "fang" that gave rise to this allegation is not from a snake.

Longevity

�֍

INFORMATION on the greatest age attained by the higher animals is gathered from three sources: domesticated individuals, wild ones existing in captivity, and wild ones living under natural conditions. Data from these three sources are not strictly comparable. The drastic artificial selection that goes with long domestication eventually affects the genetic make-up and with it, probably, the potential for longevity. Captivity, under the best of conditions, provides a better chance for survival by removing the dangers posed by natural enemies. In sharp contrast, some species are not suited to confinement and die sooner than they would in the wilds.

George J. Wallace, who compiled data on birds, emphasizes the relatively short life span of many birds living under natural conditions; it may be but a fraction of the potential span. As we might expect, Wallace's records of absolute longevity are based on captives. In his list of twenty-six species, only nine lived 30 or more years, the highest of these being a European eagle owl (68 years). Widely circulated accounts of various birds that survived a century or more are discredited.

François Bourlière has published a comparable list of about a hundred species of mammals. Sixteen failed to exceed 10 years, whereas nine lived 30 and more years. A captive Indian elephant leads with a 69-year record. Man, of course, is the champion among mammals and should be placed between the elephant and the turtles. Without this longevity, he could not have achieved such dominance.

As no reptiles or amphibians have been domesticated and we know little about their longevity under natural conditions, our data will be based almost entirely on captives. As in other groups, certain species do not long survive confinement, but experienced keepers will in time reduce the number of these. A few decades ago Stanley S. Flower made an extensive survey of the duration of life of vertebrates, and we have him to thank for nearly all that we know about reptile and amphibian longevity.

Turtles take the prize not only among reptiles but among all the vertebrates as well. Several kinds are known to pass the 50-year mark, and individuals of two species have reached venerable ages: one, living under natural conditions, attained 138 years, and another, a captive, reached 152 years; the first represented a small species (box turtle, *Terrapene*), the second a giant tortoise (*Testudo*). In turtles, there seems to be no marked correlation between size and life span. In regard to longevity, it is hard to choose among the crocodilians (crocodiles, alligators, and relatives), lizards, and salamanders; an individual of at least one species of each has been known to pass the age of 50. The frogs (including toads) rate after all these and are about on a par with snakes; individuals of two kinds of toads (*Bufo*) have attained the ages of 36 and 40 years, and a bell toad (*Bombina*) has made the 20-year mark.

In respect to snakes, we find that individuals of at least eighteen species have attained an age of 20 or more years; in nearly every case the record is based on a captive. The black-lipped cobra has first place with 29 years; the anaconda comes next with 28. Several additional kinds approach the 20-year mark. For a group, the rattlers are distinguished in having received special attention in a zoo unusually well equipped to deal with them; twenty individuals representing ten species have survived for 10 or more years in the San Diego Zoo, though only one attained the age of 20. It is possible that highly dangerous species, such as the larger rattlers, or physically powerful ones, such as our six giants, are exceptions to the general rule that captive conditions grant a longer life than do natural ones.

As about half of the 20-year species belong to the family of boas and pythons, these may seem to be especially long-lived. It must not be forgotten, however, that the value of the giant snakes causes them to receive special attention; it is one thing to replace a common garter snake, and another to do the same for a big python; the cost of replacement in the first case would be but a fraction of a veterinarian's fee. Only the private owner would let sentiment enter into the matter and spend money and effort on the small, common specimen.

Consideration of our giants one by one adds a few interesting facts to the foregoing picture.

Anaconda: There are many records of captive anacondas that survived less than 10 years, and a few interesting reports bearing on longevity. The champion lived in the National Zoological Park, Washington, from August 17, 1899, to August 26, 1927. Another individual received at the same time did exceptionally well, with 16 years and 2½ months to its credit. An anaconda lived in the possession of Hans Schweizer and two other owners for 22 years, and two have reached the 14-year mark in the Philadelphia Zoological Garden. In spite of these last records, this species is reputed to be hard to keep more than a few years.

Boa constrictor: An individual from Brazil once lived in the Zoological Garden of Bristol, England, for 23 years, 3 months, and 23 days, establishing the record for a species that seldom survives 10 years of captivity; among 100 received at the National Zoological Park, only one survived 10 years. However, the San Diego Zoo managed to keep an individual alive for 18 years and 10 months, and Schweizer had one for 15 years and another for 20 years.

African rock python: One of these giants at the Philadelphia Zoological Garden missed the 20-year mark by less than two months, and another was kept in the Zoological Garden of Bristol, England, for 18 years.

Indian python: This favorite of zoo curators often lasts from 10 to 15 years, as published records for some fifteen individuals show. Schweizer kept an Indian python for 24 years; one lived in the San Diego Zoo for 22 years and 9 months; and Flower's 1937 report lists one that survived 19 years of captivity in the London Zoological Gardens. Sylvia has now been a pet for 14 years.

Reticulate python: The Indian python has a slight edge on this giant both in the number that have lived the usual 10 to 15 years and in the maximum. Two reticulate pythons survived 21 years and a few months, one in the Jardin des Plantes, Paris, the other in the London Zoological Gardens. Another London specimen missed the 20-year period by only a week, whereas one attained just 20 years in the St. Louis Zoo. In the San Diego Zoo, another lived nearly 18 years.

Destroyers
of the Giants

✳

Pupil that closes to a vertical slit. African sedge viper (*Atheris squamigera*). (Courtesy Staten Island Zoo. Photograph by Charles R. Hackenbrock)

Round pupil. Trans-Pecos rat snake (*Elaphe subocularis*), a species of the southwestern United States and adjacent Mexico. (Courtesy Staten Island Zoo. Photograph by Charles R. Hackenbrock)

Head of Boa Constrictor. Note that the stripe extends even into the eye itself. This augments the stripe's "disruptive" effect. (Courtesy Staten Island Zoo. Photograph by Charles R. Hackenbrock)

Enemies and Defense
Against Them

THE ENEMIES of snakes are legion. Disregarding parasites, which are dealt with in another chapter, we find snake destroyers in all the groups of higher animals, and even among the larger and more voracious invertebrates, such as spiders, crayfishes, and insects. The snakes killed by these lower forms of life, virtually all small species or the young of larger ones, are few. But the toll taken by the vertebrate enemies is tremendous.

Where man, the enemy of enemies, builds his cities and suburbs, whole populations of snakes can be wiped out, and, indeed, only a few species fail to succumb. Man is by far the most fickle enemy; he is the only one that destroys and worships at the same time. In millennia gone by, man and snake struck a balance. Man's populations were not great, he had not yet covered the earth, and his reverence for snakes kept him from being a constant menace. As time went by and he expanded his range and activities, there was less and less room for snakes. Modern man destroys them inadvertently in two ways: he eliminates their haunts and his machines kill them by the millions, both in fields and on roads. Recent studies show that animals can far better withstand depletion of populations than elimination of haunts. Education is now doing a great deal to counteract the wanton killing of snakes, and may be a reasonably good substitute for the reverence that once served the same end.

Next to man, snakes are their own worst enemy. There are hundreds of kinds of snake-eating snakes. Because of its small diameter and its lack of protruding anatomical parts, a snake is ideally shaped to be swallowed by another. However, this does not imply cannibalism—a snake rarely eats its own species.

The list of mammals that eat snakes is no doubt longer than that of snake-eating snakes, but only because there are a great many more kinds of mammals. Carnivorous mammals are apt to have broad appetites, with the result that an appreciable number of species of snakes in every temperate or tropical region are occasional victims. Then, too, certain mammals destroy snakes without being impelled by hunger.

Birds, particularly birds of prey, follow mammals and snakes as the most destructive enemies of snakes. Various families, such as the cuckoos, have snake-eating species scattered among them. Numerous hawks and eagles subsist partly on snakes. An account of the killing of a bull snake (*Pituophis catenifer*) by a red-tailed hawk is quoted by Henry S. Fitch, and may be taken as typical. The hawk took off from a horizontal limb, and with wings half folded, dropped straight down 250 feet to knock the 5-foot snake from the rock on which it was discovered. Subsequent examination showed that the bird had seized the snake at mid-body, then by the neck; after the seizure it bit the neck and the head until the reptile became helpless. The hawk then began to eat the head. This attack took place in December, when the weather was cool and the snake not fully active.

When we come to the giant snakes, the only new factor that must be considered is size. These reptiles begin life free from the attacks of small animals that cannot overcome snakes more than 20 inches long. The elimination of these enemies still leaves a formidable list, however; we have just learned that a red-tailed hawk, a species 2 feet or less in length, does not hesitate to tackle a snake 5 feet long.

A python or boa, then, starts life with a great many enemies, though every foot added to its length cuts off many of these. By the time it reaches 12 feet, there are yet fewer animals to fear, whereas at 20 and more feet, the list would be extremely short. Even a human being thinks twice before facing such a reptile; at least, he did so until stimulated recently by the desire to collect skins for the leather market.

There are astonishingly few reliable firsthand accounts of actual attacks on giant snakes of good size. After many years of observation and study in the wilds of British Guiana and Venezuela, William Beebe was able to report only one enemy of the anaconda and boa constrictor: a black jungle racer (*Pseudoboa cloelia*) 6 feet long. It had seized a young boa constrictor in the thatched roof of an Indian benab. This aggressor, a notorious eater of snakes both venomous and harmless, is also known as the mussurana. Only young boa constrictors and anacondas would be overpowered by it.

Crocodiles must be included among the other reptile enemies of the giant snakes; an African rock python was once taken from the stomach of a crocodile 10 feet long. If a crocodile were lucky enough to seize a python by the head, the teeth would quickly pierce the skull. The crocodilian trick of revolving rapidly on its own axis to twist off head or limb could not be effective; a python would wrap itself about the aggressor and "roll with the punch."

Animals that co-operate with one another in their attacks on great snakes have an easier time. Herbert S. Dickey saw about forty peccaries slaughter a "great snake" with ease, cutting it into shreds with their sharp hoofs. This is consistent with the snake-killing habits of wart hogs as reported by Charles R. S. Pitman, except that such concerted action is not part of the story; a wart hog killed and ripped to bits an African rock python 12 feet long.

Concerted action is not always effective, if we may judge by R. M. Isemonger's account of a conflict between an African rock python and a troop of baboons. The giant had coiled about a baby baboon when Isemonger arrived. The baboons, though frightened, crowded about the reptile, making a great commotion. Now and then an especially bold member would dash in to give the snake a nip, but would quickly retreat. The troop finally gave up and left the infant to its fate. Isemonger met the python later, and its wounds had healed. A somewhat similar event is described by R. Hoier, who saw a young kob being devoured by an African rock python while the mother remained helpless near by, showing signs of great distress, as well she might. Female antelopes of this kind, though of good size, are hornless, which probably explains why the mother kob could do nothing in this situation.

Jim Corbett writes of coming upon an Indian python 17½ feet long that had just been killed by a pair of otters. Although he did not witness the actual killing, he explains that otters overcome pythons by attacking from two sides; when the reptile turns toward one attacker, the other rushes in to score a bite. Corbett believed that otters kill these large reptiles but do not eat them.

It is not surprising that hyenas eat pythons. In Africa, Hoier repeatedly found the remains of pythons that had been partly eaten by hyenas. Just how the victims are overcome is not recorded. Evidence of the eating of Indian pythons by tigers is given by Frank Wall: the tail of one of these snakes was taken from the stomach of one tiger and the intestine of another contained a tapeworm of a species that lives in pythons. Alfred Russel Wallace, while carrying on his memorable exploration of the East Indies, was told by a Dyak chief that the orangutan kills an attacking python by first seizing it with both hands and then biting it. Verification of this habit would be welcome.

DEFENSES

The foregoing may cause some readers to wonder how any snake manages to survive the onslaught of such a multitude of hungry creatures. A snake may circumvent an enemy in many ways: by concealment, by flight, by arousal of fear (warning or bluffing), or by genuine aggression. The harmless snake can be said to "bluff," whereas the venomous one "warns." Each individual constantly has to rely on one or more of these methods. We must not, however, think of the snake as coolly considering just which trick to pull out of its bag, as a human being might; the snake is very largely controlled by instinctive reactions, which operate automatically.

The principal method of avoiding danger is through concealment. By and large, a snake will come to rest in such a way that it is hidden. Try to find a pet after it has escaped in either the house, the yard, or a field, and observe captives in cages that afford ample chance for concealment. The very shape of a snake allows it to disappear in most natural surroundings, for so many parts of plants are also long and slender. Next to shape comes color; the basic evolution of pattern in snakes seems to be toward protective coloration. They have only a few types of patterns, and these are nearly always repetitive, one part looking like another. The vast majority of species are either blotched, striped, cross-banded, or uniformly colored, and, under the proper circumstances, each of these types of coloration facilitates concealment.

On islands near Lake Erie's Ohio shore, common water snakes (*Natrix sipedon*) with a cross-banded pattern are conspicuous against the rocky substratum. Joseph H. Camin and Paul R. Ehrlich's studies of large populations strongly suggest that the usual banded pattern of this widely distributed species has been reduced on the islands, the adults there being largely without it. Constant migration from the mainland has somewhat obscured the picture, preventing the establishment of an unbanded population that would presumably be relatively safe from the depredations of preying birds.

Watch a striped snake glide through the grass: your eye, failing to follow the snake in its forward motion, will move tailward; as the stripes are closer together toward the posterior end, their convergence will make the snake less and less evident until it seems to vanish. Much the same will happen with a banded snake, and, of course, the bands have a disruptive effect by breaking up the outline of the snake. Blotches are even more effective; blotched snakes, such as our giants, are often slow-moving (the anaconda is spotted rather than blotched). Thus, there is method in what might appear to be the heterogeneous madness of snake patterns, which have evolved toward those that promote the frustration of enemies. In some snakes even the coloration of the extended tongue matches that of the head.

In flight the snake is at a great disadvantage because of its slow progression; nearly all enemies among the birds and mammals can overtake a snake with ease. Little is known about how snake-eating snakes secure their prey, though it is likely that chemoreception is heavily relied upon.

Before treating passive action, the name I have applied to warning and bluffing taken together, it must be emphasized that snakes are bluffers rather than fighters. This will come as a surprise to many people who have heard stories of the danger from a snake bite, the aggressiveness of cobras and mambas, and the ability of giant species to kill formidable mammals. Belief in the ferocity of snakes and in their love of combat is connected with a popular notion that all life is based on "the law of the jungle," evolution being nothing but the "survival of the fittest," the fit being the fiercest. The animal world is not essentially different from the human world; there is a lot of strife, but there is also a great deal of co-operation and genuine effort to avoid strife. Snakes generally substantiate the theory that "he who fights and runs away will live to fight another day."

It is hard to imagine just how a creature with such a simple form can bluff successfully. Let us see what the snake has done along the line of making the most of a slender shape. First I shall describe bluffing and warning with the forward part of the body, next with the rear end, and finally by the whole animal.

Behaving like a dangerous snake by assuming the proper pose and actually going through the motion of striking, with the mouth closed, is one effective maneuver. Some actually bite, but in a distinctly halfhearted manner. The head and neck of certain species are spread by the elevation of the ribs, as in the cobras, or the neck may be inflated rather than flattened. The startling effect of either act is augmented when bright colors are thus made to appear. Inflating and flattening of the head and forebody, seen in unrelated snakes from various parts of the world, are among the most impressive serpentine tricks of bluffing, especially when accompanied by hissing.

Hissing is rightly thought of as a typical way for a snake to assert itself, and few are the species of reasonable size which do not use it. The hiss may be more than a simple exhalation. In British Guiana, Beebe noted that a wild boa constrictor slightly more than 12 feet long could be heard distinctly at a distance of 100 feet, and one hiss could last half a minute; it sounded like steam escaping from a radiator. He describes this snake as filling its lungs before hissing, but the Indian python can hiss on the intake as well, an ability enabling it to make a continuous noise.

The most common use of the tail is merely shaking or vibrating it. This seems to be a harmless act, and yet in dry vegetation it can make a startling noise, and its extreme development in the rattlesnakes is known to all; many a harmless snake has been let alone because the noise of its tail was mistaken for the sound of a rattle. On a par with vibrating the tail is raising a bad odor with excreta or a secretion from special glands in the base of the tail. Substances from either source can be irritating to the human eye, although it must be admitted that little concrete evidence is available on just how effective these products are when used against enemies other than man. Both products may be ejected a few inches, but their discharge is usually accompanied by a slashing about of the rear end of the snake, an act that spreads the disagreeable matter far and wide.

The tip of the tail in some snakes ends in a spine, which may be pressed against a captor. The effect is frightening, but injury does not result; no snake has a venom gland connected with the spine, the "stinging snake" being purely mythical. A few snakes have a blunt tail shaped and even colored like the head, a condition that may confuse an antagonist by causing it to seize the wrong end; this headlike tail of some species is moved about or even made to "strike" like a real head. Other species raise and curl the tail to show bright colors on its lower side, thus making an alarming display. Strangest of all uses made by the rear end of a snake is what has been called "cloaca popping," the production of sounds by alternating protrusions and retractions of the cloaca, which involves drawing in and expelling air.

So much for heads and tails. Several clever methods of defense which use the entire body may be based on structure as well as behavior. The most remarkable exponent of whole-body action is the saw-scaled viper (*Echis carinatus*) of northern Africa and southern Asia. In this true viper many of the scales on the sides are set obliquely and mounted with saw-toothed keels, one to each scale. When aroused, the viper throws its body into a figure eight and moves so that the keeled scales are rubbed together. The sides of the body, which is inflated, are set in vibration and a distinctly audible sound is produced. If several of these snakes confined in a pot are aroused, the noise made by them is like that of violently boiling water.

The flattening or inflating of the head and neck may be extended to the entire body. Both of these processes often bring suddenly to view colors not ordinarily seen. The mud snake (*Farancia*) of the southeastern United States will first curl the tail, which is brightly colored on the underside, and if further annoyed, will greatly extend the display by turning up the similarly decorated belly. A simple defensive device of many snakes (among them pythons of more than one small species) is merely to roll into a tight ball, the head concealed and protected by the coils. To unroll one of these serpentine balls without causing injury is next to impossible. A large giant rolled into a mass would be an impressive sight, but I have never found any indication that these snakes use the method.

In spite of frightening stories about king cobras, mambas, taipans, and so on, there is no snake that "attacks on sight." Each of the alleged ferocious species has been later robbed of its formidable reputation. Yet it is just as false to say that various large snakes, harmless and otherwise, will *never* attack. Scattered through the literature are records of rare cases of aggression by species that ordinarily retreat or merely hold their ground; it might be only one individual out of a thousand, but even that small percentage invalidates flat assertions.

Among some 2,500 species of snakes known to science, a few can be provoked to attack or may do so without provocation when guarding eggs; an undetermined number have been known to attack only so rarely that for all ordinary purposes they are counted as devoid of such behavior. The vast majority either flee or stand their ground. This paragraph has been written from the point of view of man because information on the actions of snakes faced by other enemies is still scarce. When it comes to the giant snakes, the whole matter is obscured by the possibility that their attacks on man are attempts to satisfy hunger rather than to drive an enemy away.

The defensive versatility of the snake is largely expended in ingenious ways of bluffing, and I have already shown that every part of the body is put to use. No such variety of method is evident in true aggression; even constriction is used for overcoming prey rather than in dealing with enemies. We can therefore disregard all but the anterior end, popular stories of stinging tails notwithstanding. Biting is the standard way, and any animal supplied with as many as six rows of teeth may well rely on them. Snakes may bite by simple sideswipes (but these enable the jaws to reach only adjacent objects); by elevating the head and forebody to make jabs forward and (necessarily) downward; or by throwing the forebody into lateral S curves and then straightening it. The usual way is to bite and let go at once, though there are variations, such as chewing, holding on while the forebody is rapidly jerked from side to side and the flesh of the victim torn by the recurved teeth.

The method of methods is injection of venom by means of large teeth, either grooved or made like hypodermic needles. The venom glands evolved from ordinary salivary glands. The boas and pythons, as I have said, are not venomous.

The giant snakes seem to rely on size, the ability to inflict a painful bite, and hissing. Nature has endowed them with protective coloration of sorts, and this may be as valuable in securing food as in protection from danger. Five of the giants have a blotched body pattern, which makes them inconspicuous, and the "disruptive" head pattern of some does the same; a stripe passing through a snake's eye renders it invisible and keeps an observer from recognizing what he sees as a head. The boa constrictor's head pattern is strikingly disruptive, and so is that of the Indian python. The relatively dark blotching of the giants' bodies illustrates Golger's rule: animals of warm, humid regions tend to have dark patterns. The anaconda does not fit this picture as well as the others; different factors may influence coloration in an animal so aquatic.

The constricting muscles of the giants are not ordinarily brought into play during acts of pure defense. This significant fact is hard to believe. But those who run a chance of encountering boas or pythons in the wilds should take this to heart. The big snake surprised in its native haunts will merely strike at the intruder after the manner of most other snakes; only when closely pressed or actually seized will it bring its coils into play. Nature has thus robbed these powerful reptiles of much potential terror for their enemies.

Parasites and Sickness

✳

SNAKES GET SICK about as often as do other higher animals. But the numerous references to maladies of the giant snakes are so scattered and often so casual that no one has collated them. The majority of worthwhile observations have been made on captives in valuable collections under the care of pathologists as well as keepers.

The frequent mention of diseased captive giants in zoo reports does not necessarily mean that these reptiles are delicate. A zoo that has paid a big price for a large snake will go to some trouble to find out what may be making it sick or what has killed it, whereas illness or death of an ordinary, small specimen will simply be ignored. On the other hand, experimental studies based on such smaller snakes have yielded by far the more valuable information; it has been possible to study these snakes in great numbers, for they are readily available in quantity and cost little or nothing.

PARASITES

Snakes have not been neglected by harmful parasites. Representatives of eight groups (five classes and three lesser assortments) of such visitors make use of snakes. These fall into two types: those that live on the outside (ectoparasites) and those that dwell within (endoparasites).

Clinging to the surface of an animal is apparently the beginning of parasitism. From the skin it is a short step to gill, mouth, nasal passage, or bladder, and thence to the true interior. Some parasites (flukes) actually show these stages, with those living in body cavities that freely communicate with the outside still having the simple life histories of the free-living species. But the intruder must change drastically to become properly adapted; what it does to the host is mild compared with what happens to itself. Parasites satisfied with life on the exterior of hosts may have to do little more than develop hooks or suckers for hanging on, whereas those that live within usually undergo such drastic changes as degeneration of the nervous, muscular, and digestive systems, or even loss of some of these. The reproductive system, in contrast, often becomes so highly developed that a great deal of energy is used up in producing quantities of eggs. Sexless reproduction may be resorted to.

The giant snakes are apparently inhabited by parasites similar to those that live in or on other snakes. As the individual parasite grows to be the same size in any host, a large python would support an immensely greater number than could an adult of a small species. However, the relation of giant snake to parasite appears to be in no other way unusual.

The studies of large numbers of wild snakes (of many species) have yielded valuable information about parasitism, but no such investigations of the giants have been made. Much of our knowledge of parasitism in giant snakes is based on captives, and such knowledge is unreliable because captivity may greatly modify the effects of parasites. The delicate balance between parasite and host may be upset by any drastic change in living conditions. This change can easily throw the balance in favor of the parasite.

There is trouble in deciding when a parasitized snake is "sick." Only a thin line can be drawn between an animal made ill by parasites and one merely inhabited by them. Moreover, there are some definitely harmless and even beneficial parasites that inhabit complex animals such as the snakes.

MITES AND TICKS

The ectoparasites of snakes are mites and ticks. A smooth, limbless creature, especially one with the habit of shedding its skin periodically, would seem to make a poor home for this type of parasite, yet snake ticks and mites are by no means rare.

One of the clearest cases of a parasitic menace to snakes is a mite of the genus *Ophionyssus*. Early in the nineteenth century a specimen was found on a captive snake in Italy, and in 1844 the species was formally described (as *Ophionyssus natricis*). It became widespread in collections, where it proved to be a serious menace, but it could not be found in a wild state. Had it evolved on snakes living in captivity? Joseph H. Camin made a thorough experimental study of its life history, which involves several stages, and revealed that considerable moisture is necessary for certain stages, a point of great importance in the control of this pest.

The mite lives on snake blood, yet spends much time off the host. Some females may fail to mate but, nevertheless, lay eggs that hatch into males.

In 1956 adult mites were found on six of eleven species of snakes collected in Giza Province, Egypt. One of the species proved to be the Egyptian cobra. The flowered snake (*Coluber florulentus*) was most heavily infested, only one among thirty-one specimens being free from mites; the average per snake was 39, the maximum 109. Its mites were usually in the eye sockets and beneath the head, neck, and chin scales. Some mites were actively running about, not lodged beneath the scales.

It seems likely that this mite originated in Africa and was introduced to collections of snakes made by the Egyptians and other early peoples of Mediterranean border lands. Serpent worship was, perhaps, the original incentive to confine snakes. From this region the mite spread to other parts of the world, improving its lot by making the most of cage life. Rapid build-up of populations would result from better places in which to hide and breed (uniform conditions of humidity and an abundance of crevices), opportunities for perennial activity, and other factors.

The discovery of this species on wild snakes is so recent that information about its effects in nature is unavailable. It is now thought of only as a threat to captives. The mite's advantage apparently increases in cages, though it sometimes defeats its own ends by destroying whole collections. Its double punch is the ability to suck blood from the host as well as transmit bacteria, one type of which, *Proteus hydrophilus,* causes blood poisoning that may be fatal in a matter of days.

Camin made an intensive experimental study of this bacterium, which was first isolated in 1891, from frog blood. He used ninety-four snakes of eleven common forms native to the United States. Thirty-six died of the induced infection, and the germs in question were actually found in the blood of twenty-eight. Death took place from five hours to twenty-one days after infection, with three and a half days as the average period. The mite itself probably plays only a passive role as mechanical vector of the bacterium, and the infective period is perhaps less than forty-eight hours. Without the mites, Camin was unable to transmit the infection from snake to snake, even by feeding the bacteria orally. The disease can be completely controlled through eradication of the mite.

After infection, the snake grows sluggish, and its normal reflexes, such as rearing and darting out the tongue, slow down or cease entirely. Some snakes simply become weak and die. The majority of individuals have convulsions, thrashing about the cage approximately an hour prior to death. The violent movements cease a short time before the end, when the mouth opens and closes, the victim apparently gasping for breath just before the heart stops.

Autopsy reveals internal bleeding in all organs. The free blood is readily visible through the skin of amphibians and fishes, whereas it is hidden by the skin of snakes; the origin of the names "red leg" of frogs and "red sore" of fishes is obvious. This bacterium also harms, but to a lesser degree, mammals, birds, and salamanders.

Of all the parasites that we shall consider, the tick is probably the most unpopular, because it is big, conspicuous, and hard to dislodge. One species, *Amblyomma dissimile*, known as the iguana tick, ranges widely over tropical America. The adult lives on the boa constrictor, as well as other snakes, lizards, toads, and possibly mammals. The larvae and nymphs have been experimentally engorged on bovines. In the Old World, ticks of the genus *Aponomma* have been found on the African rock python and the Indian python. Like the mite, the tick thrives on the blood of its host.

INTERNAL PARASITES

The internal parasites of our giant snakes and other reptiles fall into three groups: one-celled animals (protozoa), "worms" (flukes or trematodes, tapeworms or cestodes, and roundworms or nematodes), and arthropods (linguatulids or "tongue worms"). Four great phyla of the animal kingdom are represented, as the flukes and tapeworms belong to the flatworm phylum, whereas the roundworms constitute a phylum apart. Man himself is commonly inhabited by countless numbers of all of these parasites except the linguatulids; in many cases, the species found in man are related to those of reptiles. Linguatulids are a special case; though primarily parasites of reptiles, they are able to live in man, and they occasionally do. Thus, when it comes to parasites, we might say that man and reptile *have* much in common: they are "brothers under the skin."

PROTOZOA

The one-celled animals are, by count of individuals, the most numerous of creatures, all the larger animals being veritable incubators for millions of them; there are even protozoa that live in protozoa. Some fifteen thousand kinds have been described, and a great many more are still unknown to science. The protozoa are divided into some five classes, only two of which include common parasites of reptiles. Every student has seen amoebas in classroom demonstrations, and their mode of feeding and moving about by means of pseudopods is known to all of us. Several kinds have been found in reptiles; one of them (*Entamoeba invadens*) has been shown to produce, in captives, a fatal type of amoebiasis much like that caused by the common amoeba of man.

This amoeba was studied by Herbert L. Ratcliffe and Quentin M. Geiman. They found a "spontaneous" form in many species of lizards and snakes, one of the snakes being the boa constrictor. By "spontaneous" they mean that the amoeba appears in collections without detectable origin. When mature cysts isolated from one kind of water snake (*Natrix*) and from a species of lizard (*Varanus*) were fed to three kinds of water snakes, they produced amoebiasis in them, yet a lizard (*Anolis*) and the American alligator seemed to be immune. All the inoculated snakes lost appetite and most of them died, some in thirteen days, others in seventy-seven. Examination of many freshly caught water snakes, as well as the frogs they eat, failed to reveal any clue to the source of infection. However, some of these water snakes developed the disease during a few months of captivity in cages that were initially clean. This is, obviously, a type of infection that can be transmitted through lack of cleanliness, feces being a potential source.

This amoebiasis primarily attacked the colon and liver, whereas harm to the stomach and small intestine was secondary; in some cases, only the stomach and liver were damaged. The liver was entered via the portal vein. Lesions appeared in the organs concerned; the inflamed tissues finally decomposed.

The second protozoan assortment of reptile parasites belongs to the class Sporozoa, so-called because of reproduction by means of spores or sporozoites. The nucleus of an individual divides many times, the parent finally falling apart into a great number of offspring. The malarial parasite of man and other higher vertebrates is the most familiar sporozoan; its bad effects are experienced by countless thousands of human beings. But no one knows just what haemogregarines do to their reptile hosts. This technical name for such parasites derives from the fact that they live in red blood cells.

FLUKES

Coming to the internal parasites with multi-cellular bodies, we first consider the "worms" known as flukes or trematodes. These are parasitic on all vertebrates. Everybody has heard of "blood flukes" (schistosomes) and "liver flukes." The latter cause serious sickness in man and are widespread in Old World countries.

As already pointed out, not all flukes are endoparasitic, but those of snakes and other essentially terrestrial animals have become so. Flukes are usually flat and always have unsegmented bodies protected by a thick cuticle, and are fitted with one or more suckers for attachment to the host. Specialized sense organs are lacking, though a digestive tract is present; the reproductive system may be as complex as that of the higher animals.

Flukes are incredibly numerous when counted either by species or by individuals. George R. La Rue found a population of garter snakes in western Texas in which the broad rule that parasites do not seriously impair the health of hosts was violated. One heavily infested snake harbored almost a million larval trematodes, chiefly located in the posterior third of the body. Muscles, lymph spaces, fat bodies, and other structures were invaded. Each larva was about one fiftieth of an inch long and only half as wide. If a relatively small snake can carry a million, consider the millions that a large python might support.

A few facts about one well-known group of snake flukes will suffice to illustrate the complexity of trematode parasitism. The "reniferids" live in the upper digestive and respiratory tracts and do not ordinarily harm the host. The snake must acquire the parasite by eating a frog or salamander, as these amphibians carry the larval stage. Snails of the genus *Physa* are also involved. Thus, these flukes follow a snake-snail-amphibian-snake cycle. A captive snake may be kept free of infection by feeding it on amphibians that have never been exposed to snails. When freed in the ingested amphibian by partial digestion, the parasite larva migrates from the small intestine to some organ, each species having its peculiar preference: esophagus, throat, mouth, intestine, ureter, kidney, liver, gall bladder, trachea, or lung. A careful study of parasites may reveal much about the feeding habits of the hosts. For example, snakes that eat nothing but mammals will not harbor reniferid trematodes. Among rattlesnakes, only members of the genus *Sistrurus* (pygmy rattlers) have them; these, unlike rattlesnakes in general, include amphibians in their diet.

TAPEWORMS

Tapeworms, or cestodes, make up the second group of internal parasites. So familiar are tapeworms that they even enter into humor; an exceptionally thin person is often accused of having a "worm" that is robbing him of nourishment. Tapeworms, in contrast to flukes, do just that; having no mouth, they simply absorb some of the host's food rather than devour its tissues.

The body is covered with a cuticle and, in many kinds, is made up of sections rather than true segments; the sections are added just behind the head, not at the rear. Each section contains both male and female elements, and these may fertilize the same or another individual. At least two hosts are necessary for the life cycle, which may be complex.

So widespread and numerous are tapeworms that every vertebrate probably has one or more species. Of about two hundred species of reptile hosts, by far the greater number are lizards and snakes, some of which are credited with several kinds of tapeworms. Among the snakes affected are the anaconda, the boa constrictor, and at least two of our giant pythons.

Obviously, the study of reptile tapeworms has just begun. Judging by the amount of available information, cestodes are not as interesting to study as are the flukes, perhaps because tapeworms almost always live in the intestine and do not present problems equal to those of parasites that take up an abode in many parts of the host.

ROUNDWORMS

The last of the three groups of "worms" parasitic on reptiles are the nematodes, or roundworms. Many roundworms look like animated bits of thread; hence the name "nema," a Greek word meaning "thread."

Roundworms are numerous almost beyond conception in the water (salt and fresh) as well as the land areas of the world. A specialist once said that if our planet met with disaster, the surface of the earth could be reasonably well reconstructed if all nematodes escaped destruction and were left in place. Millions of free-living individuals may be found in a single shovelful of garden soil or matter from the debris of a lake, pond, or shallow ocean. Animal as well as plant tissues are inhabited by these ubiquitous creatures. Nearly all human beings are destined to harbor some at one time or another, and a common intestinal roundworm of man grows to be more than a foot long. Needless to add, too many of this kind can have serious effects, although one man passed more than five thousand roundworms of a smaller species (pinworms) as the result of a single treatment, and there is no record that he died of pinworms. Hookworms and trichina worms (the latter causes the disease known as trichinosis), are nematodes that infest man. In elephantiasis, enlargement of some part of the body is caused by a species of roundworm. About fifty different kinds have been found in man, some producing no bad effects.

Roundworms, some of which are barely discernible to the naked eye, have unsegmented bodies covered with a cuticle. They possess sense organs, and the sexes are usually separate. The development is direct, without a well-marked metamorphosis. Reproduction is not always by means of eggs. The several orders recognized are divided into more than fifty families.

Although nematodes must inhabit innumerable species of snakes, definite references are few. Various parts of the body may be invaded. Paul D. Harwood studied seventy-two snakes of seventeen species caught in southeastern Texas. Nematodes were found in twelve species in lungs, stomachs, and recta. Eight of the seventeen species harbored trematodes, whereas only three had cestodes. This gives some idea of the comparative abundance of nematodes. These parasites often live just under the skin of snakes and raise pimples readily visible from the outside. Such infections may become severe enough to cause death. Pythons have been recorded as hosts.

LINGUATULIDS

The most astonishing of reptile parasites are the linguatulids, so inappropriately known as "tongue worms." They are, moreover, the only parasitic group that finds its greatest development in reptiles; all of them, as adults, live in or near the lungs of reptiles (with the exception of a few found in the nasal passages of mammals).

Linguatulids, some fifty species of which have been described, are degenerate arachnids closely related to ticks and mites; all of these are members of the phylum Arthropoda, the animals with jointed legs. The adult linguatulids themselves are wormlike in form, with cylindrical bodies blunt at the head end. They present a ringed appearance due to raised folds around the body. The mouth is on the lower side of the head between two pairs of hooks. These hooks, which are the linguatulid's means of attaching itself to the host, are the parasite's most characteristic feature. Adult linguatulids attain the astonishing length of seven inches, and a single snake has been known to harbor 158 individuals.

The normal life history involves an intermediate host, usually a fish or mammal, which is the home of the larvae. Some of the mammalian hosts are common opossums, hedgehogs, bats, armadillos, rats, squirrels, muskrats, mongooses, raccoons, skunks, and monkeys. The reptile may become infected when it preys on any of these. Eggs of the linguatulid pass to the exterior from the reptile's lungs (or their vicinity) via the alimentary tract and are eventually consumed by the intermediary host with food or drink.

Fred R. Irvine brought together several interesting records of an appreciable number of people of western Africa infected by larval linguatulids, which do not normally cause illness. Fatal results have, nevertheless, been reported. The adult parasites are common in many of the large African snakes. Irvine, who also accumulated records from various other parts of the world, was unable to determine accurately the origin of the human infections, but he believes that they are most common among snake-eating peoples, who may devour raw snake flesh for food, for ceremonial purposes, or for both.

PARASITISM IN THE GIANTS

Collation of some forty references, though based far too much on studies of captives, allows me to make a few generalizations. For the anaconda, only blood parasites and tapeworms are among the records. With its markedly aquatic habits and special food preferences, this snake should harbor parasites somewhat different in nature from those of the other giants. Oddly enough, the references to parasites of the boa constrictor (blood parasites, amoebas, flukes, and tapeworms) are relatively rare. The African rock python and the Indian python are alike in having an equal number of references and the same parasites: ticks, blood parasites, tapeworms, roundworms, and linguatulids. There are somewhat fewer records for the reticulate python; this snake is inhabited by similar parasites, though records of ticks are lacking. For the amethystine python there is only a single record of infection (by *Entamoeba* and *Ophidascaris*). This paucity is to be expected for a snake so rarely seen in captivity.

Almost certainly, it will eventually be found that the giants, with the exception of the anaconda (because of its greater aquatic tendencies), harbor much the same array of parasitic types, though there will be many differences in the actual species. The basic reason is, of course, a marked similarity in feeding habits, for all the internal parasites, except the haemogregarines, are transmitted through food. Similarity in habitat also has its effect.

TUBERCULOSIS

Among the other maladies that take a toll of snakes—at least of many in captivity—are tuberculosis, mouth rot, "enteritis," and pneumonia.

Tuberculosis of a (captive) snake was recorded as long ago as

1889 and has been reported many times since in numerous species, among them pythons and boas. In 1929, Joseph D. Aronson gave a summary that included an Indian python with tubercles in the lung, stomach, and esophagus; a reticulate python with nodules in the region of the pancreas; and a boa constrictor with various organs affected.

He was able to study in detail four garter snakes (*Thamnophis sirtalis*) that died in the Philadelphia Zoological Garden; the spleen in two was enlarged and set with grayish tubercles, the lung in three had patches of consolidation, and the livers of all were tubercular. From three of the snakes a pure culture of an acid-fast bacterium was isolated. Aronson described this organism as different from the one previously known to attack snakes, and, therefore, new.

Mammals and birds were resistant to this and other bacteria that infest ectotherms ("cold-blooded" animals). There is some evidence that, on the other hand, reptiles may become infected by exposure to human beings with tuberculosis. Patently, much is to be learned about the relation between the bacterium causing this disease in endotherms ("warm-blooded" animals) and that producing it in ectotherms.

MOUTH ROT

Another threat to captive snakes, and perhaps the worst of all, is mouth rot, which is also called canker mouth and osteomyelitis. It is a bacterial infection found only in confined snakes. There seems to be some question about the organism that causes it, but the symptoms are readily recognized. Pinkish-white spots appear in the mouth, and the appetite vanishes; a cheesy substance is exuded by the swollen tissues and the mouth remains partly open, until, in advanced stages, obstruction of the oral cavity and even destruction of the jaw bones ensue. Two forms have been distinguished; the chronic type may require months to do what the quick kind does in a few days.

A snake's mouth, in contrast to the body and tail, is subject to injury as well as infection, and any damage to it can have serious results. This is, in some measure, because the process of eating is too complex to be carried out unless the swallowing apparatus is in good condition. Some keepers of reptiles believe that mouth rot often follows injury to the snout, teeth, or gums.

"ENTERITIS" AND OTHER DISEASES

Perhaps the best information available on reptile mortality comes from the reports by veterinarians of large zoos. One of the big killers always listed in such reports is "enteritis," but much more work will have to be done on reptile pathology before this malady can be properly diagnosed. Snakes are especially subject to intestinal disorders, and these are due to many different types of organisms. The effects of the endoparasitic diseases already considered, with the exception of mouth rot, more or less include intestinal disorders and might be reported as enteritis. Pneumonia, no doubt, causes a good number of deaths among captive snakes.

Although there are other diseases of snakes, a collection that can be kept free of snake mites and the bacterium transmitted by them, and free of amoebiasis, tuberculosis, "enteritis" (of unknown origin), mouth rot, and pneumonia, will have a very low rate of mortality.

It is noteworthy that zoos in temperate climates always report an increased number of deaths during the warmest months of the year. This increase could be blamed either on high temperatures or on the influx of specimens following spring emergence; many of these new arrivals fail to adapt to life in captivity, and succumb, not at once as a mammal or bird might, but weeks or even months later. The relative importance of these two possible causes of death remains to be determined.

Relation to Man

❈

Man's Study of
the Giants

SNAKES AROUSE more extreme emotion in man than does any other type of animal. Much of the emotion is unreasoning fear—fear often so overpowering that it produces shock, thus complicating the result of a harmless bite or simply an encounter in the wilds.

A vast superstructure of imagination has been built around snakes, and it has reached incredible proportions in the form of myths, folklore, tall tales, and misconceptions of size, shape, and habits. Man's attitude toward snakes ranges from worshipping them, at one extreme, to treating them as prey, at the other. In contrast to the worshippers, there are many people who relish python meat or seek the hides of giant snakes for leather.

The association between man and giant snake possibly began in Africa, and it must be as old as these two animals themselves. If man emerged from Africa and wandered eastward, he came in contact with the Indian, the reticulate, and the amethystine pythons, in the order named. It was not until comparatively recent times that he met the boa constrictor and the anaconda. Presumably, the migrants from northeastern Asia were unfamiliar with any snake of gigantic size; only Asiatics that came to the New

World on boats could have known such creatures, and the consensus is that few migrants arrived by way of such a route.

The history of this man-snake association may be divided into three periods: the prehistoric, the early historic, and the scientific. The prehistoric and historic periods were largely concerned with ophiolatry (serpent worship), which I shall take up in the next chapter. The main purpose of this chapter is to amplify the third, or recent, period.

The truly scientific study of the animals of the world began about two centuries ago when the renowned Swedish naturalist Carolus Linnaeus (Carl von Linné) paved the way by introducing a practical scheme for naming and classifying on a universal scale the vast array of species. The tenth edition of his great work, *Systema naturae*, dated 1758, became the foundation of systematic zoology. Many lay readers believe that the Linnaean system of assigning names of Latin and Greek origin to animals is an imposition, but it made possible a task of staggering proportions. Any difficulty in learning these new names is insignificant compared with the confusion that existed when a single species had many names in one language; if its distribution was extensive, it had scores of additional ones in other languages. Only in very recent years has the Linnaean method met with some serious adverse criticism.

Since Linnaeus collected animals from all over the world, it is not surprising that he named the three most familiar of the giants—the anaconda, the boa constrictor, and the Indian python—calling them "Boa murina," "Boa Constrictor," and "Coluber Molurus." The next to be introduced to science was the African rock python. It was named in honor of Albert Seba, whose four-volume account of his personal collection, published in 1734, served as a source book for Linnaeus and other early naturalists. In 1788, Johann Friedrich Gmelin, member of the German family to which so many famous scientists belonged, christened it *Coluber Sebae*. The reticulate and amethystine pythons came last: Johann Gottlob

Schneider named them *Boa Reticulata* and *Boa Amethistina* in 1801.

Refinements of classification have been responsible for changes in the names of the genera, whereas the original species names have been altered only to satisfy the rules of Latin grammar. The names as currently used are given on page 18.

I have already discussed the origin of "anaconda," the only puzzling common name among the six. The Indian python bears the name (*molurus*) of a Greek serpent of uncertain identity; the Latin word *murinus* means "mouse" and "resembling a mouse"; *reticulatus* and *amethystinus* refer, respectively, to pattern and color; *constrictor* is obvious in meaning. The generic terms *Python* and *Eunectes* are worthy of note. The former is borrowed from Greek mythology, Python being the monster killed by Apollo near Delphi; *eunectes* is a Greek word meaning "swimmer."

The six giants received comprehensive treatment in the stupendous ten-volume *Erpétologie générale ou histoire naturelle complète des reptiles*, written by André-Marie-Constant Duméril and Gabriel Bibron (and Duméril's son, after Bibron's death). This, the crowning work of a century of studies, which were made largely in France, was based on the museum collections in the Jardin des Plantes, Paris, and included details of classification, structure, habits, and even physiology of all known reptiles and amphibians. The first volume appeared in 1834, the last in 1854. A comparable treatment today would require scores of volumes. A fold-in table and approximately sixty-four pages of Volume VI were devoted to the six giants alone.

Belonging to this same early era was the effort by Georg Jan and Ferdinand Sordelli, of Italy, to illustrate the snakes of the world in elaborate style (several minutely detailed drawings to a species). The result was their *Iconographie générale des ophidiens*, published from 1860 to 1881 in fifty *livraisons*, each with six plates. A large percentage of the snakes known at that time was included, the six giants among them.

The center of study of herpetology eventually passed from the Continent to England, where it reached a peak in another account of living reptiles and amphibians. George Albert Boulenger, of the British Museum, accomplished this feat in a series of nine volumes variously entitled *Catalogue of . . . in the British Museum (Natural History)*. Three of the volumes were devoted to snakes, the giants, of course, coming in for their share (eight pages). Boulenger restricted himself to routine descriptions with just enough detail to back up his scheme of classification. The science of herpetology had grown so during the last half of his century that the comprehensive approach of the Dumérils and Bibron was already out of the question. Boulenger's volumes appeared over a stretch of many years (1882–96). Since his day, no one has made appreciable progress on even a bare catalogue of herpetology.

The Austrian herpetologist Franz Werner (1867–1939) had a lifetime interest in the giant snakes and published many papers on them. He observed them in captivity and studied them in museum collections. His major contribution to herpetology is a two-volume account for laymen of living reptiles and amphibians, published in 1912 and 1913 as part of the fourth edition of Brehm's *Tierleben*. Treatment of the giants covered thirty pages.

Frank Wall (1868–1950) was for years the chief authority on the snakes of India. He wrote a comprehensive scientific paper on the reticulate python and devoted many pages of his *Snakes of Ceylon* to the Indian python. As a member of the Indian Medical Service, he was stationed in various parts of that country and thus was able to learn about its snakes firsthand. His work has been referred to often in the foregoing chapters.

Wall's laurels passed to Malcolm Smith (1875–1958), who wrote the volume on snakes in *The Fauna of British India* series (1943). For many years he was attached to the court of Siam as court physician, and wild pythons lived in his Bangkok compound.

Olive Griffith Stull began a taxonomic study of the boas and pythons and published "A Check List of the Family Boidae" in

1935. Gustav Lederer, also frequently quoted in this volume, has intensively observed giant snakes in captivity for many years and has written numerous papers on them. Herndon G. Dowling's recent review of the classification of snakes includes, of course, a discussion of the Boidae.

Worship

✺

SERPENT WORSHIP has existed so long and over so much of the earth that the snake must be rated as the most revered of creatures. This will astonish many readers, for ophiolatry has all but vanished from the Western world, where modern Christianity and animal worship are incompatible. Reverence for snakes is also hard to reconcile with the widespread fear and hatred of them.

The snake has a simple shape, one not like that of man. Now, man is vain, and we should expect him to be stimulated by an animal formed in his own image, not one both low and limbless. Clearly, then, it is not shape that impresses him, but the behavior and abilities of snakes. From a vast literature on the subject, I have gleaned the following explanations.

Foremost is the periodic shedding of the entire covering of the body, even the part that covers the eyes. This act is more readily observed in snakes than in any other large animals that might come to the notice of the untutored mind. Ascribing great significance to shedding may seem farfetched, until we recall the tremendous importance of religion and the universal desire of man to retain his youth and live forever. The shedding of the skin must have been regarded by early man as symbolic of rebirth, or of eternal youth —perhaps even as a suggestion of life after extinction of the physical self.

A second factor is the crawling of the snake, in either a straight

A conveniently shaped meal. The prey of this western milk snake, a skink, is shaped for easy swallowing. The shorter and thicker the victim, the greater the stretch of the predator. (Courtesy Walker Van Riper, Denver Museum of Natural History)

African Rock Python after swallowing a goat. (Photograph, Chicago Natural History Museum)

Reticulate Python brooding eggs. Plastic reproduction, an example of the technique developed in the Chicago Natural History Museum by the late Leon L. Walters. (Photograph, Chicago Natural History Museum)

or an undulating line. Both types suggest flowing water; the latter, lightning as well as water (lightning itself was undoubtedly a symbol of water). The undulating snake also brings to mind the winding river or stream. The association of the crawling snake with water is harder to comprehend than is the association of shedding with renewal or prolongation of life, but there can be little doubt of the existence of both. This association is especially obscure to those who enjoy the abundance of water that modern technology has brought. When migrating early man found vast stretches of the earth uninhabitable because of aridity, water must have become fantastically important to him, and anything suggesting it would have been seized upon as a symbol. Serpent worship is a conspicuous element in religions found in the more arid parts of the world—Egypt, the drier parts of North America, and much of Australia, for example.

Finally and most obviously, many snakes deeply impressed man by the infliction of deadly bites. This ability in a creature of insignificant size would, by suggesting supernatural powers, arouse both fear and reverence. This explanation obviously does not apply to our giant snakes. (Most venomous snakes are of small or moderate dimensions; only the king cobra, as I pointed out earlier, has a length approximating that of the giants.)

It is risky, though tempting, to rate the importance of these three attributes and to say that they are the sole bases for man's special respect; perhaps the unwinking eye, the ability to move without apparent effort, and other qualities also enter the picture.

Pre-literate man probably lacked the feeling of superiority to animals that is so evident in highly developed civilizations of today. Men who hunted wary mammals and found difficulty in killing them had no reason to feel much smarter. Evidence of respect is found in the omnipresence of totem animals, using "totem" in the broadest sense, not merely as belief in descent from this or that creature. Given deep respect, the step thence to outright worship is not so great.

It is reasonable to infer that worship of animals is ancient enough to predate worship of heavenly bodies, weather, and seasonal changes. European cave art presents ample evidence of the antiquity of animal worship. Traces of respect for animals and a feeling of community with them may be seen in children, especially as they listen with awe to tales of their animal heroes.

The absence of a concern for animals in the teachings of Christ is puzzling, to say the least, and accounts for the feeling among Christian peoples that animal worship is an oddity; in China, the prevalence of Buddhism has counteracted the neglect of animals by Confucius, who, like Christ, was concerned largely with man's relation to man.

IN AUSTRALIA AND SOUTHERN ASIA

Let us now review the nature and geographical distribution of ophiolatry, especially the worship of giant snakes. Beginning with Australia, we meet one of the most picturesque of mythical snakes, the rainbow serpent, a gigantic and gaudy inhabitant of permanent streams and water holes. This creature, perhaps the most important nature deity of many tribes, is associated with the powers of nature, chiefly in connection with rain and water. Specifically, it represents this element, so vital to the inhabitants of Australia's great deserts. The rainbow serpent plays a part in the initiation ceremonies of some tribes and may even be the chief source of the magical powers of medicine men; other persons dare not approach its haunts for fear of being devoured.

Belief in the rainbow serpent is also found among the Arapesh, of New Guinea, though in a somewhat modified form. For example, it is not so definitely associated with the rainbow; in Australia, the serpent sometimes appears in this form. Perhaps such modification is a natural outcome of being transported to a country with heavy rainfall. There is also abundant evidence of serpent worship in other regions to the north of Australia.

Snakes have been worshipped as long and as thoroughly in southern Asia as anywhere, except perhaps Africa and adjacent regions. Worship in Asia reached its greatest development in India, where snake temples, still commonly seen, are the centers of many regular and elaborate festivals. Plowing is forbidden on a day set aside for propitiation of snakes, and tempting food in many forms is offered to them.

Snake worship in India, an element of the Hindu religion, seems to center on the "hooded serpent" (the cobra) rather than on giant serpents. The cobra is the totem of a "race" known as the "Solar race." Serpent demigods are deified Solar chiefs. There is a close connection between snake worship and tree worship, just as there is between serpents and water. Serpent chiefs were even supposed to rule countries in or under this element.

Snake charming, apparently an offshoot of this religious form, has actually stolen the show, because its followers commercialized their art and now seek out the tourist to make what meager profit they can; the student of true serpent worship must search elsewhere for its manifestations. Snake charmers often carry pythons as part of their exhibits, but these large snakes have never been a special object of worship in India.

IN THE NEAR EAST

The Mediterranean region is another center, though serpent worship has suffered a great decline there in recent centuries because of the opposition of Christianity. In spite of this, there was veneration of serpents by the Ophites, a semi-Christian sect, and we have the Biblical record of the worship of the Brazen Serpent. Snakes were revered in ancient Babylon and Egypt; serpent images are to be found in nearly all Egyptian temples. The Minoans of ancient Crete developed a very high culture, the chief deity of which, the Earth Mother, was shown in constant association with the serpent, an obvious phallic symbol. Greek mythology is full of references to snakes, and thousands of tourists annually visit the famous temple of Asclepius at Epidaurus, where snakes were kept and even reputedly used in shock treatment of mental patients. In Western medicine, the snake remains to this day the symbol of the art of healing. Robert E. Charles, a student of Greek culture both modern and ancient, writes me from Greece that he has little difficulty in finding remnants of reverence for the serpent in both Greece and Crete. The form it now exhibits is belief that snakes bring good fortune and, therefore, should not be molested even when they invade human habitations; also, saucers of milk are often put out for them. Other cultures centering on the Mediterranean Sea necessarily absorbed the Classical attitude toward the serpent, and, indeed, many of them may have developed it independently.

IN THE NEW WORLD

Presumably, the early immigrants from Asia brought serpent worship to the New World, but subsequent high development in the Americas gave it new and, at times, gory aspects. Though generally widespread in North America, reverence for the serpent skyrocketed in Central America and Mexico, a fact clearly illustrated by the ubiquity of the serpent motif in the temple art of these countries. Hundreds of gigantic stones were carved in the form of snakes, chiefly the famous Quetzalcoatl, feathered serpent god, "culture hero extraordinary," and symbol of power. The rattlesnake has been the model for many carvings, its gigantic fangs and rattle executed in admirable detail. In other cases, the serpent motif may be worked into complex reliefs. A façade of the Nunnery Quadrangle at Uxmal, Yucatán, is 160 feet long and has two entwined feathered serpents running through its entire length. The wide-open jaws of one of these hold a human head. In ancient Mexico a wooden instrument carved in the form of a snake was used for holding down the heads of sacrificial victims having their hearts cut out. This gruesome element seems to have been a specialty of the Aztecs; the later Mayan culture took it from them. Living snakes also received attention, if we can judge from the frequent reference to them by the early explorers.

IN AFRICA

I have purposely saved the treatment of serpent worship in tropical and southern Africa for last. Nowhere else on earth has the giant snake in the flesh been elevated to the exalted position that it enjoyed from one side to the other of this continent. There can be little doubt that the African rock python was the species most widely worshipped. Wilfrid D. Hambly's monograph on African serpent worship includes a map of Africa giving sixty tribe and locality names; there are two points of concentration, one centering roughly on Dahomey and Nigeria, the other on eastern central Africa, though many names are widely scattered.

The origin of this relation of man to big snake is lost in antiquity: pythons and man may have been in more continuous close association here than in any other part of the world. The advance of Western concepts did, of course, cause snake worship to decline sharply, and, no doubt, it is doomed to rapid extinction. The time factor will be ignored here; we are interested only in the worship as it existed before marked European influence.

Worship of the python god Danh-gbi, of Whydah, Dahomey, is the best example for us. Danh-gbi, god of wisdom and earthly bliss, was the great benefactor of mankind; he had a profound influence on agriculture and was commonly invoked on behalf of the king, who headed the priesthood. The first man, born blind, owed his sight to the beneficence of this god. Initiated priests acquired a knowledge of poisons and antidotes. Children who touched or were touched by a python had to be taken over for a year and taught the songs and dances of the cult at the expense of their parents.

As in many other snake cults, women held a special position. An appreciable percentage of them became priestesses; these once numbered as many as two thousand in temples observed by one man. These so-called wives of the god entered into sexual relations with the priests and worshippers, the offspring of such unions being considered the children of the python god. Elaborate festivals were held in which the pythons were carried about the streets in the wake of priestesses, who busied themselves by noisily clubbing to death any stray animals, such as dogs, pigs, and fowl. This was done to prevent these creatures from annoying the god. Even little girls were seized, to become, after proper training, brides of the god. This capture of girls was not as bad as it sounds; some pious parents purposely left their children exposed. The sacrifice of human beings to Danh-gbi was not unknown.

It is little wonder that molestation of pythons was a crime. Even the accidental killing of one might be punished by burning to death. At times, the offender was given an ordeal by fire and water with some chance of coming through alive. He was put in a hole beneath a hut made of dry fagots and thatched with grass treated with palm oil to make it burn readily. After fastening the doors, the priests set the structure on fire, allowing the victim to escape as best he could. If he succeeded, they followed him to the nearest water, beating him and throwing clods at him. Thirteen days later, the death of the python was commemorated by a service.

In the early days, the Europeans of western Africa were not exempt from these customs, and, indeed, even now animal collectors find it expedient to leave the pythons alone. Early treaties between the British and the kings of Nigeria often included clauses forbidding, under penalty of heavy fines, the molestation of pythons. If a python invaded a compound, a priest had to be called; at times, it was noticed that the python seemed prone to visit European dwellings, a fact certainly correlated with the large fee demanded by the priest who removed the snake. One foreign agent who had the temerity to kill a python in his house was tied up by the thumbs, spat upon, and, stripped of his clothes, otherwise maltreated. So strong was the feeling against this man that the British officials did not deem it wise to pursue the matter.

Finally, we may note that, according to Hambly, the hypothetical seat of origin of python worship is Uganda, where it occurs in "most perfect detail." He goes on to list three lines of important evidence: "Here there are sacred cows for supplying milk to the python. The rites by which the royal dead pass into pythons are well established. There is clearer evidence respecting the supplications of childless people." Hambly traces the migrations of python-worshipping peoples from east to west across the continent, thus adding support to his thesis. As the African rock python is the only giant of eastern Africa, it must have been the original object of worship.

Thus, we see that serpents have come in for their full share of veneration. At one time or another they have been looked upon as deities, protectors or progenitors of races and tribes, begetters of human life, possessors of vast wisdom and power, guardians of property, wells, and springs. With all this in mind, it is hard to account for the term "lowly serpent"; why not "exalted" rather than "lowly"?

Beliefs

ALTHOUGH SCIENCE encourages an objective view of nature, it has made no startling headway against snake lore, which persists among all races and types of mankind. Perhaps thousands of beliefs have been conjured up about giant snakes, and many of these have crystallized into serpent worship, the subject of the preceding chapter. Here I shall consider beliefs that cannot be classified as religious.

To begin I shall paraphrase and slightly embellish some admonitions quoted by Walter Rose from a missionary magazine published in Africa, and evidently meant to apply to the African rock python: You must remember not to run when attacked, because "the python can move faster." Instead of trying to escape, you simply lie flat on your back with legs extended and together, arms also straight and held against your sides. While the python looks you over and attempts to force his head beneath you, just keep cool and do not move, else he may succeed, which would enable him to get around you for a squeeze. After a period of frustration, he will tire and decide to swallow you from one end, most likely beginning with a foot. This will not hurt at the start, so you must remain cool to avoid convincing him that you need a bit of a hug, a process that sooner or later becomes painful and spoils your shape. When his jaws have reached your knee, carefully take the knife from your pocket and slit the distended side of his jaw.

I would like to be able to give the origin of this highly question-able advice.

One tall tale relayed by R. M. Isemonger would be hard to surpass. It is interesting that its narrator, a European farmer who had lived in Southern Rhodesia almost fifty years, got his basic plan from a local man of African lineage, and did not mind admitting as much. A python the farmer had found constricting a duiker was about to be dispatched when the local man suggested that it be spared and allowed to "catch us another one day." The advice was followed, and the serpent was robbed of its meal. Sure enough, the python continued to overcome game and allow itself to be relieved of it, though now and then the snake was permitted to keep its prey. Other local helpers took over the plan and secured their own pythons, finally organizing a hunt. This was accomplished by staking out at sunset some twenty pythons about ten yards apart and driving game toward them. The scheme worked beautifully until a European neighbor, disturbed by the nightly commotion, came out and shot every one of the snakes. If one mind can think up such a yarn, little wonder that the collective work of millions of minds has produced the vast store of snake stories and myths.

In his book devoted mainly to South African snakes, Rose includes a chapter on myths, in which he shows that the same myths met with in North America are widespread in Africa. Among these are stealing-milk-from-cows, swallowing-young-for-protection, and other favorite yarns. One that Rose found to be associated with pythons of Africa is perhaps the most interesting, for he was able to trace it thence to the West Indies, where, of course, another kind of snake has been substituted; I met this same myth in southeastern China, where the cobra was involved. (It is easy to understand how the myth reached the West Indies from Africa, but its presence in China calls for some other explanation.) This broad distribution indicates not only great age but also that the species of snake is not the important element. There are countless versions and endless details to this story, though the essential point is the existence of a crowing snake that displays wattles and a large red comb suggesting a turkey cock or a rooster.

A story told by F. W. Fitzsimons, too long to give in full, is worth mentioning. It seems that, in southern Africa, the gall of a man who has killed a python confers great "vigour, courage, and longevity" on any who eat it. A Kaffir, well known to Fitzsimons, dared to kill a python because it had seized a favorite dog; consequently, the Kaffir was ambushed by Zulus in search of the gall of a python slayer.

Coming to Asia, I shall begin with a statement by Frank Wall which proves that even a scholar as objective as he can be deceived. In his excellent and exhaustive account of the Indian python, he cites, without comment, an incident intended to illustrate the strength of one of these giants. Getting aboard a ship lying at anchor, it encircled a water cask and constricted so effectively that the middle hoops fell onto the deck. It is inconceivable that any giant snake could exert such compression on even the weakest cask.

An article published only a little more than twenty years ago under the authorship of "Tursa" presents a curious mixture of python fact and fancy. The subject is undoubtedly the Indian python, and a few choice bits of myth from it are notable. A python, justifiably viewing as an impediment the "antlered head of the stag it has crushed," tears a strip of skin from the victim's back (being careful to leave the strip attached to the head), binds the head to a tree or sapling, and revolves the stag's body until the head, with its horns, is twisted off. The author, apparently, bases his conviction on the frequent discovery of antlered heads "in the neighbourhood of recently fed snakes." Oddly enough, he is even more impressed by irrefutable evidence of a python killing and swallowing an adult leopard, a simple feat compared with the one he, along with countless others, so firmly believes.

Tursa writes that the Nepalese, "second to none in jungle

lore," say that the python must anchor its tail about a sapling or a leg of its victim before the powers of constriction can be applied. Discovery of this myth among the Nepalese is further evidence of its wide distribution. These same people are credited with additional fascinating lore: The python prefers young bulls to cows because it realizes that the latter are valuable for the milk they produce. But the milk is being conserved for consumption by the snake itself, who "winds soothingly about the grazing beast and relieves it of its milk." Nursing Nepalese mothers are allegedly robbed in much the same way, though Tursa admits that he knows of no specific case.

A quaint belief was heard in Burma by C. G. Stewart, whose cook volunteered the information that a python, after digesting a large mammal, will "hang itself by the tail over the branch of a tree and shake its head until the indigestible bones" come up.

In 1742 a remarkable book by the Reverend Charles Owen was published in England. It brings together a great deal of information on the snakes of the world and various related subjects. A winged dragon, a snake with a regal crown, and other oddities are illustrated along with perfectly credible species, the latter executed in commendable detail. Much of one page, devoted to a reptile that can be no other than the Indian python, is packed with information, and I quote:

"MARTINIUS in his *Atlas* relates, that in the Province of *Quangsi* in *China*, there are Serpents thirty Foot long. The *Flora Sinensis* reports of the Serpent call'd *Geuto*, that it devours whole Stags, but is not very venemous. 'Tis of an ash Colour, from eighteen to twenty-four Foot long; will often seize on a Man, by leaping from a Tree, and kill him, by its violent windings about him.—The *Chinese* preserve his *Gall* to cure the Diseases of the Eyes.—*Marcus Paulus Venetus* testifies the same of the Serpents of *Carrajam*.—Some are in length ten Paces, in thickness ten Palms, and able to swallow a Man. Are taken thus: The Serpent in the Day lies in Caves of Mountains; in the Night hunts for

Prey, and then returns to its Cave, with the Weight of its Body plowing deep the Earth, being sandy in the Track it goes along: Here the Huntsmen fix strong Stakes pointed with Iron, covered with Sand; and as the Serpent travels along, the Spikes gore its Entrails, and are fasten'd therein, by which 'tis kill'd; and the Huntsmen sell the *Gall* at a great Price for Medicine, and the *Flesh* for Meat. These, continues he, may be reckon'd among *Dragons*, but are without Poison: Instead of Feet, they have Claws like those of a *Lion* or *Falcon*."

This description is typical of the science of its time in mixing truth with fable. Exaggeration of size is understandable, and such elements as ambushing from trees, constricting, the use of gall as medicine, and preying on human beings are familiar enough. Even Marco Polo turns up. The concluding statement that the creature is, after all, a dragon with claws comes as a contradiction to much that has gone before, but it gives the inevitable Chinese touch. Kwangsi, one of China's southernmost provinces, certainly lies within the range of the Indian python, which has been recorded from Yunnan, to the west, Fukien, to the northeast.

Finally, I shall give a few beliefs based on the anaconda and the boa constrictor. In his book about the lower Amazon, Algot Lange reports the local belief that the boa constrictor is venomous two months of the year. This is reminiscent of the conviction in the southeastern United States that bites of animals are more dangerous during the dog days than at other times of the year. There is a myth in South America that anacondas are particularly fond of pregnant women. Perhaps this is useful to husbands who wish to keep their young wives from wandering. Truly fantastic is the story that during the night an anaconda may turn itself into a boat with white sails.

Ethnologists and students of folklore find scientific value in working out the historical development of myths as well as the courses along which they have traveled. Many questions have yet to be answered. Does the conviction by peoples all over the world that snakes perform the same fantastic feats have more significance than merely being evidence of the powerful imaginative quality of the human mind? Did the stories spread from an ancient center of origin, or did man repeatedly invent them? The lowly serpent has been carried to unmeasured heights on the wings of fancy, and it is likely to remain aloft indefinitely.

Encounters
with Giant Snakes

As BIG-SNAKE hunting has not been developed as a sport, either an encounter with a giant is not exciting enough or the excitement of it is not enjoyable. This and the two following chapters should enable each reader to come to a conclusion; I cannot make up my mind, probably because my reaction to snakes is so far from typical.

ANACONDA

A convincing account, with photographs, of a struggle between man and anaconda has been written recently by Kurt Severin. He relates how a professional snake hunter tackled an 18-foot anaconda in the water and struggled with it until several assistants could help force it into a sack. The hunter, Mike Tsalikis, knew what he was doing; he took the absolutely necessary precaution of getting, at the very start, a grip on the neck and base of the head of the reptile. This renders it relatively helpless for two reasons: biting is prevented, and the initial stage of constriction is frustrated, depending so largely as it does on anchorage of the jaws. As explained elsewhere, the giant snakes ordinarily defend themselves primarily by biting, but when actually seized after the manner of this capture, they do not hesitate to throw their entire strength into the struggle. In this case, the snake was the attacked rather than the attacker; the hunter paddled his small boat directly under the anaconda as it basked on a large limb over the water. Thus alarmed, the snake did about all it could. It attempted to escape by plunging into the water, and, incidentally, on the hunter and his boat, which capsized.

Equally interesting is Blomberg's description of capturing an anaconda almost 23 feet long "with forks and lassos and a grim determination." Five men were involved, and all came through unscathed, though the struggle was wild.

Herbert S. Dickey writes of a prolonged contest with a 19-foot anaconda. A woman rescued her duck from the giant by clubbing it, and then baited the snake with a stuffed duck. When the anaconda returned for the bait, it was waylaid by more than one person but pursued and actually killed by a mere boy armed only with a club.

F. W. Up de Graff writes of stepping on a gigantic anaconda (30 feet long) while he was bathing. The Indians with him attacked it without hesitation, in spite of its size, and the monster was finally shot in two. The fact that the Indians had so little fear of it is significant.

The preceding does not picture the anaconda as a highly dangerous creature to persons who know its habits and exactly how it must be treated. There are many hair-raising accounts of dire struggles, but these can scarcely be rated as either objective or free of exaggeration.

BOA CONSTRICTOR

Being the smallest of the six giants, the boa constrictor is the least formidable. The vast majority of individuals fall within the size range of non-venomous snakes that can be safely tackled by the experienced hunter, providing he is strong. William Beebe writes that a specimen 12½ feet long was caught by several men who simply rushed it. Stories of prolonged struggles with boa constrictors are either fabrications or are based on the application of this name to one of the other giants, an error not infrequently made. Again it is essential that, at the very start, a firm grip be secured at the neck and base of the head.

AFRICAN ROCK PYTHON

As there is no better account of the capture of a python by the experienced than Arthur Loveridge's, I shall quote him at length. The African rock python in question, though only 14⅓ feet long, was exceptionally thick (18 inches in diameter at mid-body) and therefore powerful; it weighed 135 pounds.

"Instead of being 'nearby,' as stated, we had to walk a mile and a half through the bush before we reached the place, and when we got there the python was gone! It had been lying in a dense thicket overgrown with rank grass taller than a man; the spot where it had been was plain enough for the grass was flattened where it had lain. The thicket covered an area of about thirty feet by twenty feet and there were many similar thickets in the immediate vicinity.

"Pushing into the thicket I found that the snake had only moved some six feet further in, for I caught sight of its coils which were enormous; at midbody the girth was greater than that of an average man. I proceeded to beat down the grass and brambles till one had a clear view, and while I was so engaged the reptile struck at me open-jawed, his head going as high as my chest and once as high as my throat. Having cleared the arena, I hung the small sack on the end of the snake stick and let the snake strike the sacking half-a-dozen times; each time he struck, the sack would fall to the ground, only to be lifted again on the end of the stick. While I was engaged in recovering it, the snake struck too quickly a couple of times and to avoid the blow, I had to step back so that the force of it was spent in space; the snake flopped down but quickly withdrew its head on the defensive again. After a dozen futile attempts, in one of which he struck the end of my snake stick through the sack . . . the python became discouraged and decided to retire. As he commenced to glide away I sprang after him, planted the T-end of my stick on his neck for a second as I grasped it firmly with my hand before he had time to throw off the stick. Salimu, who had been standing by waiting for orders, now came running to seize his tail; Abedi grasped it round the middle and a temporary employee held open my duffle bag, crying continuously in the vernacular, 'It cannot go, it won't go in.' Thrusting the snake's head to the bottom of the bag, I seized the neck again from the outside, i.e., through the material. Before going in, however, he dribbled from both ends, trying, I think, to disgorge the bushbuck which he had swallowed; the result was the most appalling stench imaginable. It would have made most people sick but at the moment we had other things to think about! We just crammed and crammed that poor old python into the bag, and after we succeeded in doing this it was all we could do to lace up the opening with some cord which I had brought for the purpose."

Another spirited account of the capture of an African rock python is R. M. Isemonger's. The reptile had taken refuge in the hole of an ant bear, and Isemonger recruited several local helpers to dig it out. As hours of digging did not bring results, the tactic of stamping on the ground was tried. This caused a frightened wart hog to rush forth and create a slight diversion. Not long afterward, the python itself appeared. The recruits quickly scattered, leaving Isemonger alone to drag the snake back by the tail and stuff it into a bag. Isemonger does not definitely state that no help was needed in the final stages, but such frightened assistants could hardly have been very helpful. The reptile and bag weighed together about 150 pounds.

Wynant D. Hubbard relates how, with the aid of twelve men, he captured an African rock python 17 feet 5 inches long. He gave a five-foot forked stick to each of four men, who then used them in pinning the snake down; next eight men rushed in to help subdue it; finally it was stuffed into a bag.

Another observer of African wildlife, J. Stevenson-Hamilton, once met an individual of this same species as it crawled along. It only raised its head and hissed. Even after being wounded, the serpent showed no signs of aggression, merely moving on at the same slow rate.

INDIAN PYTHON

In his detailed account of this snake, Frank Wall wrote more than a page on its placid disposition, both as a captive and in its natural haunts, "even when attacked making no attempt to avenge offence or injury." He writes that it is a simple matter for two persons to pick up specimens from 6 to 8 feet long, and he cites the case of a 20-pound Indian python that allowed two men to capture it by grasping head and tail. It gave an ineffectual snap at the face of one captor and then permitted itself to be thrust into a bag, where it huddled without remonstrance.

Malcolm Smith recommended a clever technique for handling pythons of moderate size: "Take a bath towel and wrap it several times round the left hand so as to protect it completely. Push this into the snake's face. It will be at once seized and before the creature can free its teeth for a second bite it can be gripped round the neck and carried off." He adds that inevitably the snake's body will get wrapped around you, but that there is no need for alarm, provided the snake is not more than 12 or 13 feet long. Adult

Indian pythons may not be much longer than this, especially if they are males.

RETICULATE PYTHON

Wall was convinced that this great giant, like its lesser cousin, also has a good disposition: "It is a remarkably lethargic snake, showing little or no inclination to escape when encountered." He goes on to say that the Burmese "report it as a very harmless snake of timid disposition." A few incidents are described: a python met in the jungle of the Pegu Yoma by an officer and his party retained a coiled position even though surrounded by ten or twelve excited men, one of whom went up and cut it to death with his dah. Five individuals caught in the dense jungles of southern Tenasserim behaved in just the same way, except for a young one only 3 feet long, which, encountered on the banks of a stream, glided into the water and swam some distance under the surface.

The most notable meeting with a reticulate python in the wilds is that described by Alfred Russel Wallace. One evening he was reading on the veranda of his house on Amboina, in the East Indies, when he heard above his head a curious rustling as if some heavy animal were crawling over the thatch. Thinking little of it, he went to bed. The next afternoon, when lying on his couch, he looked up and finally made out the form of a huge snake coiled between the ridgepole and the roof. The reptile had climbed one of the house posts to take up a position there; in doing so during the night, it must have passed within a yard of Wallace's head. He called for help. Among several men who responded, one had a plan: with a noose of rattan in one hand, a long pole in the other, he poked the python out of its hiding place and, after managing to slip the noose over its head, worked the rope down its body. He then dragged the 12-foot animal out of the house, though first there was a noisy scuffle on the porch, where it coiled about chairs and posts. Grasping his victim by the tail, this resourceful man tried to strike its head against a tree. The reptile escaped and got under a dead tree lying near by, but was soon extracted. The head hitting was again attempted, this time with success. Final dispatch was easily accomplished with a hatchet. Wallace concluded that this snake was "capable of doing much mischief, and of swallowing a dog or a child." He would have been nearer to the truth if he had written "infant" rather than "child."

Frank Buck was famous as a collector of wild animals and as a writer about his experiences with them. He has given a vivid account of two captures of giant snakes, presumably reticulate pythons. One event took place on the southern part of the Malay Peninsula. Coming on a 22-foot, 250-pound specimen, Buck grabbed its tail as it crawled away, causing it to turn on him. He then held a large piece of cloth toward it, and when it bit the cloth, he seized the neck. The snake then got a coil around Buck, who was quickly aided by his three companions. The subdued snake was eventually bound to a sapling so that it could be carried.

In Buck's other encounter, the hunters did not come out so well. One of his men, upon stepping over a log and on a python only a little smaller than the first, was seized by a leg and wrapped by three coils, one about his leg, another around his body, while the tail clutched his shoulders. For a while it was doubtful who was capturing whom. Buck and the two other men struggled with the reptile and finally succeeded in unwinding it and, with the butt of a revolver, prying the jaws loose from the leg. Rattan ropes were wound first around the neck and then around various points of the body, until the creature was subdued and lay in a series of loops, each tied to the other. Thus, the reptile was rendered helpless and convenient for transportation by means of a carrying pole. Although Buck had the reputation of telling tall tales, there is nothing unreasonable in his narration of these two encounters.

A vivid description by Charles Mayer of the capture of a 32-foot giant on Sumatra has the usual signs of embellishment. The plan was to drag the monster into a staked-down crate by means of a rope tied to the neck and strung through the crate, an ingenious scheme. Two ropes were to be fixed to the tail to prevent lashing. Failure to manipulate these ropes—one was never tied, the other not pulled by the overexcited assistants—caused the plan to fail in part, with the result that Mayer's arm was bitten and the body of one of his assistants was seized by the rear portion of the snake. When the head was finally hauled into the crate, another rope was tied about the middle of the body, but this did not prevent the feared lashing, which knocked several helpers flat.

All of this could well have happened in a battle with such an oversized python, but I have omitted so far the embellishments: The man seized by the reptile allegedly was killed instantly with "nearly every bone" in his body broken and blood spouting from the mouth and ears. It is entirely possible that the man could have died instantly from shock and even hemorrhaged from constriction, but the breaking of so many bones and the spouting of blood are virtual impossibilities.

SUMMARY

After reading about scores of meetings with the legless giants of jungle and savanna, I must conclude that their secret weapon is an ability to paralyze the foe with terror. Failing this, the giant lacks the aggressive drive of creatures that launch an attack from a distance, and is not to be feared at any but the very closest range. Even here, man has little to worry about because constriction will not ordinarily be resorted to, and there is no venom in the bite. Hunting the venomous serpent is far more dangerous, and may even be worthy of being called a sport.

Attacks on Man

GIANT SNAKES *almost* never attack man with the intention of satisfying their appetite; only the three largest (the reticulate python, the African rock python, and the anaconda) have even been accused. Evidence for attacks ranges from hearsay and folk belief to little that is valid, or, let us say, from very bad to poor. A big snake that attacks a man through hunger might almost be regarded as having made a mistake like that of a zoo giant who swallows its blanket, an event that has been recorded more than once.

Stories of snakes eating men sound reasonable; giant snakes devour a great variety of other large mammals, so why not man? He is more tempting than many because of his lack of fur, hoofs, and horns. And he has relatively weak powers of defense, no claws or formidable jaws. Why, then, is he so rarely a part of the largest snakes' diet?

The answer may lie in the size and intelligence of man. Human shoulders are probably too wide for boas and pythons of average size, whereas clothes as well as other apparel cause a man to look even larger than he is. Alertness, incessant activity, and social habits make him anything but an easy victim. His ability to learn about snakes allows him not only to avoid them but to turn the tables by becoming the aggressor. Close association for perhaps hundreds of thousands of years may have created an instinct to give man a wide berth; snakes that failed to develop such an instinct have simply been eliminated.

As virtually no evidence for the killing or eating of human beings by a giant snake is of the indisputable, eyewitness type, I shall have to present the best available, beginning with the reports most widely credited by herpetologists.

Felix Kopstein, who was a competent and experienced student of the reptiles of the East Indies, related that a boy fourteen years old once disappeared on one of the islands. A search party found a reticulate python almost 17 feet long near where the boy was last seen. A lump in the snake told the sad story, which was soon corroborated by dissection of the python. Kopstein also cited a case of an adult woman being swallowed by a still larger reticulate python.

L. Coomans de Ruiter's secondhand report of the swallowing of two women originated in the same part of the world. These victims were seized while bending over doing field work. The negating detail is that, allegedly, the skulls, as well as other bones, were broken. This could, of course, be an embellishment of an essentially true account, but it does prove that the observers did not know much about pythons.

Equally convincing is Loveridge's account of the killing of a woman on Ukerewe, a small island in Lake Victoria. The culprit was a heavy African rock python just over 14 feet long but almost 16 inches in diameter. The woman had been washing and spreading clothes by a stream at a ford. A man came by, and seeing the clothes but no washer, looked around and found the victim dead in the snake's coils. He called for help, and the python was killed with four spear thrusts and two knifings. Whether it had intended to swallow the woman will never be known. She had been in poor health, having given birth only eight days before. This fact could have been partly responsible; she might have fainted from illness or at the sight of the python.

The old men of the island recalled one other fatal case; a youth had been killed years before. The strong local aversion to killing pythons may also have been a contributing factor in making these snakes of Ukerewe relatively bold.

More recently, Rolf Blomberg recounted the fate of a thirteen-year-old boy who disappeared while swimming at the mouth of the Yasuní River, a tributary of the Napo River of Peru and Ecuador. Friends saw bubbles rising where the ill-fated boy had disappeared; one of them dived, only to feel the body of what he thought was an anaconda. A day and a night of constant search by the victim's father revealed the reptile lying half in and half out of the water. It had disgorged the lost boy, and was dispatched with five shots of a rifle. From this same source comes the story of a man who was killed by an anaconda while he was swimming in the Napo River of Ecuador.

Kurt Severin adds an "authenticated" attack: A man was pulled into a river by an anaconda while he was watering cattle; the snake seized his legs, coiled around him as he stood in the water, pulled him in, and drowned him.

Other accounts of giant snakes killing humans are scarcely worth repeating. Unsuccessful direct attacks are reported more often, though scarcely more convincingly. A few of these are of some interest.

There is one by an early South American explorer. A hunter in British Guiana shot a duck, and it fell near the bank of a river. When he went to get the duck, an anaconda seized him. He called to his wife for help; when she arrived with his knife, she too was promptly seized. The hunter managed to slash the anaconda enough to make it release its hold on the pair, and they escaped without great injury. The evidence that the reptile had made a direct attack is not convincing, and the seizure of the wife as well as the man savors of embellishment.

The account by A. Watts of a man caught while passing under a large tree comes from the Congo; he escaped little the worse for wear. The snake, of course, was an African rock python; its size was not stated. This case sounds like a direct attack, though Watts was not an eyewitness.

R. W. Keays tells of a man in peninsular India who was wading in shallow water while fishing. He saw a dark, submerged object in a cavity of the bank. He thrust his leg into the cavity to identify the object and was quickly enlightened; a 9-foot Indian python bit the leg. The snake then threw three coils around the man, who managed to hold the reptile's neck and free himself, but not without the help of a friend armed with a sickle.

This last story and the one of the duck hunter are typical of "attacks" so styled without real justification. The python in the hole in the bank might readily have taken the leg for some small, edible animal, or it might have bitten without realizing that doing so would bring it into a contest with a human being.

Numerous experienced reptile men, James A. Oliver among them, believe that pythons and other giant snakes virtually never attack man with the intention of getting a meal, and never attack him for purely aggressive reasons; I have yet to find a dissenting voice. Admittedly, the evidence is not so one-sided as it is, for example, with myths about deadly stinging snakes rolling around like hoops; feeding accidents *will* happen in the best of (snake) families, and enough of these occur to keep the belief alive. The wonder is rather that more reports do not appear in newspapers; a story of this type would be just the kind to get world-wide coverage.

Fear of Giant Snakes

EVEN THE THOUGHT of meeting a giant snake face to face in the wilds is, for many of us, worse than a nightmare. This chapter examines the grounds for such an emotion.

In the Western world, where it is taught that God is to be worshipped and feared, man's fear of snakes is relatively simple, for serpent worship has nearly vanished. This fear is compounded of a knowledge that many species are venomous, plus an unreasoned dread largely independent of such knowledge. Where the snake is considered something of a god, it, too, is both worshipped and feared. For one not brought up in the tradition of animal worship, the attitude of those who have, all but defies analysis. So it is not my intention to analyze this more complex fear, but merely to describe some of its results.

Extreme fear of a snake, immeasurably complicating the result of a bite, always produces shock. This shock may even cause death; perhaps nearly all deaths that follow the bite in a matter of a few minutes are the result of fear-produced shock. This generalization holds for all parts of the world, though it seems to be most applicable to tropical Asia, where, in India and Pakistan, snakebite fatalities reach a peak and serpent worship is apparently more prevalent than in any other extensive region. The usual explanation of this high death rate is the aversion to killing sacred creatures. The late Jim Corbett, a naturalist who spent most of a long life in

India, went so far as to say that half of the thousands who die there annually of the bites of venomous snakes really "die of shock or fright, or a combination of the two when bitten by non-poisonous snakes." Even allowing for gross overestimation, Corbett's conviction is impressive.

While on Ceylon, Heinz Randow once had to transfer two large pythons for shipment, one 20, the other 25 feet long. He had many men helping him, among them a fifteen-year-old Tamil. The 20-foot python managed to seize the boy's hand in its jaws. The boy fainted dead away and remained unconscious while his hand was being removed from the jaws and some loose teeth extracted from it. The wound, which bled freely, healed in two weeks without infection, but the shock had been so profound that the boy's mind was affected; he had to be sent home to his village. The presence of friends to render immediate aid and the presumed knowledge that the snake was non-venomous should have prevented serious shock.

Modern science must be given some credit for the reduction of this fear hazard in many parts of the world; peoples brought up in a more pragmatic attitude toward natural phenomena would be less subject to such severe shock and its consequences.

Two psychologists, Harold E. and Mary C. Jones, undertook to determine whether our fear of snakes is instinctive. They performed detailed experiments with nearly 150 persons of various ages. The children had lived in cities and were not familiar with snakes. One of the snakes, about 6 feet long, was a common harmless species of the United States, and another a boa constrictor even smaller. The children up to two years of age had no fear. By the age of three or three and a half, caution was commonly shown; they paid close attention to the snake's movements, approaching and touching it tentatively. Definite fear was often recorded after the age of four, and was more pronounced in adults than in children. No differences were recorded between boys and girls.

The experimenters concluded that fear of snakes is not innate or inherited, but learned by each individual. They were convinced that what might possibly be considered the appearance of an inherited fear at an early age, rather than at birth, was, in reality, a general maturation of behavior leading to greater sensitivity and more discriminatory responses and requiring a sudden new adjustment that the individual was unprepared to make. In short, the child becomes more and more aware of his surroundings and is less willing to take chances without some investigation. This conclusion is in conformity with the modern psychological view of man as a mammal almost devoid of instincts, which we aptly speak of as "built-in reactions."

There can be no doubt that the depth of the fear of snakes varies greatly, and this, perhaps, substantiates the conclusion that it is learned; if it were instinctive, we might expect it to be uniform and harder to get rid of. In dealing with a great many individuals who were afraid, I have helped a few to overcome their fear in a matter of minutes, whereas in others there was no chance of ever eradicating it. When asked to give the reason for their fear, the usual answer is: "Because snakes are slimy." Then, if to my reply that no snake is slimy, they insist: "But I hate them anyway," I probably am dealing with a deep, unreasoned fear that cannot be overcome. Calling the snake slimy is only a way of trying to justify the fear. They seem to prefer to use the word "hate"; many persons are naturally reluctant to admit fear. The hard and fast rule is: never attempt to scare anyone and never force the matter. The indirect approach becomes more effective with small children; most of them will not enjoy being left out and will quickly decide to like whatever is being liked.

As I have already mentioned Jim Corbett, I shall use his own fear as an example of what that emotion can do to a brave man. He won fame as a chivalrous killer of man-eating tigers, and his refusal to kill for sport alone added to his stature; no tiger innocent of human blood was ever molested. He followed tigers into dense jungle to meet them at close quarters and did not hesitate literally to camp on the trail of a wounded beast. A companion of mine who hunted with him assures me that Corbett's stories are not exaggerated or overdrawn, but understated.

With admirable candor, Corbett tells of refusing to help a friend in an attempt to capture an Indian python for the Lucknow Zoo. The result was that this python, though only 17 feet 6 inches long, escaped in the open from three would-be capturers while Corbett stood by, rifle in hand. Compared with the danger posed by a wounded tiger at close quarters in a jungle, the risk in facing a small python in the open would be as one to a thousand, could we rate danger on a relative scale. Perhaps this intrepid hunter had absorbed some of the local fear of snakes. An interesting sequel to the story was the discovery on a second attempt that a pair of otters had dispatched the python, and, in contrast to Corbett, all for sport; not a bit of the body had been eaten.

I am loath to concede that a horror of snakes is an advantage to anyone. Inhabitants of the United States know that automobiles account for about one hundred lives a day, and yet the most timid look at cars without fear; they learn the traffic rules and feel safe enough. Venomous snakes can be viewed in the same way; respect for them and some knowledge of their habits will suffice. It might be argued that a mild fear of snakes is good for children too young to tell a venomous from a harmless species. As a child of four or five can learn the difference, it hardly seems necessary to instill in children of any age a fear that will have to be eliminated later; children two or three years old must be watched constantly, snakes or no snakes.

FEAR IN OTHER PRIMATES

As the non-human primates have a combined range so similar to that of the giants, it will be appropriate also to consider these close relatives of man. Both Charles Darwin and Arthur E. Brown carried on simple experiments with zoo monkeys in the nineteenth century, and concluded that these animals, with few exceptions, show marked alarm, if not fear, in the presence of snakes; it seemed to matter little whether the snakes were living, dead, or stuffed. Years later, P. Chalmers Mitchell and R. I. Pocock made still more careful experiments of the same nature, including the use of a small reticulate python, and arrived at essentially the same conclusion, with the addition that lemurs were found to be devoid of fear; they even cast hungry looks at the snakes. Walter Rose recently confirmed these results in testing a lemur and a baby vervet monkey, the latter too young ever to have seen a snake before. The lemur showed fearless interest, presumably stirred by appetite, whereas the monkey exhibited terror.

All we can conclude from the monkey and lemur behavior is that, apparently, two related groups of higher vertebrate animals have very different feelings about snakes. Lemurs are primitive primates, man and the apes the most advanced members of the order; monkeys come in between. The species of monkeys are so numerous that it will be many a day before their instinctive fears can be determined.

As apes are few in number of species and resemble man much more than do any other primates, it will be profitable to review what we know about their attitude. More than one hundred years ago W. J. Broderip described the behavior of a chimpanzee when confronted with a python: "As he jumped and danced along the dresser towards the basket, he was all gaiety and life. Suddenly he seemed to be taken aback, stopped—then cautiously advanced towards the basket, peered or rather craned over it—and instantly with a gesture of horror and aversion and the cry of Hoo! hoo! recoiled from the detested object, jumped back as far as he could, and then sprang to his keeper for protection."

Renaud Paulian experimented with a young female chimpanzee living in the Ivory Coast Republic. This pet was much more afraid of a python than were some monkeys, and fled even from parts of it. Experiments with these (a section of the body and a piece of skin) suggest that she recognized pythons by shape rather than by skin pattern.

Early in the present century, while working with the monkeys and lemurs, Mitchell and Pocock concluded that the zoo apes were afraid of snakes, the orangutans being the most fearful, the gibbons the least. One chimpanzee passed large, living nematodes, and others took alarm at these parasites in the feces of their companion, presumably mistaking them for snakes. Some fifteen years later, Mitchell, still puzzling over the problem, experimented with a young male chimp received in January, apparently just after being weaned. The following summer, this ape was confronted with a tree boa wrapped around Mitchell's arm and big enough to have two feet of head and neck protruding toward the chimp. The chimp at once allowed the tongue of the boa to touch its face and even appeared ready to kiss the reptile's mouth. This same pet became fond of playing with snakes of various kinds.

Robert M. and Ada W. Yerkes, in their large book on the great apes, dealt at some length with fear of snakes. In 1943, R. M. Yerkes again considered the subject, expressing the opinion that the very young chimpanzee is relatively indifferent when with mother or trusted caretaker. The adults, on the contrary, are greatly disturbed by snakes, usually exhibiting aggressiveness tempered with caution. He concluded that there is slight indication of specific fear in young apes, what caution there is being of the kind commonly shown when confronting any unfamiliar object. The violent reaction of the adults is presumably due to the influence of social tradition or the result of individual experience.

Although man's reaction to snakes is vastly more complex than the ape's, there is a basic similarity: the young of both are indifferent, whereas the adults are, in general, fearful. In spite of a superior intelligence, man has been unable to rid himself of an unreasoned dread of harmless snakes. One outstanding difference between man and ape is that the latter has never worshipped snakes and therefore does not exhibit man's ambivalent attitude.

Uses by Man

※

APART FROM SERVING as objects of worship, the giant snakes have been found useful to man in a number of ways. Their use as food among some peoples has been mentioned already. In addition, they are prized for their hides, and in some parts of the world they are considered to have medicinal values and are also used as aids to agriculture, especially in the extermination of harmful rodents. Then, too, they play an important role in the fields of education and entertainment.

USE AS LEATHER

In contrast to animals with limbs, the snake is constantly in extensive contact with the ground, which may be rough or smooth, dry or wet; the snake can go through water and come out dry, through mud or slime and come out clean, over jagged rocks and remain unscratched. Imagine any mammal crawling on a hairless belly; how long would its tender skin last? We should expect to find durability in leather made from the skin that the snake puts to such hard use.

Some of the qualities of snake hide are shown by a story from South America told by Herbert S. Dickey. It seems that Brazilian

Boa Constrictor. These excellent engravings were made about a hundred years ago for Jan and Sordelli's monumental iconography (Plate II, *Livraison* 5).

Anaconda arrives at zoo. (Photograph, Zoological Society of Philadelphia)

collectors had put 20 feet as the minimum length for hides that they would buy. A certain clever hunter would take a boa hide only 10 or 12 feet long and, after treating it with manatee fat and sunlight, fasten one end to a post of his house and have two men strain at the opposite end. The result was a hide that met the 20-foot requirement.

Recognizing the durability of snake hides, man has used them to a limited extent for an undetermined length of time, probably since the dawn of leather. Musical-instrument heads are a good example of an ancient use; such small-scale manufactures, however, though numerous and varied, did not constitute a threat to snakes. Modern technology overlooked the possibilities of exploitation until the leather shortage of the First World War started a relentless search. When attention turned to the tropics, the giant boas and pythons with their skins of unsurpassed beauty were discovered. In general, the smaller snakes are not worth the effort, but the wart snakes (*Acrochordus*) of the Indonesian region are the shining exception. These have a unique, granular skin that happens to make the best snake leather of all; in the trade, the name "karung" is frequently used for these water snakes. Nearly all snakes of the temperate region were saved by their small size.

Accounts of the leather industry in the United States before 1920 have little or nothing to say about any reptiles but alligators. These have been used extensively as a source of high-grade leather since at least the mid-1800's, with the result that in 1929 the species was authoritatively estimated to be abundant over only one quarter of its original range. Leather reports of the 1920's tell a different story; glowing accounts of the exceptional qualities of snake hides suddenly appear, and extensive advertising campaigns are instigated. For example, the best snakeskin is described as waterproof, dampproof, easy to clean, durable, and wear-resistant; it never cracks, chips, or peels. The cost, one advertiser said, is little more than that of other fancy leathers, and snake leather is more decorative and distinctive. Special qualities are universally recognized;

its fragile feel and the fact that it is so often backed are deceptive; the purpose of the backing, either glued or sewed on, is to give body, not strength.

A list of the useful things wholly or in part made of this leather is long; here are some items: shoe uppers, handbags, traveling bags, chair covers, auto upholstery, belts, hats, cigarette cases and lighters, cameras, fountain pens, and handle coverings for tennis rackets. Most of the leather used goes into shoes and handbags. If the acceptance of a product can be judged by the extent of the effort made to imitate it, then snake leather must be rated a success. Hides of the standard domestic mammals of the trade are commonly embossed to look like snake leather, but these must be advertised as "grained"; "boa-grained" and "python-grained" are terms often seen in leather-goods advertisements.

From the manufacturer's point of view, the one great difficulty was the development of a practical method of converting raw reptile hides into finished leather. The process finally worked out was once secret, but fairly detailed descriptions are now readily available. A large French company that pioneered a process was tanning ten thousand reptile skins daily by the late 1920's.

The standard basic operations of leather preparation are used on reptile hides, but special applications are necessary. As these are tricky, most tanneries prefer to let specialists handle snakes and other reptiles. Nevertheless, in 1952 no fewer than eighteen companies in six states of this country advertised snake leather for sale to manufacturers.

A snake killed for the market must be skinned at once. There is no difficulty in skinning, for the hide comes off readily after a slit has been made down the middle of the belly. The head and much of the tail are of no value to the leather industry. The fresh hide is commonly treated in a number of ways. It may simply be dried in the sun, a procedure that makes it hard and stiff; or salting or preserving in salty mud, which are better methods, may be employed. Hides are collected by many people who cannot be called experts as well as by some full-time hunters; finding and killing large snakes present no great problem. Traders make regular visits to the towns and villages where hunters and casual collectors live.

When the hides have been unpacked at the tannery, they must be soaked in lime water to remove the outer layer of keratinized (dead) cells. If not removed, this layer may peel off later; it is the part periodically shed by all snakes. After the required week or two of liming, the hides are soaked in a solution known as bate. This soaking, which lasts only a matter of hours, softens and removes excess alkali as well as certain undesirable proteins. The hides are now flexible, but their collagen has not been damaged. This, the principal protein of skin, gives leather its strength. Collagen may have a tensile strength approximately that of steel wire. Its gigantic molecule is the most elongated one yet isolated; if it were enlarged so that its diameter equaled that of a pencil, the molecule would be about a yard long. A fiber of leather is made up of vast numbers of these microscopic threads.

Now that the flaccid hides are ready for tanning, the difficulty begins, for the shape of the skins causes them to tangle if processed after the manner of hides more or less square. As they cannot be tumbled in large drums, slow methods calling for much handwork are required. If the natural hide is not the proper thickness, it cannot be sliced into layers as a thick cow or pig hide can, but must be shaved; the skill needed is easily imagined.

Unfortunately, the tanners have never discovered a process that allows the hide to retain its colors or its iridescence; the pattern alone persists as a mere remnant of perhaps fifteen or twenty rich hues beautifully mingled. But even this remnant has beauty, and the tanners do all in their power to enhance it by means of bleaching agents that make certain markings stand out.

The skins are next treated with oils and grease to keep them soft, and then tacked out by experts. Once dry, the hides have to be cleaned and possibly dyed.

The toughness of hide that has stood snakes in good stead for some millions of years now threatens many of them with extinction, especially the largest snakes, whose great size, in addition, makes them particularly valuable. Size has thus proved to be as fickle as has man himself; his reverence for snakes was once at least as sure a protection as legislation can now be.

It is patent that the uncontrolled slaughter of snakes for their hides is proving to be another case of killing the goose that laid the golden egg. The immediate thought of many will be that, instead of killing a goose, the hide hunters are killing two birds with one stone—exterminating dangerous animals and supplying leather at the same time. But it just happens that the snakes most valuable for leather are harmless; decimating all of the economically important species will hardly affect the menace of venomous snakes. The souvenir trade does utilize, among others, such dangerous snakes as our rattlers, but this trade is an insignificant part of the commercial-leather business. Wilfred T. Neill reports from Florida that the diamondback rattler is there holding its own against the many professional hunters catering to showmen and the local souvenir makers.

Let us look at some statistics to get a rough idea of what is taking place on a large scale. Our own official reports did not recognize even reptile hides in general as a separate category until 1929, and therefore I cannot trace the earlier history of their importation, let alone that of snakes in particular. As already indicated, the trade increased greatly during the decade that ended that year.

In 1929, we imported 1,899,000 pounds of reptile skins valued at $2,982,000 from thirty-three countries. Three countries—India, Colombia, and Mexico—contributed 1,303,000 pounds, the first two in excess of 400,000 pounds each. Judging by the later, more detailed reports, the nearly 2,000,000 pounds were made up of some 5,000,000 hides. The quantities fluctuate considerably from year to year, but these 1929 figures are representative enough. For example, the number of hides stood at about 4,500,000 for

1949; just over 8,000,000 and 6,000,000 for 1950 and 1952, respectively; about 3,250,000 for 1957. Whether this means that the supply is giving out remains to be seen. As for contributors, in 1945 Brazil sent us 1,275,000 skins, India 2,056,000, Colombia 898,000, and even little Honduras 579,000.

Reptile-hide imports of the United Kingdom run noticeably higher than ours; in 1951 the figure was roughly 12,000,000, if we allow the same hide-pound ratio that is borne out by statistics for our imports. Many other European countries also import reptile hides, but it might be tiring to go into further details. Moreover, this whole matter is confusing, for units and methods of reporting vary from country to country. A country exporting chiefly crocodilian hides will have a weight-number ratio totally different from that of a country dispatching largely snake hides. In any event, it is easy to see that tens of millions of reptiles are sacrificed annually; I would guess that half of these are snakes. Putting the estimate at a conservative 12,000,000, it is readily calculated that the earth could have each year a handsome new equatorial belt of snake hide. This, I wish to emphasize, would not have to include hides of any venomous species.

USE AS FOOD

As man regards snakes with such extremes of emotion, their use as food has not been entirely a matter of taste and digestibility; a creature that arouses reverence or horror would not appeal to the appetite. Yet these sharply contrasted emotions have afforded the snake relatively little protection; the world-wide habit of eating snakes may be as old as man himself. On the other hand, it is hard to see why man should single snakes out among the higher animals as unsuitable. A snake is readily found, caught, and killed; skinning it is easier than skinning a mammal or plucking a bird; the flesh is palatable if usually limited in quantity. The giant snakes are widely relished, the quantity of their meat being ample and its quality good.

The greatest of markets is centered at Canton, but from this we cannot conclude that the Chinese as a whole are snake eaters; this habit of the Canton region is probably a cultural inheritance from aboriginal peoples who were supplanted or absorbed by the southern Chinese centuries ago. During four years of travel in other parts of China, I saw no evidence of habitual snake eating, only collectors who sold their catch to medicine shops. Even the southeastern snake eaters think of the flesh as having tonic as well as gustatory value. A similar belief prevailed in France, as shown by the works of Madame de Sévigné in the late seventeenth century. She thought that eating vipers had given her abundant health because "they temper, purify, and refresh the blood."

Fred R. Irvine, in his recent interesting paper on snakes as food for man, devotes almost as much space to the general Asiatic region as to the rest of the world combined. In Hong Kong, according to him, feasting on snakes is somewhat seasonal; the best time is from October to January, when they are fat and easy to handle. On special occasions snake banquets are held, and no other meat is served; the guests have the choice of as many as five serpentine delicacies. Other feasts, known as dragon-and-tiger banquets, have a menu of civet cat as well as snake meat.

It is extraordinarily hard to get authentic information about the Canton snake market. Years ago, I was fortunate enough to watch the activities in one of the city retail shops. There, a half-clothed man lifted cobras out of a basket and scraped out the teeth as well as the fangs with a thin bamboo knife. The king cobra, whose range extends into extreme southern China, occasionally turns up in the markets. Not all work in Canton snake shops is dangerous; several other species of snakes, some of them entirely harmless, are commonly seen there.

Two of our giants, the reticulate and Indian pythons, are by no means so available to the Canton market as the cobra, but their flesh is said to sell at a higher price than beef, and this in a region where beef is scarce. The reticulate python is not native to China, although it is found not very far south of it; the Indian python lives in extreme southern China, but is rare, except, perhaps, on the island of Hainan. Both of these species are imported in considerable numbers and are often seen in the shops.

As the countries and the enormous archipelago south of China have been so well colonized by the Cantonese, it follows that the snake-eating habit is widespread there. With the gigantic Indian, reticulate, and amethystine pythons available in one part or another, the market can be readily supplied. Yet the Cantonese are by no means the only snake eaters. For example, Henry C. Raven, who explored this archipelago for many years, wrote that the Dyaks habitually ate python meat. He relates how in Borneo his Dyak hunters killed a python some 20 feet long as it slid into a river; as the snake was found to contain two young pigs, the hunters had a feast, which included pork. This is a novel use to make of a python.

A parallel account, by A. Watts, comes from the Congo. It seems that a goat had been devoured by an African rock python only 13 feet long and 16 inches around. Unable to escape from the goat's pen, the glutton was caught, with the result that everyone enjoyed a feast of boiled python and goat meat. This practice of eating the stomach contents of snakes is repugnant until one realizes that skinning eliminates all contamination.

Albert W. C. T. Herre and D. S. Rabor describe the eating of sea snakes in the Philippines: "Snakes that are eaten by the Japanese are spitted on a pointed bamboo. This makes the snake stiff and easy to handle. Most of the snakes are then roasted and smoked, or prepared in the same way as smoked fish. They are usually eaten with soy sauce and various condiments and are then said to be very palatable."

Before turning to other parts of the world, it should be pointed out that the vast majority of the peoples of India refrain from eating snakes for religious reasons; what little ophiophagy occurs there apparently is confined to the "hill tribes."

There is ample evidence of snake eating in Australia, where the original inhabitants enjoy not only the gigantic amethystine python but six smaller species of pythons as well. Both flesh and eggs are prized. After being stiffened over the fire, a 10-foot python may be wound in coils eighteen inches in diameter and then cooked in hot ashes. Sometimes a python is wrapped in clay without being skinned, and baked in hot ashes for about seven hours.

On New Britain, an island lying immediately east of New Guinea, an unusual variation in python treatment once occurred. The Baining of the Gazelle Peninsula used local pythons in an elaborate ceremonial dance and concluded the celebration by feasting on the unfortunate snakes. W. J. Read, who observed this annual dance about three decades ago, thought at the time that it might never be repeated because of Baining migration. Technological civilization is eliminating many such practices.

The fact that python worship reached an extreme in Africa did not prevent the consumption of pythons and other snakes as food. In Irvine's paper, Africa ranks next to Asia and the East Indies, with snake eating reported for about fifteen tribes in an area ranging from Northern Rhodesia in the south to Egypt in the north and from Kenya in the east to Ghana and the Sudanese Republic in the west. About two thirds as many countries as tribes are named. A survey in Nigeria by a nutrition expert showed snake meat to be a regular part of the diet in three districts. In Ghana, Irvine saw a man take the body of a puff adder (*Bitis lachesis*) to eat, the head to be made into medicine for snake poisoning.

The African rock python is a prize because of its size and wide distribution. The only other true pythons of Africa—the ball python (*Python regius*, 3 feet in average length) and a rare dwarf species of southwestern Africa (*Python anchietae*)—are too limited in distribution and too small to offer competition. The few boas of the continent—the sand boas (*Eryx*) and the one aberrant python (*Calabaria*)—are relatively small snakes. Various harmless and venomous snakes are, of course, also eaten, but they are nothing in comparison with rock pythons several yards long.

Oddly enough, the anaconda does not seem to have great appeal to man as food; at least I find little evidence. This does not mean that anacondas and boa constrictors are never eaten, but suggests that snake eating is not widespread and well developed in South America.

Although Europe has scarcely been mentioned, snakes were once widely eaten there. In France, the euphemism "eel" was applied to those offered in the markets. This habit has not entirely vanished. In 1928 giant-snake meat was customarily served at the annual banquet of the Société Nationale d'Acclimatation.

In the United States and the highlands of northern Mexico, the average person is apt to look upon snake eating with disgust. Laurence M. Klauber summarizes the habit in this part of the world, emphasizing rattlesnakes. The Amerindians of temperate North America ate snakes, even though snakes never became a substantial part of any Indian diet. The interesting point for us is that he lists noticeably more non-rattler-eating than rattler-eating tribes. Although he dealt in detail only with rattlesnake eaters, his figures probably hold for eaters of all snakes and may be taken as an index of the conditions in comparable parts of the world: roughly, one group of snake eaters to two abstaining. Snake worship, widespread among the Amerindians in question, accounted for some abstinence. Snakes were eaten now and then by the early settlers and often became a lifesaving emergency ration; rattlers were abundant in the dry, barren areas, where human beings were most likely to run out of food.

Canning rattlesnake meat has been a thriving, if minor, industry in Florida for about three decades; from 10,000 to 15,000 cans of rattlesnake meat have been sold annually. Incidentally, it has been calculated that 2,500 rattlers fill 15,000 cans, each reptile producing on the average a little less than 2 pounds of meat. Eaten fresh and on the spot, a 7-foot rattlesnake will yield 7½ pounds.

USE IN MEDICINE

The reverence and fear inspired in primitive man by the snake inevitably led him to use it in medicine. To him, anything with such remarkable qualities necessarily contained powerful essences. Early medicine men were forever trying to transfer these to the human body. A widespread method was to eat the source of the essence, whatever it might be, or drink some harmless liquid in which it had been soaked.

The healing power of the snake was used in different ways by various peoples. For instance, Arthur Loveridge met an old woman of Mozambique who wore a string of python vertebrae around her neck to strengthen the throat, another around her waist to do as much for the stomach. In Nigeria, necklaces of these bones have been worn against snake bite. Even an image was often considered to have its power: the Brazen Serpent that Moses set up survived for more than five centuries, to the time of Hezekiah; the God of the Jews had transferred healing power to it. The symbol of healing in Western medicine today is a serpent wound around the staff of Asclepius, a renowned Greek physician who later became the god of medicine.

The Greeks were not alone in transferring to image or man the serpent's power to heal. In southern Mexico, if a young Maya wanted to become a doctor, he retired to the forest with an instructor, who taught him the necessary incantations and practices. Finally he was sent alone to meet a boa constrictor. This reptile reared and placed its tongue in the mouth of the student to complete the initiation. The Tzeatcal Mayas had a far more fanciful initiation for the novice; he had to be swallowed by the serpent and passed out again, thus experiencing a sort of metamorphosis.

Although modern medicine is sweeping away much of the faith in snakes, a brief survey will show that this revolution is not only far from complete but astonishingly recent. Even in Europe we have to go back only a few generations to find the snake occupying an important place. In France, viper flesh was not entirely banished from official pharmacopoeias until 1884. Compound tincture of vipers, a vile concoction with a generous dash of dried viper flesh, "was much used with success" in the London plague of 1665.

"Theriaca," or treacle (not to be confused with the familiar by-product of sugar refining), included viper flesh and was prescribed in England for yet another hundred years. First described a few centuries before Christ, in the early Alexandrian period, treacle spread nearly all over the world and was referred to in China as early as A.D. 667. Originally an antidote for venomous bites of all kinds, it later became a sovereign remedy. Viper flesh was apparently always one of the important ingredients.

Renaissance professors of the University of Bologna once indulged in a heated argument about some treacle that contained the flesh of gravid vipers; had they rendered the product valueless? The whole faculty split over this pregnant problem. There are Renaissance stories of lepers being completely healed by drinking wine in which vipers had been inadvertently preserved. One leper cast off his skin like a viper, and the new one was as fresh and soft as that of a serpent which had recently shed.

Apparently, the peoples of eastern Asia failed to develop anything as complex as the treacle of Europe, with its scores and even hundreds of ingredients, but they did not neglect the snake. When I traveled in China, shops with containers of snake medicine were commonly seen, and the only competitors I had in my collecting activities were men hunting snakes to be dried or employed in making tincture. The Chinese used many species, sea snakes being especially valued, and often relied on various parts for specific ailments. These included the slough, true skin, bile, flesh, fat, head, eyeballs, eggs, and bones. The gall bladder (swallowed raw) was a popular morsel. The diseases treated were insanity, convulsions, epilepsy, poor sight, colds, sore throat, malaria, earache, toothache, deafness, arthritis, rheumatism, and others. Recent photographs of medicine shops in eastern Asia prove that the belief in the power of the snake dies hard there.

The European settlers of the United States seem to have left behind them many primitive medical concepts, with the result that in relatively recent times snakes have not been so widely used on this side of the Atlantic as they were in old Europe. In Guatemala hot snake fat (species unspecified) is applied as a poultice for colds, and snake oil is well known in Puerto Rico. During pre-Columbian days Amerindians valued snake fat, as do the Hottentots today; the latter take it from the African rock python.

"Rattlesnake oil" was once sold throughout the United States as a home remedy for numerous diseases, deafness, lumbago, toothache, sore throat, and other ailments. Later, as scientific remedies slowly replaced it, peddlers recommended it chiefly for rheumatism, and not without justification. It served as a lubricant for rubbing an affected part, the high price insuring much rubbing and, no doubt, better results.

Some part or product of a snake is still used in nearly every part of the world, and one product, venom, has not been discarded even by modern medicine, which recognizes its value in treating certain diseases, alleviation of pain, and control of bleeding.

THE SNAKE AS AN AID TO AGRICULTURE

The best detailed studies of the food habits of snakes have been made in the United States, and from these it is apparent that few snakes are pure assets and that the worst of them are not without value. Some snakes are a major factor in rodent destruction. But even the champion, the bull snake, does not have a clear slate; a small part of its diet is made up of birds and their eggs.

This relationship of snakes to agriculture may be different in the tropics, although my studies in southern China, and a few others that have been made in tropical countries, indicate no sharp contrast.

Unfortunately, no investigator has had an opportunity to examine the stomach contents of any great number of giant snakes. The average size of their prey is far below what would be expected, and the average size of the snakes themselves is much less than one might think; young and half-grown individuals make up a large part of any population living under natural conditions.

The appetite of the anaconda is broad enough to include a variety of mammals harmful to the farmer, but its aquatic habits must reduce its economic value under typical conditions. The question of its merit is also complicated by its appetite for birds and fishes. Elaborate studies would be required to determine just how beneficial it is; it might be found that its destructiveness cancels out its assistance to the farmer.

In many parts of tropical America, the boa constrictor is valued as a destroyer of rodents, and it has even been described as semi-domesticated. A relatively small size makes it more suitable than any of the other giants; although its maximum length approaches 20 feet, the average adult probably measures between 10 and 15 feet, a dimension far less startling than 20 or more feet. The few data available indicate an equal fondness for birds and mammals. Its value depends on conditions; in a situation that brings it in ready contact with injurious rodents, it can be a boon to the farmer, as a snake of its size would consume large numbers of these. On the other hand, a poultry farm is not the place for an unrestricted individual.

The boa constrictor and the renowned mongoose have had an unusual relationship centering around their economic value. The mongoose has been transported from its native Asia to various other warmer parts of the world as a rodent killer. This statement will come as a surprise to those who think the mongoose a snake killer rather than a rodent destroyer. Kipling gave the Western world its greatly exaggerated conception of the mongoose as the sworn enemy of the venomous snake; before his day, it was held in its proper role of rodent enemy. It does eat snakes, but mostly small, harmless ones, along with a great variety of other little animals. On certain islands of the Caribbean, it finally became a serious threat to poultry and birds after it had only partially performed its assigned task. The boa constrictors then became the ally of man in reducing the number of mongooses, which they seem to devour as readily as mongooses do other snakes. The tables are thus turned on Kipling's Rikki-tikki-tavi.

More than one writer on the snakes of southern Africa has reported the invaluable aid that the African rock python renders to the sugar planters by destroying the cane rat (*Thyonomys swinderenianus*). Obviously, other harmful rodents must be eaten as well. The value of the African rock python varies with its size and fondness for domestic birds and mammals. This statement applies as well to the remaining giants and will not be repeated for each.

There has been no investigation of the usefulness of the Indian python. This is all the more remarkable considering its intimacy with human beings by virtue of a wide distribution over India and Pakistan, countries with teeming millions. In 1929, R. W. Keays did mention a planter of southern India who "welcomes these creatures on his estate as they are excellent ratters and assist materially in keeping these pests of the cocoanut tree under control." Some harmfulness is implied in Frank Wall's remark that this python is frequently caught in poultry runs.

As in the case of the Indian python, there is almost no information on the economic value of the reticulate python. Its fondness for living near human habitations suggests that it has value. In cities, it could scarcely grow to gigantic proportions, and therefore would remain the proper size to eat vermin.

Ruiter reports that the Chinese of western Borneo keep pythons in the holds of boats and in warehouses to protect foodstuffs from rats and mice. It is impossible to say whether he refers to the reticulate or the Indian python or both. If the Chinese of Borneo make such use of pythons, it is a safe guess that the habit is general in Chinese colonies of the East Indies.

Due to a remote and largely insular distribution, the amethystine python, no doubt, has less economic significance than the others. The new element that it brings into the picture is an appetite for wallabies and kangaroos. In regions where these marsupials are considered pests, the amethystine python would be rated as beneficial.

Under certain conditions, giant snakes of small or moderate size can be of great use to the farmer. Control of populations could benefit agriculture and leather market alike: the hunter might be allowed to kill only individuals big enough to be a threat to large animals and less inclined to eat the small, harmful ones.

USES IN EDUCATION AND ENTERTAINMENT

Although the great majority of human beings do not live near wild giant snakes, these reptiles are familiar to all. Knowledge of them springs from ten important sources: zoos, museums, lecturers, circuses, carnivals, "charmers," theatricals, roadside exhibits, hobbyists, and the press. In general, the first three may be considered educational, the next three entertaining, the rest either educational, entertaining, or both.

ZOOLOGICAL GARDENS

Certainly more people have learned about giant snakes in zoological gardens than anywhere else.

Three thousand years ago the Chinese of the Chou Dynasty had their "Intelligence Park," and it is possible that pythons were exhibited in it; these snakes inhabited regions not so far to the south. The great menagerie assembled a few centuries before Christ at Alexandria by Ptolemy II included a gigantic snake, presumably an African rock python sent down the Nile. And at the beginning of the Christian Era, the Roman Emperor, Augustus, had a huge snake in his collection.

More recently, persons of wealth and position brought together in Europe various assortments. The Mexicans of the fifteenth and sixteenth centuries maintained collections, and snakes formed a part of Montezuma's zoological garden. Boa constrictors were available near by; so the reverence in which snakes were held must have assured these giants a place in it. The Mexican collections seem to have had religious, rather than educational, significance.

During the nineteenth century zoos sprang up like mushrooms wherever modern science had penetrated. The most interesting pioneer of this crop was the Jardin des Plantes of Paris. It was officially started in 1793 along with the Muséum d'Histoire Naturelle, at the admirable suggestion of Georges-Louis Leclerc de Buffon that museum and zoo should be part of the same endeavor.

The gardens of the Zoological Society of London were not founded until 1826, but they have, to this day, maintained an exhibition unsurpassed in variety of animals and excellence of maintenance. Their remarkably complete records show that an Indian python was received before June 1833, a boa constrictor in 1840 or 1841, an African rock python in 1843 or 1844, a reticulate python in 1848 or 1849, and a northern anaconda in 1849. Thus, we learn that for more than a century the people of London have been able to see virtually all of the big snakes.

It is safe to assert that these giants have been an important part of many zoo exhibits for almost a hundred years. Their only rivals for attention would be the notorious venomous snakes, such as cobras, mambas, puff adders, rattlesnakes, bushmasters, and ferde-lances. It would be impossible to say which type gives the novice a greater thrill: in one type it is sheer strength that impresses; in the other, power to injure with minimum effort.

The zoo movement came late in the United States. The giant snakes were first displayed before the public in "America's First Zoo," in Fairmount Park, Philadelphia. The boa constrictor arrived first, in 1875; by the end of 1894 the four other common giants had followed. The amethystine python was only recently placed on view in an American zoo (the New York Zoological Park, in 1959).

A survey made in the winter of 1959 showed eighty-two individuals of five of the giants on exhibit in eight of our major reptile collections spread from coast to coast. Four of the eight are in or near two cities, New York and Chicago. The anaconda alone was in all eight collections, though none had more than two, the total being an even dozen. In contrast, there were three times as many boa constrictors in seven collections; only our National Zoological Park, in Washington, was without one. Just half of the zoos displayed all five. Excluding the boa constrictor, the numbers of individuals of each species range from nine to fourteen, the former for the African rock python, the latter for the Indian python.

The five largest giants were reticulate pythons measuring from 19 to 24 feet, with values ranging from four hundred to a thousand dollars; a single one (not the longest) was valued at the higher figure. Many factors enter into the price put on a big snake, and length is not always the most important. The heaviest individual was a 225-pound reticulate python 19 feet long. (One reticulate python about 20 feet long was not weighed.) The longest anaconda measured only 18 feet, the longest African rock python but 14 feet.

Impressive though they be, living giant snakes, because of their inactivity, are disappointing exhibits. I can recall standing in front of cages and fervently wishing that the pythons and boas would *do* something. Small snakes are frequently fed on specified days for the edification of crowds pushing and shoving to get a good view; feeding the giants before the public is out of the question, for some persons would inevitably rebel at the sight, even if dead animals were used.

Alligators may be wrestled before spectators, and huge turtles give rides to children, but the giant snakes are left strictly alone. Although big boas and pythons often become tame, as shown by Sylvia and Blue Boy, many individuals in zoos are much too wild to permit free handling. Few keepers have the time or inclination to make pets out of their charges.

MUSEUMS

The boas and pythons do not play so important or conspicuous a role in museum exhibits as they do in zoos—partly because museums are likely to be wider in scope and partly because, until recently, the taxidermy of big reptiles was not well developed and most of the mounted giant snakes appeared much too lifeless and unnatural.

The last few decades have seen a radical change; now the largest snake can be made to look the same in an exhibit as in life. The revolution started at the Chicago Natural History Museum, where the late Leon L. Walters invented and perfected his cellulose-acetate technique. A snake is reproduced literally scale for scale in this plastic medium, the result including not a speck of the original animal. First an ordinary plaster cast is made in removable sections; then it is painted *inside* with layer after layer of liquid acetate, colored as required. It is this thick layer of acetate that will be the final model. The colored acetate is what gives the finished product its natural look; the pigment of the true skin of the living snake is similarly buried in the skin, not spread on the surface as the pigment of the ordinary plaster cast must be. Separating the thick layer of acetate from the cast requires a great deal of practice;

it is a process with many pitfalls. A major disadvantage of this new and superior method is the great amount of time required; each reproduction must be made laboriously by hand from the stage of painting inside the cast.

LECTURERS

Lectures on snakes, always popular, are responsible for the dissemination of much scientific information. Large individuals of the giant snakes are not commonly used by lecturers because of the difficulty of transporting them, but small ones are often displayed along with snakes of various ordinary-sized species.

Sylvia has a notable record: in eight and a half years she has been shown in several midwestern states to school, college, club, and church audiences totaling nearly 800,000 persons. At the beginning of this period, she measured 10 feet 9 inches and weighed 34 pounds; at the end, she was 27 inches longer and 32 pounds heavier. This docile python has never bitten anyone though she has been handled by hundreds of persons of all ages.

CIRCUSES, CARNIVALS, AND "CHARMERS"

The old traveling circus of the United States was incomplete without a giant-snake exhibit. A huge, gaudy picture outside the side-show tent often depicted a monstrous reptile performing some super-serpent feat, while a barker announced in a highly unnatural voice that the largest snake ever caught could be seen inside.

The snake usually turned out to be a boa constrictor or an Indian python of moderate size displayed by a plump woman dressed in a colorful, abbreviated costume. The average observer looked at her in awe; surely she must have incredible courage to handle such a dangerous creature. It was more likely that the snake was in too poor condition to care who handled it or how; the woman, being in no danger whatsoever, merely had to overcome any dread of snakes she might have. Some persons do this with ease.

The "charmer's" job was, perhaps, the easiest in the whole circus; acrobats, clowns, and other performers had to work at their specialties for years to become proficient, whereas the "snake charmer" could be instructed in a matter of hours.

The circus snake show, being neither permanent nor scientific, was never comparable to museum or zoo exhibits. As a rule, the specimens were bought at the beginning of the season and disposed of at its end after months of starvation, a practice made possible by the ability of the snakes to survive long fasts. Years ago, I was offered big snakes at a ridiculous price by the "living skeleton," who happened to be the manager of a large side show.

The traveling carnival was also once popular; its snake exhibits were essentially like those of the circus.

ROADSIDE EXHIBITS

I have used the past tense in the foregoing paragraphs because the place of the moribund traveling circuses and carnivals is being taken by new forms of entertainment. In contrast to the carnival or circus snake show, the roadside exhibit is a new development made possible by improvements in transportation and the consequent increase in the number of persons driving about in search of amusement. The roadside show varies in size and quality; from an educational point of view, it may be no better than the circus show, or it may be conducted on a high level. It is usually an adjunct to some other business—gasoline station, refreshment stand, or curio shop.

The roadside show is often set up in a part of the country where local snakes can be shown to travelers; desert animals may be successfully exhibited in the West to tourists from the East. For this reason, the ordinary roadside exhibit of the United States is not likely to display giant snakes of the Old World, although a boa constrictor from tropical America might well be included.

SNAKE CHARMERS OF AFRICA AND ASIA

The use of the term "snake charmer" in connection with the circus shows has been borrowed from the more legitimate application of it to the snake men of Africa and Asia, chiefly the latter. The words "snake charmer" at once bring to mind India, for there all tourists are given a chance to see the charmer at work with his rearing cobras and hissing pythons. Such charming, undoubtedly descended from ancient serpent worship, is more renowned than any other form of snake entertainment, and it is the most exciting for the spectator. The Indian python, the only python native to the Indian peninsula, is frequently included in the charmer's collection, its beauty and size being useful in impressing the audience.

THEATRICALS

Giant snakes have long been popular with certain entertainers, who begin their act with full attire and a snake but end up in little but the snake. At first, the snake draws much attention; as the act progresses, the focus of the male observers shifts until the snake becomes a definite obstruction. I refer to the python or boa as part of a strip-tease act.

Thoroughly tamed giants are required because no person is more vulnerable to the bite of a snake than the partly undressed dancer. In spite of the care that is taken, occasional accidents happen. One dancer was reported in the press as being rescued from gigantic coils by five men.

257

Gypsy Rose Lee relates a fantastic story about a friend of hers who attempted to transport a beloved python to Chicago by plane. The reptile was wrapped around the body of the woman and hidden by a big fur coat. The unfortunate reptile died en route while the dancer slept under the influence of a sedative. It took four men to uncoil the python when the sad truth was revealed; rigor mortis had set in. The dancer suffered only from the shock; her favorite had died quietly and without applying pressure.

My friend Lyman Carpenter was once asked to cure a sick giant. After doing so, he was invited to watch the dancer's act. He saw that the snake's rich colors clashed with those of her costume. On Mr. Carpenter's advice, subdued colors were substituted and the act greatly improved.

HOBBY GROUPS

Many persons—more than is generally realized—make a hobby of studying snakes. Both reptiles and amphibians have been kept for observation by hobbyists in several European countries, especially Germany, for half a century and longer. Popular journals devoted to these and other "cold-blooded" animals have long been available there. The strictly amateur groups of the United States are also indicative of the extent of the hobby. In 1959 there were twelve of these in nine states, all but three with ambition enough to have regular journals; the largest society had a membership of more than two hundred. There are other groups still more local in nature; after them come an undetermined number of individuals with a deep interest in reptiles and amphibians, most of them especially attracted to snakes.

There is, in addition to all of the above, a widespread, unsung, and unorganized group of fanciers who are, in one sense, also educators. It is made up of individualists, often unsophisticated and uneducated, who live in snake country and in some way have

learned to catch and handle snakes. I have encountered these untutored snake men in China, and I believe that they are to be found
in all parts of the world where snakes are abundant.

THE PRESS

Items about snakes are constantly appearing in the daily press, and
many of them get national and even world-wide coverage. Sunday
magazines and supplements often run articles. The information
thus broadcast is seldom reliable, and rarely is it concerned with the
giant snakes; snake-bite stories are favored.

Snakes, pythons among them, have been publicized on a higher
level in many of our monthly and weekly magazines of wide circulation. During the last twenty-three years the following articles
on giant snakes have appeared: *Harper's Magazine* had one about
the roadside exhibit in Georgia of a 220-pound python; *Collier's*
printed Frank Buck's spirited account of capturing two large
pythons; *True* magazine recently ran an article by Kurt
Severin, with color photographs, about the landing of an anaconda
18 feet long; both *The New Yorker* and *Life* devoted space to
Serata, the white Indian python; *Life* within a decade had the account of Serata, one of Sylvia, and one on the birth of twenty-
three anacondas in the Brookfield Zoo, near Chicago. Two characteristics of these seven magazine articles stand out: All,
though essentially true, were incidental reports, and none offered
general facts about giant snakes.

It is clear from the foregoing that little reliable and much ques-
tionable information is to be gleaned from the popular press. Another source is specialized, non-technical journals, such as *Natural
History*. The material in these is authentic, though one has to search
hard for articles on giant snakes. Until recently, the next recourse
was technical literature, but only herpetologists and studious hobbyists could profit by this.

Relation to Man

Now there are a few general reptile books that include basic information on the giant snakes. Reading these and articles in the best magazines, attending lectures, visiting museums, zoos, and the better roadside exhibits, are superior ways to learn about the giants. Making a hobby of snakes is far better, provided the care of the reptiles is accompanied by serious study.

Giant Pets

✳

IN THE UNITED STATES, an adult's interest in snakes is apt to be looked upon as juvenile, something that should have been outgrown. In contrast, many adults in northern European countries keep snakes as well as other types of reptiles as pets. As scores of species are available, such a hobby can become a great joy and can include learning not only about the animals themselves but about the countries from which they come. In this day of air transportation, rare kinds can be secured for the hobbyist who knows where they live.

In the United States, where it is generally young people who keep reptile pets, this hobby has several interesting side aspects. To the worried parent, it is a "state" rather than a stage and may cause great disturbance in the family life. The boy is often thought to develop a liking for snakes merely to make himself feel brave by handling a creature feared by most. That this factor enters into the picture cannot be denied; many a youthful person is inspired to participate in football or some similar activity for the same purpose. The youth who uses snakes in this way has found one of the most efficient of morale boosters and deserves to be given due credit.

A humorous aspect of this morale boosting is the fact that modern girls frequently have no fear of snakes. A marked difference between the sexes may no longer exist; I have seen a bold girl turn the tables on a not so brave boy by unexpectedly seizing a tame snake from his unsteady grasp. Some girls freely play with snakes before the age of sex consciousness, but at this age develop an apparently genuine repugnance. This change can be explained only by the girl's enjoyment of being feminine and her willingness to feign any becoming fear.

I have repeatedly told the distraught American mother that, once the ice is broken, snakes are much easier to keep than, let us say, pedigreed dogs. Snakes do not have to be fed frequently and may be left to themselves for a week or so at a time.

Snakes, including the giants, make good pets for owners who are not primarily interested in strong emotional response; a snake has no obvious way of showing attachment, and some keepers even question its ability to become "emotionally involved."

Unfortunately, few veterinarians know how to treat an ill reptile; the owner himself must learn something about the common maladies of snakes. Information about these has been given in an earlier chapter.

Although detailed directions for the care of giants do not come within the scope of this book, I shall condense into four paragraphs a translation from the single most useful paper for the keeper of large pythons and boas. (See Lederer, 1944, in the bibliography.)

Young reticulate pythons first accept, one to three times a week, grown and half-grown mice and sparrows. After a year, they prefer white rats, young rabbits, and, to a lesser degree, guinea pigs. Depending on size, they should be given one or two of these animals, either alive or dead, every eight days. Half-grown individuals take, every week or so, one or two rabbits, or from one to three guinea pigs or pigeons. Individuals 20 to 26 feet long prefer piglets weighing from thirteen to thirty-three pounds, from five to eight a year. Animals weighing more than fifty-five pounds are not usually acceptable; nor are those as small as rats and guinea pigs. Dogs, cats, she-goats, monkeys, antelopes, young deer, and birds are also eaten; sheep are often refused.

Giant Pets

A reticulate python once ate a dead, meter-long Nile monitor (*Varanus*) after the big lizard had been confined for two and a half hours in a feed container, where it must have acquired the odor of rabbits. This same python also ate another species of monitor (*V. griseus*). However, certain fishes (carp, crucian carp, *Weissfische*) were never eaten.

Most reticulate pythons have individualistic feeding habits. For example, for years a large female took only young wild boars and crosses of wild pigs with a domestic Chinese breed (*Maskenschwein*), refusing ordinary domestic pigs. Three young domestic pigs were then kept with wild ones, tainted with their odor, and darkened to match them. After this treatment, three of the altered pigs were accepted by the python in eleven weeks, no doubt because of similarity in odor rather than color. Later, ordinary domestic pigs that had not been modified were accepted. Another reticulate python for years ate only pigeons and hens; yet another, only guinea pigs. Frequently such a special habit will be abruptly given up.

Many reticulate pythons will eat dead animals; one python even devoured an old, dried, and fairly hard rabbit. Feeding exclusively on corpses causes dietary deficiency, however. Young reticulate pythons and those of medium size are usually fed dead animals still retaining some body heat; these, when presented, are moved to simulate the living condition, which causes the python to seize and constrict in the usual manner. Such reactions are natural for the snake. The use of dead animals in which decomposition has begun should be avoided because symptoms of poisoning may result.

Finally, I should like to point out that making records of snakes living in captivity can be rewarding for keepers with a scientific turn of mind and some spare time. The records can be simple or elaborate. Detailed records take a great deal of time, patience, and persistence; even the mere weighing and measuring of a snake can entail more effort than is readily imagined.

Suggested References

SYLVIA

Cowles, Raymond B., and R. L. Phelan: "Olfaction in Rattlesnakes." *Copeia*, No. 2, 1958, pp. 77–83.

Pope, Clifford H.: "A Python in the Home." *Bulletin, Chicago Natural History Museum*, Vol. 18, No. 4 (1947), pp. 4–5.

"Python Is a Boy's Pal." *Life*, May 8, 1950, p. 152.

THE BIG SIX

Dowling, Herndon G.: "Classification of the Serpentes: A Critical Review." *Copeia*, No. 1, 1959, pp. 38–52.

Dunn, Emmett R., and Roger Conant: "Notes on Anacondas, with Descriptions of Two New Species." *Proceedings, Academy Natural Sciences Philadelphia*, Vol. 88 (1936), pp. 503–6.

Stull, Olive G.: "A Check List of the Family Boidae." *Proceedings, Boston Society Natural History*, Vol. 40 (1935), pp. 387–408.

Wall, Frank: "A Popular Treatise on the Common Indian Snakes. Part XVII." *Journal, Bombay Natural History Society*, Vol. 21 (1912), pp. 447–75.

——: *The Snakes of Ceylon*. Colombo: H. R. Cottle; 1921. See pp. 48–73.

THE WORLD OF THE GIANTS

Allen, William R.: "Banana Stowaways." *Copeia*, No. 169 (1928), pp. 98–9.

Beebe, William: "Field Notes on the Snakes of Kartabo, British Guiana, and Caripito, Venezuela." *Zoologica*, Vol. 31, Part I (1946), pp. 11–52. See p. 20.

Dammerman, K. W.: "The Fauna of Krakatau 1883–1933." *Verhandelingen (Tweede Sectie), Koninklijke Nederlandische Akademie Wetenschappen*, Vol. 44 (1948), pp. 1–594.

Darlington, Philip J., Jr.: *Zoogeography: The Geographical Distribution of Animals*. New York: John Wiley & Sons; 1957.

Duellman, William E.: "The Amphibians and Reptiles of Jorullo Volcano, Michoacán, Mexico." *Occasional Papers, Museum Zoology, University Michigan*, No. 560 (1954), pp. 1–24.

Dunn, Emmett R.: "Relative Abundance of Some Panamanian Snakes." *Ecology*, Vol. 30 (1949), pp. 39–56.

Suggested References

FLOWER, STANLEY S.: "Notes on a Second Collection of Reptiles Made in the Malay Peninsula and Siam, from November 1896 to September 1898, with a List of the Species Recorded from Those Countries." *Proceedings, Zoological Society London*, 1899, pp. 600–97. See p. 654.

GILMORE, CHARLES W.: "Fossil Snakes of North America." *Special Papers, Geological Society America*, No. 9 (1938), pp. 1–96.

HOIER, R.: *A Travers Plaines et Volcans au Parc National Albert*. Brussels: Institut des Parcs Nationaux du Congo Belge; 1950. Reptiles, pp. 119–27.

HUTTON, A. F.: "Notes on the Snakes and Mammals of the High Wavy Mountains, Madura District, S. India. Part I: Snakes." *Journal, Bombay Natural History Society*, Vol. 48 (1949), pp. 454–60.

KLAUBER, LAURENCE M.: *Rattlesnakes*. Berkeley and Los Angeles: University of California Press; 1956. See Index, p. 1421, for references to dispersal.

KOPSTEIN, FELIX: "Reptilien von den Molukken und den Benachbarten Inseln." *Zoologische Mededeelingen, 's Rijks Museum van Natuurlijke Historie* (Leiden), Vol. 9 (1926), pp. 71–112. See pp. 102–3.

LAURENT, R. F.: "Contribution à l'herpétologie de la région des Grands Lacs de l'Afrique centrale. I. Généralités; II. Cheloniens; III. Ophidiens." *Annales, Musée Royal Congo Belge, Sciences Zoologiques*, Vol. 48 (1956), pp. 1–390. See p. 85.

LEWIS, THOMAS H., AND MURRAY L. JOHNSON: "Notes on a Herpetological Collection from Sinaloa, Mexico." *Herpetologica*, Vol. 12 (1956), pp. 277–80.

LEY, WILLY: *Dragons in Amber: Further Adventures of a Romantic Naturalist*. New York: The Viking Press; 1951. See pp. 295–320.

MARTIN, PAUL S.: "A Biogeography of Reptiles and Amphibians in the Gomez Farias Region, Tamaulipas, Mexico." *Miscellaneous Publications, Museum Zoology, University Michigan*, No. 101 (1958), pp. 1–102. See pp. 31, 67.

MATTHEW, WILLIAM D.: "Climate and Evolution." *Special Publications, New York Academy Sciences*, Vol. 1 (1939), pp. 1–223.

OLIVER, JAMES A.: *Snakes in Fact and Fiction*. New York: The Macmillan Company; 1958. See pp. 150–1.

PITMAN, CHARLES R. S.: *A Guide to the Snakes of Uganda*. Kampala: Uganda Society; 1938. See p. 53.

SMITH, MALCOLM: *The Fauna of British India, Ceylon and Burma, Including the Whole of the Indo-Chinese Sub-Region. Reptilia and Amphibia*. Vol. 3: *Serpentes*. London: Taylor and Francis; 1943. See p. 110.

TAYLOR, EDWARD H.: "Notes on the Herpetological Fauna of the Mexican State of Sonora." *Science Bulletin, University Kansas*, Vol. 24 (1936), pp. 475–503. See p. 489.

——: "A Brief Review of the Snakes of Costa Rica." *Science Bulletin, University Kansas*, Vol. 34 (1951), pp. 3–188.

Suggested References

Uthmöller, W.: "Beitrag zur Kenntnis der Schlangenfauna Nordost-Ost-afrikas (Tanganyika Territory). Ergebnisse der Ostafrika-Expedition Uthmöller-Bohmann. V. A. Schlangen 1." *Zoologischer Anzeiger* (Leipzig), Vol. 135 (1941), pp. 225–42.

Wall, Frank: *The Snakes of Ceylon.* Colombo: H. R. Cottle; 1921. See pp. 50, 73.

——: "The Reticulate Python. *Python reticulatus* (Schneider)." *Journal, Bombay Natural History Society,* Vol. 31 (1926), pp. 84–90.

Wallace, Alfred Russel: *The Geographical Distribution of Animals,* 2 vols. London: The Macmillan Company; 1876.

——: *Island Life.* London: The Macmillan Company; 1880. See pp. 71, 265.

Wet, J. C. de: "Snakes and Tractors on Kotapalli." *Asia,* Dec. 1927, pp. 998–1003, 1036–40.

Worrell, Eric: *Song of the Snake.* London: Angus and Robertson; 1958. See pp. 133–6.

Zimmerman, Elwood C.: *Insects of Hawaii.* Vol. 1: *Introduction.* Honolulu: University of Hawaii Press; 1948.

SENSES

Bullock, T. H., and Raymond B. Cowles: "Physiology of an Infrared Receptor: The Facial Pit of Pit Vipers." *Science,* Vol. 115 (1952), pp. 541–3.

Cowles, Raymond B., and R. L. Phelan: "Olfaction in Rattlesnakes." *Copeia,* No. 2, 1958, pp. 77–83.

Kahmann, Hermann: "Zur Chemorezeption der Schlangen." *Zoologischer Anzeiger,* Vol. 107 (1934), pp. 249–63.

——: "Zur Biologie des Gesichtssinns der Reptilien." *Zoologischer Anzeiger,* Vol. 108 (1934), pp. 311–25.

Klauber, Laurence M.: *Rattlesnakes.* Berkeley and Los Angeles: University of California Press; 1956. See pp. 350–78.

Lederer, Gustav: "Nahrungserwerb, Entwicklung, Paarung und Brutfürsorge von *Python reticulatus* (Schneider)." *Zoologische Jahrbücher* (*Anatomie*) (Jena), Vol. 68 (1944), pp. 363–98.

Lynn, W. Gardner: "The Structure and Function of the Facial Pit of the Pit Vipers." *The American Journal of Anatomy,* Vol. 49 (1931), pp. 97–139.

Milne, Lorus J., and Margery J. Milne: "Untold Eyes Are on You." *Natural History,* Vol. 56 (1947), pp. 312–19, 333–4.

Noble, G. K.: "The Sense Organs Involved in the Courtship of *Storeria, Thamnophis* and Other Snakes." *Bulletin, American Museum Natural History,* Vol. 73 (1937), pp. 673–725.

—— and A. Schmidt: "The Structure and Function of the Facial and Labial Pits of Snakes." *Proceedings, American Philosophical Society,* Vol. 77 (1937), pp. 263–88.

Suggested References

QUARANTA, JOHN V.: "How We Learn about Color Vision in Animals." *Animal Kingdom*, Vol. 57 (1954), pp. 71–4.

ROS, MARGARETE: "Die Lippengruben der Pythonen als Temperaturorgane." *Jenaische Zeitschrift für Naturwissenschaft*, Vol. 70 (1935), pp. 1–32.

WALLS, GORDON L.: "Ophthalmological Implications for the Early History of the Snakes." *Copeia*, No. 1, 1940, pp. 1–8.

——: *The Vertebrate Eye and Its Adaptive Radiation*. Bloomfield Hills, Mich.: The Cranbrook Institute of Science; 1942.

WEST, G. S.: "On the Sensory Pit of the Crotalinae." *Quarterly Journal of Microscopical Science*, New Series, Vol. 43 (1900), pp. 49–59.

STRENGTH AND CONSTRICTION

ISEMONGER, R. M.: *Snakes and Snake Catching in Southern Africa*. Cape Town: Howard Timmins; 1955. See pp. 5–6.

LEDERER, GUSTAV: "Nahrungserwerb, Entwicklung, Paarung und Brutfürsorge von *Python reticulatus* (Schneider)." *Zoologische Jahrbücher (Anatomie)* (Jena), Vol. 68 (1944), pp. 363–98.

MASH, P.: "Indian Python (*Python molurus*) Preying on Monitor Lizard (*Varanus monitor*)." *Journal, Bombay Natural History Society*, Vol. 45 (1945), pp. 249–50.

PITMAN, CHARLES R. S.: *A Guide to the Snakes of Uganda*. Kampala: Uganda Society; 1938. See p. 15.

RUITER, L. COOMANS DE: "Pythons of Reuzenslangen." *Lacerta*, Vol. 12 (1954), pp. 12–14.

SOKOLOWSKY, A.: "Die Fressleistung der Riesenschlangen." *Umschau*, Vol. 11 (1907), pp. 433–4.

VAN RIPER, WALKER: "Measuring the Speed of a Rattlesnake's Strike." *Animal Kingdom*, Vol. 57 (1954), pp. 50–3.

INTELLIGENCE

BROWN, E. E.: "Feeding Habits of the Northern Water Snake, *Natrix sipedon sipedon* Linnaeus." *Zoologica*, Vol. 43, Part II (1958), pp. 55–71.

DITMARS, RAYMOND L.: "Observations on the Mental Capacity and Habits of Poisonous Serpents." *Ninth Annual Report, New York Zoological Society*, 1905, pp. 5–24.

HEDIGER, H.: *Wildtiere in Gefangenschaft*. Basel: Benno Schwabe & Co.; 1942. See p. 82.

KELLOGG, W. N., AND W. B. POMEROY: "Maze Learning in Water Snakes *Tropidonotus fasciatus* var. *sipedon*." *Journal of Comparative Psychology*, Vol. 21 (1936), pp. 275–95.

KLAUBER, LAURENCE M.: *Rattlesnakes*. Berkeley and Los Angeles: University of California Press; 1956. See pp. 376–8.

Suggested References

LEDERER, GUSTAV: "Nahrungserwerb, Entwicklung, Paarung und Brutfürsorge von *Python reticulatus* (Schneider)." *Zoologische Jahrbücher (Anatomie)* (Jena), Vol. 68 (1944), pp. 363–98.

MERTENS, ROBERT: *Quer durch Australien.* Frankfurt am Main: Waldemar
Kramer; 1958.

MITCHELL, P. CHALMERS, AND R. I. POCOCK: "On the Feeding of Reptiles
in Captivity, with Observations on the Fear of Snakes by Other Vertebrates." *Proceedings, Zoological Society London,* 1907, pp. 785–94.

MUNRO, D. F.: "Eating Habits of Young *Coluber constrictor flaviventris.*"
Herpetologica, Vol. 5 (1949), pp. 72–3.

THORPE, W. H.: *Learning and Instinct in Animals.* Cambridge, Mass.:
Harvard University Press; 1956. See p. 296.

WOLFLE, DAEL L., AND C. S. BROWN, JR.: "A Learning Experiment with
Snakes." *Copeia,* No. 2, 1940, p. 134.

LOCOMOTION

BEEBE, WILLIAM: "Field Notes on the Snakes of Kartabo, British Guiana,
and Caripito, Venezuela." *Zoologica,* Vol. 31, Part I (1946), pp. 11–52.
See pp. 32–3.

BOGERT, CHARLES M.: "Rectilinear Locomotion in Snakes." *Copeia,* No. 4,
1947, pp. 253–4.

——: "Tree-Climbing Snakes." *Natural History,* Vol. 62 (1953), pp. 281–2.

GRAY, JAMES: "The Mechanism of Locomotion in Snakes." *The Journal
of Experimental Biology,* Vol. 23 (1946), pp. 101–20.

——: *How Animals Move.* Cambridge: University Press; 1953. See chapter
on jumping and creeping.

HOME, E.: "Observations Intended to Show That the Progressive Motion
of Snakes Is Partly Performed by Means of the Ribs." *Philosophical
Transactions, Royal Society London,* Vol. 102, Part I (1812), pp.
163–8.

KLAUBER, LAURENCE M.: *Rattlesnakes.* Berkeley and Los Angeles: University of California Press; 1956.

LISSMANN, H. W.: "Rectilinear Locomotion in a Snake (*Boa occidentalis*)."
The Journal of Experimental Biology, Vol. 26 (1950), pp. 368–79.

MOSAUER, WALTER: "How Fast Can Snakes Travel?" *Copeia,* No. 1, 1935,
pp. 6–9.

OLIVER, JAMES A.: *Snakes in Fact and Fiction.* New York: The Macmillan
Company; 1958. See pp. 72–3.

RAVEN, HENRY C.: "Adventures in Python Country." *Natural History,*
Vol. 55 (1946), pp. 38–41.

SHAW, G. E., E. O. SHEBBEARE, AND P. E. BARKER: "The Snakes of Northern
Bengal and Sikkim." *Journal, Darjeeling Natural History Society,*
Vol. 13, Part III (1939), pp. 64–73.

STEVENSON-HAMILTON, J.: *Animal Life in Africa.* New York: E. P. Dutton
& Co.; 1912.

Suggested References

ACTIVITY

ALLEE, W. C., A. E. EMERSON, O. PARK, T. PARK, AND K. P. SCHMIDT: *Principles of Animal Ecology*. Philadelphia and London: W. B. Saunders Company; 1949. See pp. 544–6.

BEEBE, WILLIAM: "Field Notes on the Snakes of Kartabo, British Guiana, and Caripito, Venezuela." *Zoologica*, Vol. 31, Part I (1946), pp. 11–52.

BLOMBERG, ROLF: "Giant Snake Hunt." *Natural History*, Vol. 65 (1956), pp. 92–7.

FLOWER, STANLEY S.: "Notes on a Second Collection of Reptiles Made in the Malay Peninsula and Siam, from November 1896 to September 1898, with a List of the Species Recorded from Those Countries." *Proceedings, Zoological Society London*, 1899, pp. 600–97. See p. 654.

JOHNSON, RICHARD M.: "An Indication of Sleep in Snakes." *Herpetologica*, Vol. 5 (1949), p. 147.

LEDERER, GUSTAV: "Nahrungserwerb, Entwicklung, Paarung und Brutfürsorge von *Python reticulatus* (Schneider)." *Zoologische Jahrbücher (Anatomie)* (Jena), Vol. 68 (1944), pp. 363–98.

LOVERIDGE, ARTHUR: "Australian Reptiles in the Museum of Comparative Zoology, Cambridge, Massachusetts." *Bulletin, Museum Comparative Zoology*, Vol. 77 (1934), pp. 243–383.

MERTENS, ROBERT: *Quer durch Australien*. Frankfurt am Main: Waldemar Kramer; 1958.

MUNRO, D. F.: "Vertical Position of the Pupil in the Crotalidae." *Herpetologica*, Vol. 5 (1949), pp. 106–8.

NICHOLLS, F.: "Pythons." *Journal, Bombay Natural History Society*, Vol. 52 (1954), p. 620.

PITMAN, CHARLES R. S.: *A Guide to the Snakes of Uganda*. Kampala: Uganda Society; 1938. See pp. 9, 59.

SHAW, G. E., E. O. SHEBBEARE, AND P. E. BARKER: "The Snakes of Northern Bengal and Sikkim." *Journal, Darjeeling Natural History Society*, Vol. 13, Part III (1939), pp. 64–73.

SMITH, MALCOLM: "A Bangkok Python." *Journal, Siam Society, Natural History Supplement*, Vol. 11, No. 1 (1937), pp. 61–2.

STEMMLER-MORATH, CARL: "Beitrag zur Gefangenschafts und Fortpflanzungsbiologie von *Python molurus* L." *Der Zoologische Garten* (Leipzig), Vol. 21 (1956), pp. 347–64.

STEVENSON-HAMILTON, J.: *Wild Life in South Africa*. London: Cassell & Co.; 1947. See p. 331.

TAYLOR, EDWARD H.: "Notes on the Herpetological Fauna of the Mexican State of Sonora." *Science Bulletin, University Kansas*, Vol. 24 (1936), pp. 475–503.

WALL, FRANK: *The Snakes of Ceylon*. Colombo: H. R. Cottle; 1921. See pp. 53–4.

Suggested References

WALLS, GORDON L.: *The Vertebrate Eye and Its Adaptive Radiation*. Bloomfield Hills, Mich.: The Cranbrook Institute of Science; 1942. See pp. 206–8, 607–8.

WORRELL, ERIC: *Song of the Snake*. London: Angus and Robertson; 1958. See pp. 134–5.

WRENICKE, C. J. T.: "Pythons." *Journal, Bombay Natural History Society*, Vol. 53 (1955), pp. 134–5.

SHEDDING

FITCH, HENRY S.: "Study of Snake Populations in Central California." *American Midland Naturalist*, Vol. 41 (1949), pp. 513–79.

KLAUBER, LAURENCE M.: *Rattlesnakes*. Berkeley and Los Angeles: University of California Press; 1956. See pp. 318–30.

LEDERER, GUSTAV: "Nahrungserwerb, Entwicklung, Paarung und Brutfürsorge von *Python reticulatus* (Schneider)." *Zoologische Jahrbücher (Anatomie)* (Jena), Vol. 68 (1944), pp. 363–98.

SHAW, CHARLES E.: "Blue Boy . . . His Life and Successor." *Zoonooz*, Vol. 27, No. 5 (1954), pp. 2–3.

WALL, FRANK: *The Snakes of Ceylon*. Colombo: H. R. Cottle; 1921. See pp. 55–6.

WHAT THEY EAT—AND HOW MUCH

BEEBE, WILLIAM: "Field Notes on the Snakes of Kartabo, British Guiana, and Caripito, Venezuela." *Zoologica*, Vol. 31, Part I (1946), pp. 11–52. See pp. 18–19, 20.

BENEDICT, FRANCIS G.: *The Physiology of Large Reptiles with Special Reference to the Heat Production of Snakes, Tortoises, Lizards and Alligators*. Washington, D.C.: Carnegie Institution of Washington; 1932. See pp. 192–5.

——: "Reptiles Used in Study of Human Physiology." *Carnegie Institution of Washington, News Service Bulletin*, Vol. 2 (1932), pp. 192–7.

DITMARS, RAYMOND L.: *Snakes of the World*. New York: The Macmillan Company; 1951. See p. 48.

FITZSIMONS, F. W.: *Snakes*. London: Hutchinson & Co.; 1932. See pp. 258–9.

FLOWER, STANLEY S.: "Notes on a Second Collection of Reptiles Made in the Malay Peninsula and Siam, from November 1896 to September 1898, with a List of the Species Recorded from Those Countries." *Proceedings, Zoological Society London*, 1899, pp. 600–97. See pp. 654–5.

GILLMORE, S. H.: "Jungle Terror: A Human Struggle in Which a Boa of the French Guiana Bush Yields His Skin." *Asia*, Apr. 1925, pp. 296–300, 332–5.

HEADLEY, H. S.: "The Record Australian Python." *The Field, The Country Gentleman's Newspaper* (London), Vol. 150, No. 3896 (1927), p. 319.

Suggested References

IRVINE, FRED R.: "Snakes as Food for Man." *British Journal of Herpetology*, Vol. 1 (1954), pp. 183–9.

KEAYS, R. W.: "An Unpleasant Experience with a Python." *Journal, Bombay Natural History Society*, Vol. 33 (1929), pp. 721–2.

KOPSTEIN, FELIX: "Reptilien von den Molukken und den Benachbarten Inseln." *Zoologische Mededeelingen, 's Rijks Museum van Natuurlijke Historie* (Leiden), Vol. 9 (1926), pp. 71–112. See pp. 102–3.

LEDERER, GUSTAV: "Nahrungserwerb, Entwicklung, Paarung und Brutfürsorge von *Python reticulatus* (Schneider)." *Zoologische Jahrbücher (Anatomie)* (Jena), Vol. 68 (1944), pp. 363–98. See pp. 375–6.

LEWIS, THOMAS H., and MURRAY L. JOHNSON: "Notes on a Herpetological Collection from Sinaloa, Mexico." *Herpetologica*, Vol. 12 (1956), pp. 277–80.

LIAT, LIM BOO: "The Natural Food of Some Malayan Snakes." *The Malay Nature Journal*, Vol. 10 (1956), pp. 139–44.

LOVERIDGE, ARTHUR: "On Two Amphibious Snakes of the Central African Lake Region." *Bulletin, Antivenin Institute America*, Vol. 5 (1931), pp. 7–12.

——: "Australian Reptiles in the Museum of Comparative Zoölogy, Cambridge, Massachusetts." *Bulletin, Museum Comparative Zoology*, Vol. 77 (1934), pp. 243–383. See p. 269.

——: "On a Second Collection of Reptiles and Amphibians Taken in Tanganyika Territory by C. J. P. Ionides, Esq." *Journal, East Africa Natural History Society*, Vol. 22 (1955), pp. 168–98. See pp. 181–2.

MOOKERJEE, S.: "Mango-fruit on the Menu of the Common Python (*Python molurus*)." *Journal, Bombay Natural History Society*, Vol. 46 (1947), p. 733.

NEILL, WILFRED T., and E. ROSS ALLEN: "Secondarily Ingested Food Items in Snakes." *Herpetologica*, Vol. 12 (1956), pp. 172–4.

OLIVER, JAMES A.: *Snakes in Fact and Fiction*. New York: The Macmillan Company; 1958. See Chap. 4.

PITMAN, CHARLES R. S.: *A Guide to the Snakes of Uganda*. Kampala: Uganda Society; 1938. See pp. 15, 19, 56–7.

POCOCK, R. I.: "A Record Australian Python." *The Field, The Country Gentleman's Newspaper* (London), Vol. 149, No. 3879 (1927), p. 707.

REICHERT, E.: "Geheilte Munfäule bei *Boa imperator*." *Blätter für Aquarien- und Terrarienkunde*, Vol. 41 (1930), pp. 324–5.

ROSE, WALTER: *Snakes—Mainly South African*. Cape Town: Maskew Miller; 1955. See pp. 26–7, 30–1.

SHAW, CHARLES E.: "Blue Boy . . . His Life and Successor." *Zoonooz*, Vol. 27, No. 5 (1954), pp. 2–3.

WALL, FRANK: *The Snakes of Ceylon*. Colombo: H. R. Cottle; 1921. See pp. 57–63.

——: "The Reticulate Python. *Python reticulatus* (Schneider)." *Journal, Bombay Natural History Society*, Vol. 31 (1926), pp. 84–90.

———: "Snakes Collected in Burma in 1925." *Journal, Bombay Natural History Society,* Vol. 31 (1926), pp. 558–66.

WEHEKIND, LUDOLF: "Notes on the Foods of the Trinidad Snakes." *British Journal of Herpetology,* Vol. 2 (1955), pp. 9–13.

WOERLE, A.: "Junge Riesenschlangen." *Die Aquarien- und Terrarien-Zeitschrift,* Vol. 7 (1954), pp. 322–4.

FEEDING HABITS

FORSYTH, W.: "Habits of the Python (*Python molurus*)." *Journal, Bombay Natural History Society,* Vol. 21 (1911), pp. 277–8.

ISEMONGER, R. M.: *Snakes and Snake Catching in Southern Africa.* Cape Town: Howard Timmins; 1955. See pp. 47–8.

JAMESON, DAVID L.: "Duplicate Feeding Habits in Snakes." *Copeia,* No. 1, 1956, pp. 54–5.

KLAUBER, LAURENCE M.: *Rattlesnakes.* Berkeley and Los Angeles: University of California Press; 1956. See pp. 611–31.

LEDERER, GUSTAV: "Nahrungserwerb, Entwicklung, Paarung und Brutfürsorge von *Python reticulatus* (Schneider)." *Zoologische Jahrbücher (Anatomie)* (Jena), Vol. 68 (1944), pp. 363–98. See p. 368.

OLIVER, JAMES A.: *Snakes in Fact and Fiction.* New York: The Macmillan Company; 1958. See Chap. 4.

ROSE, WALTER: *Snakes—Mainly South African.* Cape Town: Maskew Miller; 1955. See p. 77.

DIGESTION

AVERY, ROGER: "Common Frog Swallowed and Rejected Alive by Grass Snake." *British Journal of Herpetology,* Vol. 1 (1953), p. 173.

BENEDICT, FRANCIS G.: *The Physiology of Large Reptiles with Special Reference to the Heat Production of Snakes, Tortoises, Lizards and Alligators.* Washington, D.C.: Carnegie Institution of Washington; 1932.

BLAIN, ALEXANDER W., AND K. N. CAMPBELL: "A Study of Digestive Phenomena in Snakes with the Aid of the Roentgen Ray." *The American Journal of Roentgenology and Radium Therapy,* Vol. 48 (1942), pp. 229–39.

FITCH, HENRY S., AND H. TWINING: "Feeding Habits of the Pacific Rattlesnake." *Copeia,* No. 2, 1946, pp. 64–71.

SCHWEIZER, HANS: "Die Anakonda (*Eunectes murinus*) als Schlangenfresserin." *Die Aquarien- und Terrarien-Zeitschrift,* Vol. 6 (1953), pp. 236–8.

TSCHAMBERS, BERT: "Boa Constrictor Eats Porcupine." *Herpetologica,* Vol. 5 (1949), p. 141.

Suggested References

USE OF WATER

ALLEE, W. C., A. E. EMERSON, O. PARK, T. PARK, AND K. P. SCHMIDT: *Principles of Animal Ecology*. Philadelphia and London: W. B. Saunders Company; 1949. See pp. 183–9.

BENEDICT, FRANCIS G.: *The Physiology of Large Reptiles with Special Reference to the Heat Production of Snakes, Tortoises, Lizards and Alligators*. Washington, D.C.: Carnegie Institution of Washington; 1932.

BOGERT, CHARLES M., AND RAYMOND B. COWLES: "Results of the Archbold Expeditions. No. 58. Moisture Loss in Relation to Habitat Selection in Some Floridian Reptiles." *American Museum Novitates*, No. 1358 (1947), pp. 1–34.

PETTUS, DAVID: "Water Relationships in *Natrix sipedon*." *Copeia*, No. 3, 1958, pp. 207–11.

SMITH, HOMER W.: *From Fish to Philosopher*. Boston: Little, Brown and Company; 1953. See pp. 34, 122–4.

WOLF, A. V.: "Thirst." *Scientific American*, Vol. 194 (1956), pp. 70–6.

——: "Body Water." *Scientific American*, Vol. 199 (1958), pp. 125–32.

TEMPERATURE

BENEDICT, FRANCIS G.: *The Physiology of Large Reptiles with Special Reference to the Heat Production of Snakes, Tortoises, Lizards and Alligators*. Washington, D.C.: Carnegie Institution of Washington; 1932.

BOGERT, CHARLES M.: "Thermoregulation in Reptiles, a Factor in Evolution." *Evolution*, Vol. 3 (1949), pp. 195–211.

——: "How Reptiles Regulate Their Body Temperature." *Scientific American*, Vol. 200 (1959), pp. 105–20.

COLBERT, EDWIN H., RAYMOND B. COWLES, AND CHARLES M. BOGERT: "Rates of Temperature Increase in the Dinosaurs." *Copeia*, No. 2, 1947, pp. 141–2.

COWLES, RAYMOND B., AND CHARLES M. BOGERT: "A Preliminary Study of the Thermal Requirements of Desert Reptiles." *Bulletin, American Museum Natural History*, Vol. 83 (1944), pp. 261–96.

FITCH, HENRY S.: "Temperature Responses in Free-Living Amphibians and Reptiles of Northeastern Kansas." *University Kansas Publications, Museum Natural History*, Vol. 8 (1956), pp. 417–76.

LUETH, FRANCIS X.: "Effects of Temperature on Snakes." *Copeia*, No. 3, 1941, pp. 125–32.

SEX AND MATING

BEDDARD, F. E.: "The Rudimentary Hind-Limbs of the Boine Snakes." *Nature*, Vol. 72 (1905), p. 630.

Suggested References

BRAIN, C. K.: "Mating in the South African Mole Snake, *Pseudaspis cana* (Linnaeus)." *Copeia*, No. 1, 1959, pp. 71–2.

DAVIS, D. DWIGHT: "Courtship and Mating Behavior in Snakes." *Field Museum of Natural History, Zoological Series*, Vol. 20 (1936), pp. 257–90. See p. 259.

DOWLING, HERNDON G., AND JAY M. SAVAGE: "A Guide to the Snake Hemipenis: A Survey of Basic Structure and Systematic Characteristics." *Zoologica*, Vol. 45 (1960), pp. 17–28.

FOX, WADE: "Seminal Receptacles of Snakes." *Anatomical Record*, Vol. 124 (1956), pp. 519–40.

HOGE, ALPHONSE R.: "Dimorfismo Sexual nos Boídeos." *Memórias, Instituto Butantan*, Vol. 20 (1947), pp. 181–7.

KLAUBER, LAURENCE M.: *Rattlesnakes*. Berkeley and Los Angeles: University of California Press; 1956. See pp. 686–90, 692.

KOPSTEIN, FELIX: "Ein Beitrag zur Eierkunde und zur Fortpflanzung der malaiischen Reptilien." *Bulletin, Raffles Museum* (Singapore), No. 14 (1938), pp. 81–167. English summary, pp. 158–67; see pp. 163–4.

LAURENT, R. F.: "Contribution à l'herpétologie de la région des Grands Lacs de l'Afrique centrale. I. Généralités; II. Cheloniens; III. Ophidiens." *Annales, Musée Royal Congo Belge, Sciences Zoologiques*, Vol. 48 (1956), pp. 1–390. See p. 85.

LEDERER, GUSTAV: "Nahrungserwerb, Entwicklung, Paarung und Brutfürsorge von *Python reticulatus* (Schneider)." *Zoologische Jahrbücher* (*Anatomie*) (Jena), Vol. 68 (1944), pp. 363–98.

——: "Fortpflanzungsbiologie und Entwicklung von *Python molurus molurus* (Linné) und *Python molurus bivittatus* (Kühl)." *Die Aquarien- und Terrarien-Zeitschrift*, Vol. 9 (1956), pp. 243–8.

LEIGH, C.: "Notes on the Fauna of British India: Reptilia and Amphibia, by Malcolm Smith." *Journal, Bombay Natural History Society*, Vol. 47 (1947), pp. 390–1.

——: "Egg-laying by a Python in Captivity." *Journal, Bombay Natural History Society*, Vol. 50 (1951), p. 183.

MERTENS, ROBERT: "Über Reptilienbastarde." *Senckenbergiana*, Vol. 31 (1950), pp. 127–44.

——: "Über Reptilienbastarde, II." *Senckenbergiana Biologica*, Vol. 37 (1956), pp. 383–94.

MOLE, R. R.: "The Trinidad Snakes." *Proceedings, Zoological Society London*, 1924, pp. 235–78.

NICHOLLS, F.: "Pythons." *Journal, Bombay Natural History Society*, Vol. 52 (1954), p. 620.

NOBLE, G. K.: "The Sense Organs Involved in the Courtship of *Storeria, Thamnophis* and Other Snakes." *Bulletin, American Museum Natural History*, Vol. 73 (1937), pp. 673–725. See pp. 678, 682, 685, 690–1.

POPE, CLIFFORD H.: *The Reptiles of China—Turtles, Crocodilians, Snakes, Lizards*. Vol. 10 of *Natural History of Central Asia*. New York: The American Museum of Natural History; 1935. See pp. 436–9.

POPE, CLIFFORD H.: "Copulatory Adjustment in Snakes." *Field Museum Natural History, Zoological Series*, Vol. 24 (1941), pp. 249–52.

SHAW, G. E., E. O. SHEBBEARE, AND P. E. BARKER: "The Snakes of Northern Bengal and Sikkim." *Journal, Darjeeling Natural History Society*, Vol. 13 (1939), pp. 64–73. See p. 69.

STEMMLER-MORATH, CARL: "Beitrag zur Gefangenschafts- und Fortpflanzungsbiologie von *Python molurus* L." *Der Zoologische Garten* (Leipzig), Vol. 21 (1956), pp. 347–64. See pp. 349–51, 364.

VOLSØE, H.: "Structure and Seasonal Variation of the Male Reproductive Organs of *Vipera berus* (L.)." *Spolia Zoologica Musei Hauniensis* (Copenhagen), 1944, pp. 1–172. See pp. 18–22, 49–50.

WALL, FRANK: *The Snakes of Ceylon.* Colombo: H. R. Cottle; 1921. See p. 65.

WRENICKE, C. J. T.: "Pythons." *Journal, Bombay Natural History Society*, Vol. 153 (1955), pp. 134–5.

LAYING, BROODING, HATCHING, AND BIRTH

"Ball Python Upsets Zoological Ideas." *Science News Letter*, Apr. 26, 1941, p. 265.

BENEDICT, FRANCIS G.: *The Physiology of Large Reptiles with Special Reference to the Heat Production of Snakes, Tortoises, Lizards and Alligators.* Washington, D.C.: Carnegie Institution of Washington; 1932. See pp. 86–114.

COWLES, RAYMOND B.: "Casual Notes on the Poikilothermous Vertebrates of the Umzumbe Valley, Natal, South Africa." *Copeia*, No. 1, 1936, pp. 4–8.

FITZSIMONS, F. W.: *Pythons and Their Ways.* London: George G. Harrap & Co.; 1930. See pp. 14, 15.

FORBES, W. A.: "Observations on the Incubation of the Indian Python (*Python molurus*), with Special Regard to the Alleged Increase of Temperature During That Process." *Proceedings, Zoological Society London*, 1881, pp. 960–7.

FRITH, H. J.: "Incubator Birds." *Scientific American*, Vol. 201 (1959), pp. 52–8.

HOOVER, EARL E.: "On the Birth of *Constrictor constrictor imperator* in Captivity." *Copeia*, No. 1, 1936, p. 62.

KOPSTEIN, FELIX: "Ein Beitrag zur Eierkunde und zur Fortpflanzung der malaiischen Reptilien." *Bulletin, Raffles Museum* (Singapore), No. 14 (1938), pp. 81–167. English summary, pp. 158–67; see pp. 131, 159.

LEDERER, GUSTAV: "Nahrungserwerb, Entwicklung, Paarung und Brutfürsorge von *Python reticulatus* (Schneider)." *Zoologische Jahrbücher* (*Anatomie*) (Jena), Vol. 68 (1944), pp. 363–98.

——: "Fortpflanzungsbiologie und Entwicklung von *Python molurus molurus* (Linné) und *Python molurus bivittatus* (Kühl)." *Die Aquarien- und Terrarien-Zeitschrift*, Vol. 9 (1956), pp. 243–8.

Suggested References

LESTER, J. W.: "Snakes Common in Sierra Leone." *Zoo Life*, Vol. 10 (1955), pp. 24–7.

——: "The Breeding of the Western Boa [*Constrictor occidentalis*]." *Aquarist* (London), Vol. 12 (1947), pp. 128–30. (Data from this paper, which was not seen, are not included in the text.)

NOBLE, G. K.: "The Brooding Habit of the Blood Python and of Other Snakes." *Copeia*, No. 1, 1935, pp. 1–3.

——AND E. R. MASON: "Experiments on the Brooding Habits of the Lizards *Eumeces* and *Ophisaurus*." *American Museum Novitates*, No. 619 (1933), pp. 1–29.

PITMAN, CHARLES R. S.: *A Guide to the Snakes of Uganda*. Kampala: Uganda Society; 1938. See pp. 55–6.

SCLATER, P. L.: "Notes on the Incubation of *Python sebae*." *Proceedings, Zoological Society London*, 1862, pp. 365–8.

SMITH, MALCOLM: "A Bangkok Python." *Journal, Siam Society, Natural History Supplement*, Vol. 11 (1937), pp. 61–2.

——: *The Fauna of British India, Ceylon and Burma, Including the Whole of the Indo-Chinese Sub-Region. Reptilia and Amphibia. Vol. 3: Serpentes.* London: Taylor and Francis; 1943. See p. 110.

STEMMLER-MORATH, CARL: "Beitrag zur Gefangenschafts- und Fortpflanzungsbiologie von *Python molurus* L." *Der Zoologische Garten* (Leipzig), Vol. 21 (1956), pp. 347–64.

VALENCIENNES, ACHILLE: "Observations faites pendant l'incubation d'une femelle du Python à deux raies (*Python bivittatus*, Kuhl) pendant les mois de mai et de juin 1841." *Comptes Rendus* (Paris), Vol. 13 (1841), pp. 126–33.

WALL, FRANK: *The Snakes of Ceylon*. Colombo: H. R. Cottle; 1921. See p. 66.

——: "The Reticulate Python. *Python reticulatus* (Schneider)." *Journal, Bombay Natural History Society*, Vol. 31 (1926), pp. 84–90.

GROWTH, MATURITY, AND LENGTH

AMARAL, AFRÂNIO DO: "Serpentes Gigantes." *Boletim, Museu Paraense E. Goeldi*, Vol. 10 (1948), pp. 211–37.

BEEBE, WILLIAM: "Field Notes on the Snakes of Kartabo, British Guiana, and Caripito, Venezuela." *Zoologica*, Vol. 31, Part I (1946), pp. 11–52.

CANSDALE, G. S.: "Field Notes on Some Gold Coast Snakes." *The Nigerian Field* (London), Vol. 13, No. 2 (1948), pp. 43–50.

CARPENTER, CHARLES C.: "Comparative Ecology of the Common Garter Snake (*Thamnophis s. sirtalis*), the Ribbon Snake (*Thamnophis s. sauritus*), and Butler's Garter Snake (*Thamnophis butleri*) in Mixed Populations." *Ecological Monographs*, Vol. 22 (1952), pp. 235–58.

DEAN, S.: "Length of Python." *North Queensland Naturalist*, Vol. 22, No. 107 (1954), pp. 13–14.

Suggested References

DITMARS, RAYMOND L.: "The Big Serpents." *Bulletin, New York Zoological Society*, Vol. 1 (1904), pp. 157–63.

——: *Snakes of the World.* New York: The Macmillan Company; 1951. See p. 35.

DUNN, EMMETT R.: "Los Géneros de Anfibios y Reptiles de Colombia, III." *Caldasia*, Vol. 3 (1944), pp. 155–224.

FLOWER, STANLEY S.: "Contributions to Our Knowledge of the Duration of Life in Vertebrate Animals. 3. Reptiles." *Proceedings, Zoological Society London*, No. 60 (1925), pp. 911–81.

GILMORE, CHARLES W.: "Fossil Snakes of North America." *Special Papers, Geological Society America*, No. 9 (1938), pp. 1–96.

GRIFFIN, LAWRENCE E.: "A Catalog of the Ophidia from South America at Present (June 1916) Contained in the Carnegie Museum with Descriptions of Some New Species." *Memoirs, Carnegie Museum*, Vol. 7 (1916), pp. 163–228.

HEUVELMANS, BERNARD: *On the Track of Unknown Animals.* New York: Hill and Wang; 1959. See Chap. 13.

HOGE, ALPHONSE R.: "Notas Erpetológicas. 2. Dimorfismo Sexual nos Boídeos." *Memórias, Instituto Butantan*, Vol. 20 (1947), pp. 181–7.

KLAUBER, LAURENCE M.: *Rattlesnakes.* Berkeley and Los Angeles: University of California Press; 1956. See p. 659.

KOPSTEIN, FELIX: "Ein Beitrag zur Eierkunde und zur Fortpflanzung der malaiischen Reptilien." *Bulletin, Raffles Museum* (Singapore), No. 14 (1938), pp. 81–167. English summary, pp. 158–67; see pp. 161–2.

LEDERER, GUSTAV: "Nahrungserwerb, Entwicklung, Paarung und Brutfürsorge von *Python reticulatus* (Schneider)." *Zoologische Jahrbücher* (*Anatomie*) (Jena), Vol. 68 (1944), pp. 363–98.

——: "Fortpflanzungsbiologie und Entwicklung von *Python molurus molurus* (Linné) und *Python molurus bivittatus* (Kühl)." *Die Aquarien- und Terrarien-Zeitschrift*, Vol. 9 (1956), pp. 243–8.

LEIGH, C.: "Breeding of Pythons." *The Field, The Country Gentleman's Newspaper* (London), Dec. 19, 1936, p. 1556.

——: "Notes on the Fauna of British India: Reptilia and Amphibia, by Malcolm Smith." *Journal, Bombay Natural History Society*, Vol. 47 (1947), pp. 390–1.

LOVERIDGE, ARTHUR: "Blind Snakes and Pythons of East Africa." *Bulletin, Antivenin Institute America*, Vol. 3 (1929), pp. 14–19.

MCPHEE, DAVID R.: *Some Common Snakes and Lizards of Australia.* Brisbane: Jacaranda Press; 1959.

MERTENS, ROBERT: "Die Amphibien und Reptilien von El Salvador, auf Grund der Reisen von R. Mertens und A. Zilch." *Abhandlungen der Senckenbergischen Naturforschenden Gesellschaft*, No. 487 (1952), pp. 1–120. See p. 59.

MOLE, R. R., AND F. W. URICH: "Biological Notes upon Some of the Ophidia of Trinidad, B.W.I., with a Preliminary List of the Species Recorded from the Island." *Proceedings, Zoological Society London,* 1894, pp. 499–518.

OLIVER, JAMES A.: *The Natural History of North American Amphibians and Reptiles.* Princeton, N.J.: D. Van Nostrand Company; 1955. See pp. 282–4.

——: *Snakes in Fact and Fiction.* New York: The Macmillan Company; 1958. See Chaps. 2, 3.

PITMAN, CHARLES R. S.: *A Guide to the Snakes of Uganda.* Kampala: Uganda Society; 1938. See pp. 54–5.

QUELCH, J. J.: "The Boa-Constrictors of British Guiana." *Annals and Magazine of Natural History,* Series 7, Vol. 1 (1898), p. 296.

SCHWEIZER, HANS: "Die Anakonda (*Eunectes murinus*) als Schlangenfresserin." *Die Aquarien- und Terrarien-Zeitschrift,* Vol. 6 (1953), pp. 236–8.

SIMPSON, GEORGE GAYLORD: "A New Fossil Snake from the Notostylops Beds of Patagonia." *Bulletin, American Museum Natural History,* Vol. 67 (1933), pp. 1–22.

SOMANADER, S. V. O.: "The Ceylon Python." *Loris* (Colombo), Vol. 2, No. 5 (1941), pp. 283–5.

VOLSØE, H.: "Structure and Seasonal Variation of the Male Reproductive Organs of *Vipera berus* (L.)." *Spolia Zoologica Musei Huanensis* (Copenhagen), 1944, pp. 1–172. See pp. 35–6.

WALL, FRANK: *The Snakes of Ceylon.* Colombo: H. R. Cottle; 1921. See pp. 66–9.

——: "The Reticulate Python. *Python reticulatus* (Schneider)." *Journal, Bombay Natural History Society,* Vol. 31 (1926), pp. 558–66.

WOERLE, A.: "Junge Riesenschlangen." *Die Aquarien- und Terrarien-Zeitschrift,* Vol. 7 (1954), pp. 322–4.

WUNDER, W.: "Nestbau und Brutpflege bei Reptilien." *Ergebnisse der Biologie* (Berlin), Vol. 10 (1934), pp. 1–36.

LONGEVITY

BOURLIÈRE, FRANÇOIS: *The Natural History of Mammals.* New York: Alfred A. Knopf; 1954. See pp. 201–2.

FLOWER, STANLEY S.: "Contributions to Our Knowledge of the Duration of Life in Vertebrate Animals. 3. Reptiles." *Proceedings, Zoological Society London,* No. 60 (1925), pp. 911–81.

——: "Further Notes on the Duration of Life in Animals. 2. Amphibians." *Proceedings, Zoological Society London,* Part II (1936), pp. 369–94.

——: "Further Notes on the Duration of Life in Animals. 3. Reptiles." *Proceedings, Zoological Society London,* Series A, Part I (1937), pp. 1–39.

KLAUBER, LAURENCE M.: *Rattlesnakes.* Berkeley and Los Angeles: University of California Press; 1956. See pp. 307–9.

Suggested References

MERTENS, ROBERT: *La Vie des amphibiens et reptiles*. Paris: Horizons de France; 1959. See pp. 181–2.

OLIVER, JAMES A.: *The Natural History of North American Amphibians and Reptiles*. Princeton, N.J.: D. Van Nostrand Company; 1955. See pp. 288–96.

PERKINS, C. B.: "Longevity of Snakes in Captivity in the United States as of January 1, 1955." *Copeia*, No. 3, 1955, p. 262.

SCHWEIZER, HANS: "Die Anakonda (*Eunectes murinus*) als Schlangenfresserin." *Die Aquarien- und Terrarien-Zeitschrift*, Vol. 6 (1953), pp. 236–8.

SHAW, CHARLES E.: "Longevity of Snakes in Captivity in the United States as of January 1, 1957." *Copeia*, No. 4, 1957, p. 310.

——: "Longevity of Snakes in the United States as of January 1, 1959." *Copeia*, No. 4, 1959, pp. 336–7.

WALLACE, GEORGE J.: *An Introduction to Ornithology*. New York: The Macmillan Company; 1955. See pp. 205–6.

ENEMIES AND DEFENSE AGAINST THEM

BEEBE, WILLIAM: "Field Notes on the Snakes of Kartabo, British Guiana, and Caripito, Venezuela." *Zoologica*, Vol. 31, Part I (1946), pp. 11–52.

CAMIN, JOSEPH H., AND PAUL R. EHRLICH: "Natural Selection in Water Snakes (*Natrix sipedon* L.) on Islands in Lake Erie." *Evolution*, Vol. 12 (1958), pp. 504–11.

CORBETT, JIM: *Jungle Lore*. New York: Oxford University Press; 1953. See pp. 40–1.

COTT, HUGH B.: *Adaptive Coloration in Animals*. London: Methuen & Co.; 1940 (reprinted 1957). See pp. 57, 88, 197, Fig. 11, and Pl. 24.

DAVIS, D. DWIGHT: "Flash Display of Aposematic Colors in *Farancia* and Other Snakes." *Copeia*, No. 3, 1948, pp. 208–11.

DICKEY, HERBERT S.: *My Jungle Book*. Boston: Little, Brown; 1932. See pp. 220–1.

FITCH, HENRY S.: "Study of Snake Populations in Central California." *The American Midland Naturalist*, Vol. 41 (1949), pp. 513–79. See p. 559.

HOIER, R.: *A Travers Plaines et Volcans au Parc National Albert*. Brussels: Institut des Parcs Nationaux du Congo Belge; 1950. See pp. 119–27 for section on reptiles; also p. 70 for reference to hyena.

ISEMONGER, R. M.: *Snakes and Snake Catching in Southern Africa*. Cape Town: Howard Timmins; 1955. See p. 48.

KLAUBER, LAURENCE M.: *Rattlesnakes*. Berkeley and Los Angeles: University of California Press; 1956. See Index, p. 1423, for references to enemies.

MERTENS, ROBERT: "Die Warn- und Droh-Reaktionen der Reptilien." *Abhandlungen, Senckenbergischen Naturforschenden Gesellschaft*, Vol. 471 (1946), pp. 1–108.

Suggested References

MOHR, J. C. VAN DER MEER: "Notiz über Seeschlangen." *Miscellanea Zoologica Sumatrana*, Vol. 23 (1927), pp. 1–2.

PITMAN, CHARLES R. S.: *A Guide to the Snakes of Uganda*. Kampala: Uganda Society; 1938. See p. 57.

PORTMANN, ADOLF: *Animal Camouflage*. Ann Arbor, Mich.: University of Michigan Press; 1959.

PROCTOR, JOAN B.: "Unrecorded Characters Seen in Living Snakes, and Description of a New Tree-Frog." *Proceedings, Zoological Society London*, Part IV (1924), pp. 1125–9.

SKUTCH, ALEXANDER F.: "The Laughing Reptile Hunter of Tropical America." *Animal Kingdom*, Vol. 63 (1960), pp. 115–19.

WALL, FRANK: *The Snakes of Ceylon*. Colombo: H. R. Cottle; 1921. See p. 57.

PARASITES AND SICKNESS

ARONSON, JOSEPH D.: "Spontaneous Tuberculosis in Snakes. N. Sp. *Mycobacterium thamnopheos*." *The Journal of Infectious Diseases*, Vol. 44 (1929), pp. 215–23.

——: "The Occurrence of Tuberculosis in Cold-Blooded Animals." *Transactions, Twenty-seventh Annual Meeting of the National Tuberculosis Association*, Vol. 27 (1931), pp. 184–7.

BISHOPP, F. C., AND H. L. TREMBLEY: "Distribution and Hosts of Certain North American Ticks." *Journal of Parasitology*, Vol. 31 (1945), pp. 1–54.

BUCHSBAUM, RALPH: *Animals Without Backbones. An Introduction to the Invertebrates*. Chicago: The University of Chicago Press; 2nd ed., 1948.

BURTSCHER, J.: "Über die Mundfäule der Schlangen." *Der Zoologische Garten*, Vol. 4 (1931), pp. 235–44.

BYRD, ELON E., MALCOLM V. PARKER, AND ROBERT J. REIBER: "Taxonomic Studies on the Genus *Styphlodora* Looss, 1899 (Trematoda: Styphlodorinae), with Descriptions of Four New Species." *Transactions, American Microscopical Society*, Vol. 59 (1940), pp. 294–326.

CAMIN, JOSEPH H.: "Mite Transmission of a Hemorrhagic Septicemia in Snakes." *Journal of Parasitology*, Vol. 34 (1948), pp. 345–54.

——: "Observations on the Life History and Sensory Behavior of the Snake Mite, *Ophionyssus natricis* (Gervais) (Acarina: Macronyssidae)." *The Chicago Academy of Sciences*, Special Publication No. 10 (1953), pp. 1–75.

CHITWOOD, B. G., AND M. B. CHITWOOD: *An Introduction to Nematology*. Section 1: "Anatomy." Baltimore: B. G. Chitwood, publisher; revised, 1950.

FINNEGAN, SUSAN: "On a New Species of Mite of the Family Heterozerconidae Parasitic on a Snake." *Proceedings, Zoological Society London*, 1931, pp. 1349–57.

FITCH, HENRY S.: "Natural History of the Six-lined Racerunner (*Cnemi-*

dophorus sexlineatus)." *University Kansas Publications, Museum Natural History*, Vol. 11 (1958), pp. 11–62. See pp. 53–4.

GOODMAN, JOHN D.: "Some Aspects of the Role of Parasitology in Herpetology." *Herpetologica*, Vol. 7 (1951), pp. 65–7.

HARWOOD, PAUL D.: "The Helminths Parasitic in the Amphibia and Reptilia of Houston, Texas, and Vicinity." *Proceedings, United States National Museum*, Vol. 81, Art. 17 (1932), pp. 1–71.

HILL, HOWARD R.: "The Occurrence of Linguatulids in Pythons." *Bulletin, Southern California Academy Sciences*, Vol. 33 (1934), pp. 117–22.

——: "New Host Records of the Linguatulid, *Kiricephalus coarctatus* (Diesing) in the United States." *Bulletin, Southern California Academy Sciences*, Vol. 34 (1935), pp. 226–7.

HUGHES, R. CHESTER, JOHN R. BAKER, AND C. BENTON DAWSON: "The Tapeworms of Reptiles, Part 1." *The American Midland Naturalist*, Vol. 25 (1941), pp. 454–68.

——: "The Tapeworms of Reptiles, Part 2. Host Catalogue." *The Wasmann Collector*, Vol. 4 (1941), pp. 97–104.

IRVINE, FRED R.: "Snakes as Food for Man." *British Journal of Herpetology*, Vol. 1 (1954), pp. 183–9.

LA RUE, GEORGE R.: "Two New Larval Trematodes from *Thamnophis marciana* and *Thamnophis Eques*." *Occasional Papers, Museum Zoology, University Michigan*, No. 35 (1917), pp. 1–12.

LOVELL, REGINALD: "The Bacteriological Findings in Certain Fatal Cases of Enteritis Occurring in the Gardens during 1928." *Proceedings, London Zoological Society*, 1929, pp. 623–32.

POPE, CLIFFORD H.: "Reptiles." In *The Care and Breeding of Laboratory Animals*, edited by Edmond J. Farris. New York: John Wiley & Sons; 1950.

RADFORD, CHARLES D.: "The Mites (Acarina) Parasitic on Mammals, Birds, and Reptiles." *Parasitology*, Vol. 40 (1950), pp. 366–94.

RATCLIFFE, HERBERT L., AND QUENTIN M. GEIMAN: "Amebiasis in Reptiles." *Science*, Vol. 79 (1934), pp. 324–5.

SCHROEDER, CHARLES R.: "Report of the Veterinarian." *New York Zoological Society, Forty-second Annual Report* (1938), pp. 18–27.

——: "Report of the Hospital and Laboratory of the New York Zoological Park, 1938. Mortality Statistics of the Society's Collection." *Zoologica*, Vol. 24 (1939), pp. 265–83.

WALL, FRANK: "The Reticulate Python. *Python reticulatus* (Schneider)." *Journal, Bombay Natural History Society*, Vol. 31 (1926), pp. 84–90.

YUNKER, CONRAD: "Studies on the Snake Mite *Ophionyssus natricis*, in Nature." *Science*, Vol. 124 (1956), pp. 979–80.

MAN'S STUDY OF THE GIANTS

DOWLING, HERNDON G.: "Classification of the Serpentes: A Critical Review." *Copeia*, No. 1, 1959, pp. 38–52.

Suggested References

MAYR, ERNST, E. GORTON LINSLEY, AND ROBERT L. USINGER: *Methods and Principles of Systematic Zoology*. New York: McGraw-Hill Book Company; 1953.

ROLLINS, REED C., AND OTHERS: "Symposium on Linnaeus and Nomenclatural Codes." *Systematic Zoology*, Vol. 8 (1959), pp. 2–3.

SCHMIDT, KARL P.: "Herpetology." *A Century of Progress in the Natural Sciences, 1853–1953*. San Francisco: California Academy of Sciences; 1955.

SMITH, MALCOLM: *The Fauna of British India, Ceylon and Burma, Including the Whole of the Indo-Chinese Sub-Region. Reptilia and Amphibia*. Vol. 3: *Serpentes*. London: Taylor and Francis; 1943.

STULL, OLIVE GRIFFITH: "A Check List of the Family Boidae." *Proceedings, Boston Society Natural History*, Vol. 40 (1935), pp. 387–408.

WALL, FRANK: *The Snakes of Ceylon*. Colombo: H. R. Cottle; 1921.

——: "The Reticulate Python. *Python reticulatus* (Schneider)." *Journal, Bombay Natural History Society*, Vol. 31 (1926), pp. 84–90.

WETTSTEIN, OTTO V.: "Franz Werner als Mensch und Forscher." *Annalen, Naturhistorischen Museums in Wien*, Vol. 51 (1941), pp. 8–53.

WORSHIP

ARMSTRONG, EDWARD A.: *The Folklore of Birds*. London: Collins; 1958. See Chap. 1.

COOK, STANLEY ARTHUR: "Serpent Cults." *Encyclopaedia Britannica*, Vol. 20 (1955), pp. 369–71.

FERGUSSON, JAMES E.: *Tree and Serpent Worship*. London: India Museum, W. H. Allen and Co., publishers to the India office; 1868.

FRAZER, JAMES G.: *The Golden Bough*. Abridged edition. New York: The Macmillan Company; 1922.

HAMBLY, WILFRID D.: "Serpent Worship in Africa." *Field Museum of Natural History, Anthropological Series*, Vol. 21 (1931), pp. 1–85.

HOWEY, M. OLDFIELD: *The Encircled Serpent*. New York: Arthur Richmond Company; 1955. See Chaps. 25, 30.

MEAD, MARGARET: "The Marsalai Cult Among the Arapesh, with Special Reference to the Rainbow Serpent Beliefs of the Australian Aboriginals." *Oceania*, Vol. 4 (1933), pp. 37–53.

MORLEY, SYLVANUS GRISWOLD: *The Ancient Maya*. Stanford University, Cal.: Stanford University Press; 1946. See pp. 210–11.

OLDHAM, C. F.: *The Sun and the Serpent*. London: Archibald Constable & Co., 1905.

RADCLIFFE-BROWN, A. R.: "The Rainbow-serpent Myth in South-east Australia." *Oceania*, Vol. 1 (1930–1), pp. 342–7.

READ, JOHN: *Through Alchemy to Chemistry*. London: G. Bell and Sons; 1957.

SAYCE, A. H.: "Serpent-Worship in Ancient and Modern Egypt." *Contemporary Review*, Oct. 1893, pp. 523–30.

Suggested References

VAILLANT, GEORGE C.: *Aztecs of Mexico*. Garden City, N.Y.: Doubleday, Doran & Company; 1941.

WELSFORD, ENID, W. CROOKE, AND J. A. MacCULLOCH: "Serpent-Worship." *Encyclopaedia of Religion and Ethics* (New York), Vol. 11 (1928), pp. 399–423.

BELIEFS

DICKEY, HERBERT S.: *My Jungle Book*. Boston: Little, Brown; 1932. See p. 216.

FITZSIMONS, F. W.: *Pythons and Their Ways*. London: George G. Harrap & Co.; 1930. See Chap. 6.

FREIBERG, MARCOS A.: *Vida de Batracios y Reptiles Sudamericanos*. Buenos Aires: Cesarini Hnos.; 1954. See p. 93.

ISEMONGER, R. M.: *Snakes and Snake Catching in Southern Africa*. Cape Town: Howard Timmins; 1955. See pp. 55–6.

LANGE, ALGOT: *The Lower Amazon*. New York: G. P. Putnam's Sons; 1914.

OWEN, CHARLES: *An Essay Towards a Natural History of Serpents*. London: "Sold by John Gray"; 1742. See p. 146.

ROSE, WALTER: *The Reptiles and Amphibians of Southern Africa*. Cape Town: Maskew Miller; 1950. See pp. 261–2.

——: *Snakes—Mainly South African*. Cape Town: Maskew Miller; 1955. See Chap. 19.

STEWART, C. G.: "Feeding Habits of the Python (*Python molurus*)." *Journal, Bombay Natural History Society*, Vol. 25 (1917), pp. 150–1.

TURSA: "Pythons." *Blackwood's Magazine* (London), Vol. 242 (1937), pp. 384–94.

WALL, FRANK: *The Snakes of Ceylon*. Colombo: H. R. Cottle; 1921. See p. 53.

ENCOUNTERS WITH GIANT SNAKES

BEEBE, WILLIAM: "Field Notes on the Snakes of Kartabo, British Guiana, and Caripito, Venezuela." *Zoologica*, Vol. 31, Part I (1946), pp. 11–52.

BLOMBERG, ROLF: "Giant Snake Hunt." *Natural History*, Vol. 65 (1956), pp. 92–7.

BUCK, FRANK, WITH FERRIN FRASER: "Snake in the Grass." *Collier's*, Jan. 11, 1936, pp. 18, 52–3.

DICKEY, HERBERT S.: *My Jungle Book*. Boston: Little, Brown; 1932. See pp. 219–20.

HUBBARD, WYNANT D.: *Wild Animals*. New York: D. Appleton & Co.; 1926. See pp. 40–3.

ISEMONGER, R. M.: *Snakes and Snake Catching in Southern Africa*. Cape Town: Howard Timmins; 1955. See p. 9.

LOVERIDGE, ARTHUR: "On Two Amphibious Snakes of the Central African Lake Region." *Bulletin, Antivenin Institute America*, Vol. 5 (1931), pp. 7–12.

Suggested References

MAYER, CHARLES: "Recruiting for the Menagerie." *Asia*, Oct. 1920, pp. 849–54.

OLIVER, JAMES A.: *Snakes in Fact and Fiction*. New York: The Macmillan Company; 1958. See pp. 11–15.

SEVERIN, KURT: "Eighteen Feet of Death." *True*, June 1958, pp. 69–71.

SMITH, MALCOLM: "A Bangkok Python." *Journal, Siam Society, Natural History Supplement*, Vol. 11 (1937), pp. 61–2.

STEVENSON-HAMILTON, J.: *Wild Life in South Africa*. London: Cassell & Co.; 1947. See p. 331.

UP DE GRAFF, F. W.: *Head Hunters of the Amazon*. New York: Duffield and Company; 1923.

WALL, FRANK: *The Snakes of Ceylon*. Colombo: H. R. Cottle; 1921. See pp. 51–2.

——: "The Reticulate Python. *Python reticulatus* (Schneider)." *Journal, Bombay Natural History Society*, Vol. 31 (1926), pp. 558–66.

WALLACE, ALFRED RUSSEL: *The Malay Archipelago*. London: The Macmillan Company; 1922. See pp. 227–8.

ATTACKS ON MAN

BLOMBERG, ROLF: "Giant Snake Hunt." *Natural History*, Vol. 65 (1956), pp. 92–7.

CUTRIGHT, P. R.: *Great Naturalists Explore South America*. New York: The Macmillan Company; 1940. See pp. 243–4.

KEAYS, R. W.: "An Unpleasant Experience with a Python." *Journal, Bombay Natural History Society*, Vol. 33 (1929), pp. 721–2.

KOPSTEIN, FELIX: "Over het Verslinden van Menschen door *Python reticulatus*." *Tropische Natuur*, Vol. 4 (1927), pp. 65–7.

LOVERIDGE, ARTHUR: "On Two Amphibious Snakes of the Central African Lake Region." *Bulletin, Antivenin Institute America*, Vol. 5 (1931), pp. 7–12.

OLIVER, JAMES A.: *Snakes in Fact and Fiction*. New York: The Macmillan Company; 1958. See pp. 46–9.

RUITER, L. COOMANS DE: "Pythons of Reuzenslangen." *Lacerta*, Vol. 12 (1954), pp. 12–14.

SEVERIN, KURT: "Eighteen Feet of Death." *True*, June 1958, pp. 69–71.

WATTS, A.: "Pythons in the Belgian Congo," *The Field, The Country Gentleman's Newspaper* (London), Vol. 145, No. 3774 (1925), p. 647.

FEAR OF GIANT SNAKES

BRODERIP, W. J.: "Observations on the Habits, etc., of a Male Chimpanzee, *Troglodytes niger*, Geoff., Now Living in the Menagerie of the Zoological Society of London." *Proceedings, Zoological Society London*, 1835, pp. 160–8.

Suggested References

BROWN, ARTHUR E.: "The Serpent and the Ape." *The American Naturalist,* Vol. 12 (1878), pp. 225–8.

CORBETT, JIM: *Jungle Lore.* New York: Oxford University Press; 1953.

JONES, HAROLD E., AND MARY C. JONES: "Maturation and Emotion: Fear of Snakes." *Childhood Education,* Vol. 5 (1928), pp. 136–43.

MITCHELL, P. CHALMERS: "Monkeys and the Fear of Snakes." *Proceedings, Zoological Society London,* Part II (1922), pp. 347–8.

—— AND R. I. POCOCK: "On the Feeding of Reptiles in Captivity with Observations on the Fear of Snakes by Other Vertebrates." *Proceedings, Zoological Society London,* 1907, pp. 785–94.

PAULIAN, RENAUD: *Un Naturaliste en Côte-d'Ivoire.* Paris: Stock; 1949. See pp. 128–33.

RANDOW, HEINZ: *Zoo Hunt in Ceylon.* Garden City, N.Y.: Doubleday & Co.; 1958.

ROSE, WALTER: *Snakes—Mainly South African.* Cape Town: Maskew Miller; 1955.

YERKES, ROBERT M.: *Chimpanzees: A Laboratory Colony.* New Haven: Yale University Press; 1943.

—— AND ADA W. YERKES: *The Great Apes. A Study of Anthropoid Life.* New Haven: Yale University Press; 1929.

USES BY MAN

"A Fad Two Years Ago—A Staple Today." *Printers' Ink,* Vol. 145 (Dec. 20, 1928), pp. 10, 12.

AHL, ERNST: "Reptilienfette (einschliesslich Reptilieneieröle)." *Rohstoffe des Tierreichs,* Lief. 3 (1929), pp. 68–74.

BUCK, FRANK, WITH FERRIN FRASER: "Snake in the Grass." *Collier's,* Jan. 11, 1936, pp. 18, 52–3.

"Busy Chicago Anaconda." *Life,* Sept. 2, 1946, pp. 126–8.

CARNEGIE, THOMAS M., JR.: "Park Here for the Python." *Harper's Magazine,* Feb. 1942, pp. 299–307.

CASTIGLIONI, ARTURO: "The Serpent in Medicine." *Ciba Symposia,* Vol. 3 (1942). See pp. 1161–2, 1171–2, 1174, 1177–9, 1179–81, 1185.

DICKEY, HERBERT S.: *My Jungle Book.* Boston: Little, Brown; 1932. See pp. 222–3.

FLOWER, STANLEY S.: "Contributions to our Knowledge of the Duration of Life in Vertebrate Animals. 3. Reptiles." *Proceedings, Zoological Society London,* No. 60 (1925), pp. 911–81.

——: *List of the Vertebrated Animals Exhibited in the Gardens of the Zoological Society of London, 1828–1927.* Reptiles, Vol. 3, pp. 1–272. London: Zoological Society; 1929.

——: "Further Notes on the Duration of Life in Animals. 3. Reptiles." *Proceedings, Zoological Society London,* Series A, Part I (1937), pp. 1–39.

Foreign Commerce and Navigation of the United States. Calendar years 1929 and following.

Suggested References

GRANT, CHAPMAN: "Notes on *Epicrates inornatus* (Reinhardt)." *Copeia*, No. 4, 1933, pp. 224–5.

HERRE, ALBERT W. C. T., AND D. S. RABOR: "Notes on Philippine Sea Snakes of the Genus *Laticauda*." *Copeia*, No. 4, 1949, pp. 282–4.

IRVINE, FRED R.: "Snakes as Food for Man." *British Journal of Herpetology*, Vol. 1 (1954), pp. 183–9.

KEAYS, R. W.: "An Unpleasant Experience with a Python." *Journal, Bombay Natural History Society*, Vol. 33 (1929), pp. 721–2.

KLAUBER, LAURENCE M.: *Rattlesnakes*. Berkeley and Los Angeles: University of California Press; 1956. See pp. 580–4, 1022–5.

LEE, GYPSY ROSE: *Gypsy; A Memoir*. New York: Harper & Brothers; 1957.

LOVERIDGE, ARTHUR: "Zoological Results of a Fifth Expedition to East Africa. III. Reptiles from Nyasaland and Tete." *Bulletin, Museum Comparative Zoology*, Vol. 110 (1953), pp. 143–322.

"New Yorkers Ogle a White Python." *Life*, Nov. 28, 1955, pp. 8–9.

OLIVER, JAMES A.: "Is the Mongoose a Snake Killer?" *Natural History*, Vol. 64 (1955), pp. 426–9.

"Python Party." *The New Yorker*, Oct. 22, 1955, pp. 33–4.

RAVEN, HENRY C.: "Adventures in Python Country." *Natural History*, Vol. 55 (1946), pp. 38–41.

READ, W. J.: "A Snake Dance of the Baining." *Oceania*, Vol. 2 (1931–2), pp. 232–6.

RUITER, L. COOMANS DE: "Pythons of Reuzenslangen." *Lacerta*, Vol. 12 (1954), pp. 12–14.

SEVERIN, KURT: "Eighteen Feet of Death." *True*, June 1958, pp. 69–71.

"There Are No Snakes in Ireland . . ." *The Rohm & Haas Reporter*, Vol. 6, No. 6 (1948), pp. 4–7, 17.

UHLER, F. M., C. COTTAM, AND T. E. CLARKE: "Food of Snakes of the George Washington National Forest, Virginia." *Transactions, Fourth North American Wildlife Conference*, 1939, pp. 605–22.

WALL, FRANK: *The Snakes of Ceylon*. Colombo: H. R. Cottle; 1921. See p. 54.

WALTERS, LEON L.: "New Uses of Celluloid and Similar Material in Taxidermy." *Field Museum of Natural History*, No. 230 (1925), pp. 1–20.

WAMBSGANSS, MARGARET E.: "Exotic Hides and Skins from 'South-of-Border' Resource." *Foreign Commerce Weekly*, Vol. 27 (May 24, 1947), pp. 8, 24.

WATTS, A.: "Pythons in the Belgian Congo." *The Field, The Country Gentleman's Newspaper* (London), Vol. 145, No. 3774 (1925), p. 647.

GIANT PETS

ALLEN, E. ROSS, AND WILFRED T. NEILL: "Keep Them Alive!" *Ross Allen's Reptile Institute* (Silver Springs, Fla.), Special Publication No. 1 (1950), pp. 1–24.

Suggested References

HOOPES, ISABEL: "Reptiles in the Home Zoo." *New England Museum of Natural History*, Special Publication No. 1 (1936), pp. 1–64.

LEDERER, GUSTAV: "Nahrungserwerb, Entwicklung, Paarung und Brutfürsorge von *Python reticulatus* (Schneider)." *Zoologische Jahrbücher* (*Anatomie*) (Jena), Vol. 68 (1944), pp. 363–98.

——: "Fortpflanzungsbiologie und Entwicklung von *Python molurus molurus* (Linné) und *Python molurus bivittatus* (Kühl)." *Die Aquarien- und Terrarien-Zeitschrift*, Vol. 9 (1956), pp. 243–8.

OLIVER, JAMES A.: *The Natural History of North American Amphibians and Reptiles*. Princeton, N.J.: D. Van Nostrand Company; 1955. See Chap. 13.

POPE, CLIFFORD H.: *Snakes Alive and How They Live*. New York: The Viking Press; 1937. See Chap. 17.

——: "Reptiles." In *The Care and Breeding of Laboratory Animals*, edited by Edmond J. Farris. New York: John Wiley & Sons; 1950.

——: *Reptiles Round the World*. New York: Alfred A. Knopf; 1957. See chapter entitled "Reptiles as Pets."

SMITH, HOBART M.: *Snakes as Pets*. Fond du Lac, Wis.: All-Pets Books, Inc.; 1953.

STEMMLER-MORATH, CARL: "Beitrag zur Gefangenschafts- und Fortpflanzungsbiologie von *Python molurus* L." *Der Zoologische Garten* (Leipzig), Vol. 21 (1956), pp. 347–64.

WERNER, FRANZ: "Über die Lebensweise von Riesenschlangen im Terrarium." *Der Zoologische Garten* (Leipzig), New Series, Vol. 11 (1939), pp. 165–82.

Index

Only major references to the six giants are entered below.

Acrochordus, 237

Activity, 62–7

African rock python: length, range, habits, and name, 15–16; habitat and habits, 27–8; strength, 46; rate of crawling, 60; time of activity, 65; food preferences, 80–1; food capacity, 86–7; lurking for prey, 90–1; handling of multiple prey, 94; sexual differences, 117–18; nesting sites, 128–9; laying season and pre-hatching period, 133; hatching, 134; eggs, 135; size of clutches, 138; brooding in nature, 141–2; brooding in captivity, 143, 144–5, 145–6, 147; growth, 151; size at birth, rate of growth, and maximum length, 157–8; longevity, 168–9; enemies, 175–6; parasites, 194; worship of, 209–11; encounters with, 220–2; attacks on man, 226, 227–8; economic value, 248, 250; numbers of in zoos of the United States, 253

Aggregation, 64–6, 123–4

Agriculture, snakes as aid to, 248–51

Alligator, American, 188

Alligators, 140, 237

Amblyomma dissimile, 187

Ameivas, 79

American Museum of Natural History, 86

America's First Zoo, 253

Amethystine python: name, relationship, and range, 17; distribution and habitat, 30–1; temperament, 52–3; time of activity, 66–7; food preferences, 83; food capacity, 88; nesting site, 129; nineteen eggs in clutch of,

Amethystine python (*continued*)
140; size at hatching, growth, and maximum length, 163–4; parasite of, 194

Amoebas, 194

Amoebiasis, 188

Amphibians, 108, 148

Anaconda: method of reproduction, 12; name, range, and subspecies, 15; distribution and habitat, 25, 26; time of activity and aggregation, 64–5; shedding, 73; food preferences, 78–9; food capacity, 86; courtship, 120; breeding season, 123; size of clutches, 137; growth, 150–1; size at birth, rate of growth, and maximum length, 153–5; longevity, 168; parasites, 194; beliefs based on, 216; encounters with, 218–19; attacks on man, 228; economic value, 249; numbers of in zoos of the United States, 253

Anaconda, southern, 15

Ancistrodon, 152

Anolis, 140, 188

Aponomma, 187

Asclepius, 208, 246

Attacks on man, 226–9

Aztecs, 209

Bacterium, 186, 195

Basel Zoological Garden, 145

Baumann, F. E., 118

Béart, Mr. and Mrs. C., 158

Beliefs, 212–17

Bibron, G., 163

Biting, 181–2

Bitis lachesis, 244

i

Index

Blue Boy, 72, 85, 88, 163
Bluffing, 178–9
Boa(s):
  Madagascar, 89
  rosy, 60
  sand, 245
  tree, 235
  water, 15
Boa constrictor: method of reproduction, 12; name, range, and subspecies, 14; distribution and habitat, 25–7; time of activity, 65; food preferences, 79–80; food capacity, 86; rate of digestion, 100–1; water loss, 107; sexual differences, 118; courtship, 120–1; breeding season, 123; size of clutches, 137; growth, 150–1; size at birth, rate of growth, and maximum length, 153, 155–7; longevity, 168; enemy of, 175; hissing, 179; parasites, 194; encounters with, 219–20; economic value, 249; relation of mongoose to, 249–50; numbers of in zoos of the United States, 253
Boa constrictor:
  constrictor, 124
  imperator, 14, 156
  occidentalis, 124
Boidae, 11, 13, 40, 141
Boinae, 13
Bombina, 167
Bone breaking, 47–9
Breeding, 123–4
Brooding, 132, 140–7
Brookfield Zoo, 73, 153–4, 259
Bufo, 167
Bullfrog, 93–4
Bushmaster, 10

Caiman, 78
Calabaria, 245
Canker mouth, 195–6
Carnivals, 255–6
Carpenter, L., 258
Cestodes, 190–1, 192
Charles, R. E., 208
Chemoreception, 42–3
Chicago Natural History Museum, 254
Christianity, 204, 207
Circuses, 255–6
Climbing, 61

Cloaca, 102, 129
Cloaca popping, 180
Clutches, size of, 136–404
Cnemidophorus, 79
Coachwhip, 11
Cobra(s), 213, 242, 257
  black-lipped, 167
  Indian, 141
  king, 10, 52, 242
Cold-blooded animals, 110–11
Collagen, 240
Coloration, protective, 177, 182
Coluber:
  constrictor, 55
  florulentus, 185
Colubridae, 36
Colubrids, 141
Constriction, 47–9, 225
Constrictor, 12
Copulation, 122–3
Corallus hortulanus, 55
Cottonmouth, 152
Courtship, 119–21
Crawling, 204–5
Crocodiles, 140, 175
Crocodilians, 167
Ctenosaura, 79

Darwin, Charles, 19, 52, 234
Defenses, 176–82
Dehydration, 108–9
Dent, 66
Development, internal, 125–7
Dhaman, 10
Digestion, 99–104
Dispersal, 20–1
Distribution of giants, 18, 22, 25–31
Dowling, H. G., 145–6
Drinking, 105–6
Drymarchon corais, 101

Ecdysis, *see* Shedding
Echis carinatus, 180
Ectoparasites, 184, 185
Ectothermic animals, 111
Education, 251–5
Egg, the, 134–6
Egg tooth, 134
Elaphe obsoleta, 142
Elapids, 141
Elimination, 102–4
Encounters, 217–25

Index

Endothermic animals, 111
Enemies, 173–6
Entamoeba, 194
  invadens, 188
Enteritis, 196
Eryx, 245
Esophagus, 100–1
Eunectes, 201
  murinus, 15
  murinus gigas, 15
  notaeus, 15
Excrement, 102–4
Eye, 35–9

Farancia, 180
  abacura, 141
Fear of giant snakes, 230–5
Fear of snakes in primates, 233–5
Feeding:
  capacity, 85–8
  frequency, 88–9
  habits, 90–5
Fertilization, delayed, 124–5
Fishes, 79
Flukes, 189–90, 194
Food:
  finding, 90–1
  preferences, 78–83
  use of snakes as, 241–6
Fossils:
  Boidae, 22
  snake, 164
Frog(s), 167, 190

Gall bladder, 248
Gestation, 124
Gigantophis garstini, 164–5
Gland(s):
  pituitary, 71
  sweat, 107
  thyroid, 71
God, python, Danh-gbi, 209–10
Golger's rule, 182
Growth, 70–1, 148–64

Habitats, 23–31
Haemogregarines, 189
Hagenbeck, J., 84
Handling giant snakes, 46–7
Hatching, 134
Hearing, 39
Heinroth, O., 55
Hershey Zoo, 159

Hessey, D., 4
Hibernation, 71–2
Hide(s), 152, 236, 240–1
Hissing, 179
Hormones, 71
Hybridization, 124

Iguana, Mexican, 64
Incubation, 140–7
Indian python: popularity and range, 16–17; distribution and habitat, 28–9; crawling rate, 60; climbing, 61; time of activity and aggregation, 65–6; shedding frequency, 72; eating of mangoes, 78; food preferences, 81–2; food capacity, 87; fasting experiment with, 89; attack on deer, 90; time required to swallow rats, 94–5; handling multiple prey, 95; elimination, 103; rate of digestion, 104; percentage of water in, 105; water loss by, 107; sexual differences, 117–18; courtship, 120–1; duration of copulation, 122; penis, 123; breeding, 123–4; delayed fertilization, 124–5; internal development, 125–6; behavior of gravid female, 129; laying, 131–2; laying season and pre-hatching period, 133; hatching, 134; eggs, 135–6; size of clutches, 139; incubation in captivity, 143, 144, 145; quivering, 146–7; growth, 151; size at birth, rate of growth, and maximum length, 158–61; longevity, 169; enemies, 176; hissing, 179; parasites, 194; tuberculosis in, 195; old account of, 215–16; encounters with, 222–3; attacks on man, 229; fear of man by, 233; numbers of in zoos of the United States, 253
Indians, 219
Instincts, 232
Institute for Medical Research, 82
Intelligence, 51–5
Intestines, 100–1
Ionides, J. P., 81

Jacobson's organ, 42–3
Jardin des Plantes, 143, 169, 201, 252
Jaws, 91, 99
Johnson, L., 8

Index

Kamudi, water, 15
Karung, 237
Kauffeld, C., 155
Kidneys, 102, 108
Kipling, R., 250

Lamon, R., 154
Lampropeltis, 12
Laying, 130–2
Leather, 236–41
Length, maximum, 150–1, 152–3
Lepers, 247
Leptophis, 61
Leptotyphlopidae, 11
Liasis amethystinus, 17
Lichanura roseofusca, 60
Linguatulids, 192–3, 194
Lizards, 110, 140, 167, 187
  earless, 112
  spiny, 112
Locomotion, 56–61
London Zoological Gardens, 143, 144, 169, 252
Longevity, 166–9

Madtsoia bai, 164–5
Mamba, 10
Man:
  as enemy of snakes, 173–4
  relation of to giant snakes, 197–263
Mangoes, 78
Markets, 242
Mating, 119–23
Mayan culture, 209
McPhee, D. R., 163
Measurement(s), taking, 6, 148–9
Medicine, use of snakes in, 246–8
Metabolism, 106
Mites, 185–7
Molurus, 201
Mongoose, 249–50
Monitor, Nile, 263
Mouth rot, 195–6
Museums, exhibits of giant snakes in, 254

National Zoological Park, 133, 144, 159, 163, 168, 253
Natrix, 119–20, 188
  natrix, 101
  sipedon, 54, 93–4, 107, 177
Neill, W. T., 240

Nematodes, 191–2
Nests, 128–9
New York Zoological Park, 145, 253
Nostrils, 100

Ophidascaris, 194
Ophiolatry, 204–11
Ophionyssus natricis, 185
Ophites, 207
Osteomyelitis, 195–6

Paine, G., 159
Parasites, 183–4
  blood, 194
  internal, 187–94
Pattern, disruptive, 178, 182
Penis, 121
Perkins, R. M., 121
Pets, giant snakes as, 262–3
Philadelphia Zoological Garden, 168, 195
Physa, 190
Pits, facial and labial, 39–42
Pittendrigh, C. F., 156
Pituophis catenifer, 174
Pit vipers, facial pits of, 40, 41
Placenta, 127
Pneumonia, 196
Pope, W., 6
Porcupine, prehensile-tailed, 80
Pre-hatching period, 133
Prey:
  seizing, 91–2
  size of, 83–5
Primates, fear of snakes in, 233–5
Proteus hydrophilus, 186
Protozoa, 188–9
Pseudoboa cloelia, 175
Puff adder, 244
Pyloric valve, 100–1
Python, 201
  amethystinus, 17
  amethystinus kinghorni, 30
  anchietae, 244
  molurus, 16–17
  molurus bivittatus, 17, 124
  molurus molurus, 124, 158–9
  regius, 244
  reticulatus, 17
  sebae, 15–16
Python(s):
  ball, 244

iv

Python(s) (*continued*)
blood, 121, 141
green, 141
Indian rock, 16
regal, 141
Sumatran blood, 145
Pythons, vertebrae of, 246
Pythoninae, 13

Quetzalcoatl, 208
Quivers, 131, 145, 146-7

Race runner, 79
Racer, black jungle, 175
Rattlesnake:
diamondback, 240
Pacific, 71, 125
prairie, 123, 152
pygmy, 190
western, 103
Rattlesnake oil, 248
Rattlesnakes: reaction to human odor, 8; sensitivity to odor, 43; speed of strike, 45; intelligence, 52, 53; time of activity, 63; frequency of shedding, 71; shedding process, 72; food hunting, 91; heat tolerance, 111; duration of copulation, 122; hybridization, 124; period of internal development, 125; growth before maturity, 150; age at maturity, 152; longevity, 167-8; parasites, 190; as model for carvings, 208; as food, 245-6
Raven, H. C., 163
Reniferids, 190
Reproduction, 115-27
organs of, 121-2
Reptiles, 108, 111, 126, 142, 148
Age of, 164
Reticulate python: size and range, 17; distribution and habitat, 29-30; ability to find concealed food, 43; time of activity, 66; shedding, 72-3; food preferences, 82; size of prey, 84; food capacity, 87-8; handling multiple prey, 95; sexual differences, 117-18; courtship, 120; duration of copulation, 122; breeding, 123; laying, 129-30; laying season and pre-hatching period, 133; eggs, 135; size of clutches, 139-40; growth, 150,

Reticulate python (*continued*)
151; size at birth, rate of growth, and maximum length, 161-3; longevity, 169; parasites, 194; encounters with, 223-5; attacks on man, 226, 227; numbers of in zoos of the United States, 253; directions for feeding, 262-3
Robichaux, L., 163-4
Ross Allen Reptile Institute, 81
Roundworms, 191-2, 194

St. Louis Zoo, 169
Salamanders, 167, 187, 190
Saliva, 101-2
San Diego Zoo, 71, 72, 125, 167, 168, 169
Scales, 69
Sclater, P. L., 23
Senses, 35-43
Serata, 259
Serpent, Brazen, 207, 246
Serpent(s):
feathered, 208-9
rainbow, 206-7
Serpent worship, 204-11, 257
Sévigné, Madame de, 242
Sex recognition, 118-19
Sexual dimorphism, 117-18
Shedding, 68-74, 204
Shock resulting from bites, 230
Sidewinder, 57
Sistrurus, 190
Skin(s), 99, 107, 152
Sleep, 63-4
Smell, 42-3
Snails, 190
Snake(s):
bull, 11, 174, 249
common garter, 152
common water, 54, 93-4, 107, 177
crowing, 214
flowered, 185
fresh-water, 20
garter, 118, 119-20, 125, 150, 189, 195
grass, 101
indigo, 11, 101
keeled rat, 10
king, 12
lined, 152
mud, 141, 142, 180
rat, 11
red-bellied, 152

Snake(s) (*continued*)
  ribbon, 150, 152
  sea, 141, 243, 247
  wart, 237
  water, 37, 119–20, 188
  worm, 11
Snake charmers, 255–6, 257
Snake charming, 207
Snake fat, 248
Snake oil, 248
Snake shops, 242
Snake temples, 207
Snedigar, R., 73
Société Nationale d'Acclimatation, 245
Sparring contests, 119
Speed, overland, 59–60
Sporozoa, 189
Spurs, 69, 117–18, 120–1, 131
Staten Island Zoo, 155
Stomach, 100–1
Storeria, 152
Strength, 44–7
Sucuriú, 15
Swallowing, 93–5
Swimming, 60–1
Sylvia: history of, 3–9; breathing method, 41–2; swallows boy's toe, 45; crawling, 58, 59; shedding, 72, 73; amount eaten and growth, 85; eating of rats, 87; time required to swallow rats, 94–5; shaping prey, 94; frequency of elimination, 103; growth, 159–61; fourteen years as pet, 169; *Life* article about, 259; use of in lectures, 255

Tail, use of in defense, 179
Tanning, 239–40
Tapeworms, 190–1, 194
Taste, 42
Teeth, 91, 99
Tegus, 79
Temperature, 110–13
Temple of Asclepius, 208
Terrapene, 167
Testudo, 167
Thamnophis, 118, 119–20, 125, 150, 195
Theriaca, 247
Throat, 99–100
Tick, iguana, 187
Ticks, 187, 194

Toad, bell, 167
Toads, 81, 167, 187
Tongue, 42, 99, 105
Tongue worms, 192–3
Tortoise, giant, 167
Touch, 43
Treacle, 247
Trematodes, 189–90, 192
Trimeresurus monticola, 141
Tropidoclonion, 152
Tropidophis melanurus, 59
Tsalikis, M., 218
Tuberculosis, 194–5
Turtle, box, 167
Turtles, 78, 140, 142, 167
Typhlopidae, 11

United States National Museum, 163
Urea, 102, 108
Uric acid, 102, 108
Urine, 102, 103
Uses of snakes by man, 236–63

Varanus, 188, 263
  griseus, 263
  monitor, 48
Vertebral column, 49–50
Viper(s):
  common, of Europe, 123
  European, 118, 119
  Gaboon, 89
  saw-scaled, 180
Viper(s), 141, 242
  tincture of, 247
Vipera berus, 123
Vision, 35–9

Wallace, A. R., 176
Warm-blooded animals, 110–11
Warning, 178–9
Water:
  retention and loss of, 106–8
  use of, 105–9
Weighing, 149
Werner, F., 202
Wiley, G. O., 52
Worship, 204–11

Zoogeographic regions, 23
Zoological Garden of Bristol, 168, 169
Zoological gardens, 251–4

A NOTE ABOUT THE AUTHOR

CLIFFORD H. POPE was born in Washington, Georgia, in 1899. After graduating from the University of Virginia, he spent the years 1921–6 in China as Herpetologist of the Chinese Division of the Central Asiatic Expeditions led by Roy Chapman Andrews, and later became Assistant Curator of Herpetology at The American Museum of Natural History. In 1940 Mr. Pope joined the Chicago Natural History Museum, where he soon became Curator of the Division of Amphibians and Reptiles, a post that he held until 1953. During this period he led three scientific expeditions to Mexico, and many others to various parts of the United States. He is a past president of the American Society of Ichthyologists and Herpetologists, and the author of a number of books on reptiles for the general reader and the specialist alike. Perhaps the best known of these are *Turtles of the United States and Canada* (1939), *The Reptile World* (1955), and *Reptiles Round the World* (1957). Mr. Pope now lives with his wife in Escondido, California.

A NOTE ON THE TYPE

THE TEXT of this book was set on the Linotype in JANSON, a recutting made direct from the type cast from matrices long thought to have been made by Anton Janson, a Dutchman who was a practicing type-founder in Leipzig during the years 1668–1687. However, it has been conclusively demonstrated that these types are actually the work of Nicholas Kis (1650–1702), a Hungarian who learned his trade most probably from the master Dutch type-founder Dirk Voskens. The type is an excellent example of the influential and sturdy Dutch types that prevailed in England prior to the development by William Caslon of his own incomparable designs, which he evolved from these Dutch faces. The Dutch in their turn had been influenced by Claude Garamond in France. The general tone of Janson, however, is darker than Garamond and has a sturdiness and substance quite different from its predecessors.